POLITICAL CHANGE

Political Change

Collected Essays

David E. Apter

Department of Political Science, Yale University

FRANK CASS : LONDON

First published 1973 in Great Britain by
FRANK CASS AND COMPANY LIMITED
67 Great Russell Street, London WC1B 3BT, England

and in United States of America by
FRANK CASS AND COMPANY LIMITED
c/o International Scholarly Book Services, Inc.
P.O. Box 4347, Portland, Oregon 97208

Copyright © 1973 DAVID E. APTER

ISBN 0 7146 2941 3

Library of Congress Catalog Card No. 72–92953

Printed in Great Britain by
Billing & Sons Limited, Guildford and London

Contents

Preface   ix

1 Some Opening Comments   1

2 The Old Anarchism and the New   11

3 Radicalization and Embourgeoisement: Hypotheses
   for a Comparative Study of History   23

4 Political Studies and the Search for a Framework   61

5 Government   73

6 Why Political Systems Change   102

7 Development and the Political Process: A Plan for a
   Constitution   118
   (*with Martin R. Doornbos*)

8 Political Theories and Political Practices: A Critique
   of Overseas Aid as Social Engineering   147

9 Comparative Government: Developing New Nations   180
   (*with Charles Andrain*)

   Index   239

For B. S. A.

Preface*

It is a commonplace that analysis in the social sciences requires precise notational constructs whose empirical referents are capable of locating appropriate descriptive events. Theory, based on relationships between these constructs and phrased in the form of hypotheses or propositions, must be transformed into verification in the first instance or used to discover or locate either new events or new relationships in the second. Those are the objects of theory which, accordingly, is both a cause and method of discovery. As a cause it is creative; as a method didactic. The problem in the social sciences has been to improve the quality of the relationship between the creative and didactic sides and produce more interesting and verifiable hypotheses and propositions.

The literature dealing with this problem has grown in recent years and become increasingly technical. On the didactic side this has been accompanied by a certain pomposity about the exercise itself. Abstractions begin to lose touch with events, the empirical referents are uncertain, and the multiplicity of interpretations of events makes the exercise suspect. A need for simplicity becomes evident as the urge to theory is an urge to abstraction. What is needed is a return to a more understandable language of description, whether in words or numbers, to improve the fit between event, discovery, and generalization. Otherwise "big issues" become impenetrable and dense. Indeed, one reaction to formalization and the retreat into specialized languages by theoreticians has been the rise of simplifying totalistic theories. Marxism prospers today not only because of its integrity and appropriateness as a theory, but in the absence of more satisfying alternatives. Moreover, without some such simplifying theory or theories, specialization has the effect of destroying the professionality of a field by elevating the sub-specialities within it. Each theorist presents his own idiosyncratic reformulation which leads away rather than towards a corpus of cumulative propositions. Indeed, the disciplines of social science today are witness to that process. So divided are they within and shredded between that it becomes more significant to speak of styles of research than disciplines, i.e.

* I would like to thank the Warden and Fellows of St. Antony's College, Oxford, who made it possible for me to edit these essays; my wife, who corrected the proofs; and Diana Maxwell, who prepared the index.

stochastic, gaming, functionalist, sociology of knowledge, and not political science, sociology, anthropology, etc.

One reaction to such tendencies is the elevation of techniques of analysis into theoretical questions so that the imprecise, the qualitative, and the open-ended become suspect. Another consequence is a distinct loss of the authority which knowledge itself implies, i.e. the validity of rational analysis as a means of solving problems. Theorists, in order to compensate for this inflate the marginal significance of their subject-matter, with the result that they say too much that is trivial. Students confronted with the morass are at best bewildered, and at worst see it as a game. One plays the game not for the intrinsic rewards of intellectual work, but because it is a way of entering the academic universe, a way of earning a living and obtaining the privileges of university life. They then repeat the very same process for a new generation of students. As a result, a very unhappy situation has grown up in the universities, in which the growth of the social sciences can be correlated with its lack of credibility and a trivialization of the enterprise.

What is the cure for such a deplorable trend? Obviously there is no one single solution. Some of the predicaments are intrinsic to the enterprise. One is to push aside some of the more didactic efforts. But another is that we need a shrewder creativity. Both these require a certain modesty. It is simply not true that we use terms that have exact empirical referents. It is not true that our concepts derive from bundles of events in which the process of abstraction can be made explicit, i.e. from events to classes of events, and from classes to universalized processes. It is not true that our abstractions lead to many discoveries. If the logic of didactic criticism is that we should become more and more precise, that same precision is a contributing factor to the absurd situation which obtains today. How do we go about resolving the predicament of making the precise less didactic and creativity more practical? One answer is better "intermediate" categories, those capable of descriptive and quantitative referents, which relate to more generalized theoretical systems in ways which centre about a problematic focus derived from human predicaments. This brings me to comment on my own work. I have been interested in certain fundamental human predicaments that centre about the problem of choice and development, and that are embodied in changing functions and meanings of social institutions. The first task is to locate predicaments or contradictions of choice brought about by developmental change. The second is to treat the relations between them as a continuous process. A third is to translate this process into the concrete context of politics and, particularly, the variable capacities of political systems. The fourth is to use a comparative method in order to discover a pattern or "syndrome" capable of providing generalizations about the process, and the capacities of political systems in a system. Whether one begins or ends in the events of everyday life, in a sense does not matter. It is more a function of taste and preference than scientific orthodoxy. But the point is one must begin or end there.

These essays are between creativity and didactics. Some are "experiments" in the mind, as it were plundering history for purpose. Others seek criteria for a politics of development. Still others are more analytical, seeking criteria for theory, as in the articles on political studies, and on political systems. In all, however, there is a common thread, the creation and use of intermediate categories and their applications to real-life historical or contemporary development situations.

One could very well argue that these essays are illustrations of the difficulties and weaknesses of the social sciences which I have just described. That is a very disturbing question and I find it intimidating. One solution is to give up this kind of theorizing, which I have been tempted to do many times. (And, periodically, I do.) I vastly prefer the pleasures of field work, the heightened intensity of feelings and awareness that come with it, the recognition of multiple realities, sometimes by sheer intuition and sometimes by painful and laboured analysis. What turns me back to the more analytical again and again is the need, having gone this far, to perfect, simplify and perhaps reorganize ideas so that they do in fact serve to make new realities observable and generalizable. In effect, theory in social analysis becomes a kind of sociology of one's own knowledge. Such knowledge cannot be acquired entirely in a private manner because a necessary corrective is criticism and conflict with one's peers—the sociology of the knowledge itself. This, in turn, leads to continuous revision and refinement of categories, the rejection of most, the preservation of only a few. At the end there is perhaps not only the prospect of new discovery in events, but also the discovery of what truth and what consequences might be contained in the theory itself.[1]

All these essays were written over the last three or four years, picking up where my earlier essays, published in *Some Conceptual Approaches to the Study of Modernization*, leave off. Just as those essays were the background materials for a theoretical book, *The Politics of Modernization*, so these form the basis of more recent thinking embodied in *Choice and the Politics of Allocation*. Thus I have tried to synthesize, simplify, and make more empirical, the theories on which I have been working. Just as a reader, *Comparative Politics* (with Harry Eckstein) stands behind the materials of the earlier theory book, so a new reader, *Contemporary Analytical*

Theory (with Charles Andrain) stands behind the new theoretical volume. The future tasks are two. The first will be to apply these new theories to monographic studies in a world of events and, second, to deal more fully with the behavioural dimensions of politics in terms of the structural constraints presently developed. These are tasks for the future.

Oxford   D. APTER
May, 1972

REFERENCES

1   See the discussion of such matters in Alfred Schutz, *Reflections on the Problem of Relevance* (New Haven: Yale University Press, 1970), pp. 78–86.

1

Some Opening Comments*

It is difficult to think of one's work as an entity, public, separated, divorced from one's self. Theory, the least finished or completed of any intellectual task, and most in need of public disclosure, is rarely equal to it. One publishes books and articles fully conscious that (despite the finality of the printed word, its standing as a matter of record) a word can be mute, especially when the ideas expressed are undergoing continuous revision.

Let me say straightaway what is evident in even the most cursory examination of my work. I am interested in big themes in human affairs; it is not merely a matter of drama. But what interests me is revolution, choice, political hope, the missed opportunity; I want to understand what lies behind drama itself, what gives an event its force and impact. Big events in this sense are larger in human affairs than themselves, for they are fissionable. They set off chain reactions. Independence for Ghana meant independence for Africa. A revolutionary moment in one society has repercussions in others. Cuba changes a great deal about Latin America, but how, to what effect, and through what subsequent transformations—these are what we mean by big questions.

I see these questions centring around two highly generalized and related topics. One is the consequence of development, the expansion of choice. Another is how to control development, shape it, and make it serve men's purposes. If development has been my consistent concern, for these large reasons, the management of it by human beings is for me the central political problem. Choice, development, order—these are the results of countless pressures, demands, concerns. Political choice is perhaps different from other kinds because it means that some men, with power, are able to determine the conditions under which other men can choose, and further restrict and define their alternatives.

Such interests are obviously classic in their proportions, and very old. To try to say something new, or (to use a somewhat over-

* Reprinted from *Comparative Political Studies*, Volume 3, Number 3 (October 1970), pp. 323–32, by permission of the publisher, Sage Publications, Inc.

worked term these days) relevant, about such matters takes one on a long and rather difficult research path. There have been many blind alleys and false steps. What begins as promising turns out to be cumbersome, or obvious, or worse, ridiculous. I knew this would be the case from the start, so that my first concern was to search through the literature for an appropriate method. The first genuine theory which captured my interest and most deeply affected my thinking was the Marxist. I was attracted to Marxism for many reasons. It provided historical depth, a clear pattern of causality, a progressive concept of change, and a moral conclusion. All these critical elements in a powerful and generalized theory set a standard against which all others can be evaluated (see Sachs, n.d.: 392–406).

One weakness in Marxian theory is the limited attention paid to "superstructure". As well, I seemed to find more empirical complexity in emergent real-life situations than a Marxian system would admit. My attempt to deal with the second problem led me to study economics and particularly economic theory, while an interest in the first, the problem of superstructure brought me into contact with the great historical sociologists and lawyers, Maine, Maitland, Vinogradoff, Weber, Durkheim, Pareto, Toennies. The formalized economic models had the necessary parsimony, and *a priori* power, which seemed to me one goal of theory. On the other hand dealing with the normative complexities of human society, the leads and lags of culture, personality and organization, represented the challenge for political sociology. This is why in my work I have tried to make use of both traditions, including some highly formalized expressions but only those which seem to preserve the richness of complexity and not do it too much violence.

Creating such theory is more easily said than done. Weber, Durkheim, and Pareto (particularly the first two) fascinated me because they linked the study of predispositions, residues, attitudes, convictions, faiths, and ideologies (all treated as more than mere superstructure) to the primitive relations of class, elite, occupation, capitalism, and development. These formed the phenomena of analysis in sharp contrast to the political science of my day, which dealt with epiphenomena: courts and constitutions, formal instruments of democratic government, and so on. That discipline—all important—failed to ask the right questions or, worse, assumed that they were already answered while the work of some of those outside the field, such as anthropologists like Fortes and Evans-Pritchard, Firth, Geertz, and Fallers all seemed to have more important things to say about politics than most political scientists.

Moreover, much of their work was specifically designed to bridge the gap between "behaviour" and "structure" while the political behaviourists themselves were more engrossed and preoccupied with matters of method than of substance. It was not an insufficient sympathy for what they were doing which dissuaded me from following directly in the behavioural tradition. In a sense, I felt very much a part of the movement. But behaviourism in a strict sense was just beginning. I preferred the more "evolutionary" developmental personality theory like that offered by Harry Stack Sullivan to the more experimental learning theorists. The former related the substance of behaviour to the substance of structure and combined them in the concept of roles. Such notions were compatible too with the kind of work represented by George Herbert Mead, who was a very early influence on my thinking.

I cite these not as a sort of intellectual odyssey (which would certainly be out of place here), but to clarify my conception of the political, which is very broad indeed. For me, politics is the interplay of three social dimensions—normative, structural, and behavioural. They are ingredients of choice, the critical centre of all social life. These may be strained and tense in their relations as in times of great complexity and change, or may, at promontory moments in history, be highly integrated. It is the ebb and flow of the relations between these three dimensions which for me is the substance of politics. Since my point of view is developmental, it links the relations between these dimensions to ongoing processes. The means people devise with which to cope under such conditions are the objects of analysis, including the instruments of government and the effects of their institutional structure on the choices people can make for themselves. That is why I suggest that politics for me is a study of the way in which social choice occurs.

With such interests, it is perhaps not surprising that I became very much influenced by Talcott Parsons and, more directly, by Marion Levy. Parsons' original means–ends schema was based on the action of choice. Levy's structural–functional analysis was a codification of variables both structural and behavioural which, as a minimal and irreducible set, had abstracted political implications, individually for each function and structure and collectively, i.e. as a system. This was particularly useful as a departure point for comparing highly discrete units both ecologically and over time. The crucial research unit was "role" following the work of Parsons, Merton, Newcomb, Nadel, a category which can be seen in sets or congeries from an organizational point of view and as the embodiment of normative prescriptions from an institutional point of view. Development, choice, structural–functional analysis, and role and societies as concrete units formed the original context of my first field work in what was then the Gold Coast during the academic

year 1952–53. Going back to the book I wrote as a result of that
period, which was also my Ph.D. dissertation, I am amazed at the
number of concerns which, explicitly stated then, remain with me
to the present. (See Apter, 1972.)

Ghana was for many reasons the ideal case study. From the
standpoint of my interest in tradition, forces of change, the contrast
between ethnic and national life, and the emergence of a highly
organized nationalist movement as a political instrument, the
devolution of political authority by staged steps seemed not like a
ballet but a drama in which all the epic qualities of human beings
were organized, harnessed, and brought together in a new and
independent polity. Participants generated ideas, enthusiasm, and
moral purpose. These combined in a universalized goal, independence,
would have important and infectious consequences not only in
Africa but in the United States as well. A black population was
performing the act of destroying white political power for the first
time and doing it with grace and power. Such epic themes can be
found in history, but it is rare that one can study them firsthand.
One also saw the other side of such epic phenomena. That which is
bright and exciting at one stage may become corrupt and hurtful
at another. One must also be prepared to study why things fall
apart, and why it is that the emergence of hope and innocence in a
new polity is so often followed by despair and cynicism.

One is not drawn to the dramatic case for a single reason. In a real
sense, each time a situation arises which one sees as possessing
universalized moral significance, it gives one pause. The urge is
to enquire into its true meanings. This is what I call the "sociological
moment", when there is a heightening of awareness, a quickening
of processes, and an anticipatory sense on the part of the observer
that here is a "real" event. Such movements are the most exciting
in social life and social science. The mundane may well be more
important to study on a day-to-day basis. But these sociological
moments serve to redefine purposes, to underscore our humanity.
Africa did this in the late 'fifties and the early 'sixties. Latin America
will do this, I think, in the 'seventies. Indeed, this is one reason, as
well as the marvellous complexity and texture of social structure
there, that I am drawn to Argentina, Chile, and Peru, for my
current research interests.

Of course, such sociological moments can also be very misleading.
Precisely what gives them their brilliance is the insubstantiality of
their events. When lustre fails, it is impossible to recapture the
moment itself, or reconstruct it. Today's generation of scholars,
for example, is hard put to take Nkrumah and the Convention
People's Party seriously. Some are inclined to dismiss the entire

period as silly and vainglorious—a period in which all parties took in each other's rhetorical washing, but did little more.

All this helps to make one conscious of error, not simply that of erroneous interpretation, but of purely idiosyncratic conclusions fobbed off as scientific generalization. Who in such settings could really control his analysis? Data were inevitably sketchy. A global approach, whether dressed up in the language of structural–functional analysis or some other, would remain useful only superficially. One needed to know more—that is, to understand more deeply the specific context of events—a pull toward what is called "area studies". One also wanted to be sure that the facts were right and suitably gathered, a pull in the direction of quantitative and statistical analysis. In the first instance, I decided to do more intensive field work in a particular part of an African country (on Buganda in Uganda), and in the second to try to formulate a more suitable and focused analytical system of my own.

The second is much harder to do than the first and infinitely less enjoyable. Field work is exciting. It is like working with the pieces of a jigsaw puzzle. One gradually discerns a pattern. The rules for finding the pieces and interpreting the pattern—these are much more complex. For one thing, broad themes and large units are hard to fit into a narrow quantitative mode as such and need to be translated into indicator variables. These, while they may be capable of being programmed and manipulated, are rarely generalizable for the macro unit. Thus the search for ultimately quantitative, indicator variables capable of standing as surrogates for analytical ones became a long-term concern.

Such matters obviously run into problems of all kinds. A good highly generalized theory, particularly of a structural sort, should demarcate predictable boundaries around some type of social action. Needed first in this kind of political sociology are the sort which operate on a purely logical level, using formal abstractions to define the rules of relationship. Second, a "socio-logical" level should "fit" inside the formal categories so that substantive concepts having both logical and empirical relationships can lead to a third or descriptive level in which the categories are quantitative. In my own analysis, I have not been able to work out such a synthesis satisfactorily, but it has been one of my efforts. I have not been able to organize a purely formal model, although I have come close to one by combining two formalized sets of relationships—one dialectical, which I use for the analysis of norms; the other functional, which I use for the analysis of structures. The substantive or socio-logical categories are equity of allocation in relation to allocation itself, and generalized values in relation to political norms. Discrepancies between the first two create political "informa-tion", while discrepancies between the second generate crises in legitimacy. These are translated descriptively into such categories as stratification, ideology, participation, and the like.

Obviously it is impossible to go into such matters in any detail here. I cite these to suggest the direction my thinking has gone. At the same time, because there is a variety of new mathematical and quantitative techniques, the logico-empirical and the more quantita-tive, which approach to favour (or produce the more interesting results), becomes a nice question. Perhaps the real answer is that both will if the researcher is himself "interesting"; that is, capable of locating important regularities of behaviour. For the rest, it is a matter of style and insight. I myself think that if one could combine, say, certain types of factor or regression analysis or time series to abstract variables for which quantitative surrogates can be found, this would give us an important leg up on control and understanding in the social sciences.

Experimentalism in small groups might then be more readily transferable to large units and not in the metaphorical sense accepted by systems theorists. For example, one of the propositions which has emerged from my own analysis is that there is an inverse relationship between coercion and information. I suggested that the relationship itself was linear, but of course I have no genuine evidence of that. Partly the idea was suggested to me when, studying Ghana over a long period of time and interviewing political leaders whom I had known for many years, I realized that whereas they once had had a sure sense of what the public wanted and felt, now they did not and did not know whom to trust. They spied on each other, felt betrayed, became jealous, and often became dangerous. It occurred to me that the more authoritarian the regime became (often in attempts to carry out policy), the more various echelons of leaders passed up to their superiors that information which was pleasing to the regime, while they falsified or repressed that which was not. In effect the more authoritarian the policy, the more misinformed was the government. Those inclined to give honest information became dangerous and were eliminated. As decisions were taken in a climate of increasing uncertainty, greater and greater coercion was applied. Similar evidence for this "macro-proposition" seemed to follow many other situations: Indonesia, for example, Mali, and so on. Perhaps the extreme case was the USSR, but it also fit with small group experiments where comparisons were made between authoritarian and participant work groups.

It would be very nice indeed if such a proposition turned out to be experimentally correct on both macro and micro levels. It might even have the persuasiveness of a very highly formalized model like that of "supply and demand" in economics, i.e. in identifying *a priori* optima for decision-making. One might be able to locate alternative mixtures of coercion and information appropriate for political systems, identifying points of equilibrium at various stages of development.

To be useful, such variables would not only need to be tied specifically to development as a process, but also to political systems types of a sufficiently abstract character to have predictable effects on the use of coercion and information. It was this in mind which led me to formalize the various political systems types I employ, i.e. mobilization, reconciliation, theocratic, and bureaucratic systems. Using such variables, it is possible to treat development as a linear process in one sense, but having multilinear consequences.

This brings up another question. If one lacks good experimental techniques, how does one test a theory, especially of the "nesting box" variety aimed at here? There is no simple answer. Over time, specific predictions may be wrong. It is then necessary to ask whether the mistake was an error in theory (omission of a variable, for example) or of fact. More properly, however, what one asks of a formal level of theory is that it be logically correct while at an empirical level one asks that it be "true". Perhaps a brief diagram will clarify what I mean (see Figure 1).

	Type of Functionality	Degree of Isomorphism
Formal	Logic	Congruence (Functional and Dialectical)
Socio-logical	Structures	Comparison (Analytical)
Descriptive	Consequence	Measurement (Descriptive Indicator)

Figure 1. The Integration of Formal and Empirical Theory

Each of the three levels of analysis shown in Figure 1—formal, socio-logical, and descriptive—should follow the same pattern, since they are on a descending order of generalization. However, the tests applied to them are different. Descriptive categories have diverse consequences, and the clustering of them is particularly subject to quantitative analysis. Socio-logical categories abstract structural implications for any given system enabling the comparative method to be employed. Formal categories using arbitrary definitions are logically related by dialectical or functional rules. Ideally if we begin at the "top", i.e., at the most formal, we should not be content until we have arrived at the "bottom", i.e. the most descriptive. This is why it is so important to maintain an intimate relationship of formal modelling and field work.

Of course there are other modes of "testing". One common form is sheer publication. In the academic profession, it is publish or perish all right, but not in the sense usually attributed to that shibboleth. To write is to communicate ideas so that they can be attacked, rethought, and modified. This is necessary if we are to remain open to ideas. Verbal criticisms lack the publicity, the embarrassing demonstration of vulnerability that written ones have. One reads, squirms, and reacts.

It also becomes necessary to create one's own map or conceptual guide to the bewildering array of materials which are produced in this manner, if only because sheer volume is likely to be overwhelming. My map centres around the problem of choice. If norms, structures, and behaviour constitute its elements, then any combination of two should locate or identify the third. From the analysis of norms and structures, it should be possible to infer the behavioural, i.e. the choices which individuals will make given a range. The combination of norms and behaviour will allow the articulation of structure, i.e. roles and role sets. The combination of structure and behaviour will allow the inferring of norms.

Such mapping I have attempted in a number of essays. Some of these have been reprinted in *Some Conceptual Approaches to the Study of Modernization* (Apter, 1968). The attempt to put these together in a rather loose way was made in *The Politics of Modernization* (Apter, 1965), These, as I described them, were theories for burning. They were attempts to clarify and sharpen what a good theory ought to be about, especially when dealing with complex developmental phenomena at a macro level. For the past four years I have been trying to make such theories more systematic, simpler, on the one hand more analytical, and on the other more concrete. (Apter, 1971).

As already indicated, the problem of the expansion and control of choice is my central concern. Using a highly abstract analytical system, with development and order as dependent variables, I have derived a series of behavioural propositions which can be compared in modernizing and industrial societies. The present theory is based on two analytical dimensions, the relations between norms and structures. How these are affected by the need to expand choice by means of increased development, as well as to contain choice within a system of order, constitutes a central political concern.

Two behavioural variables are employed in the theory. Modernizing societies are preoccupied with development for "embourgeoise-ment" while highly industrialized societies, searching for new normative priorities, have become increasingly radicalized. Radicali-zation from above and embourgeoisement from below are seen as interwoven in all societies, the relations between them forming the substance of political life.

The link between these behavioural tendencies and the larger structural changes which occur in contemporary society is examined in terms of several operational categories. These, descriptive in character, are surrogate terms for the abstract relationships defined by the model. They include categories for the comparative analysis of stratification, elite access and competition, and the changing pattern of norms as a dialectical process. Each of the descriptive categories is designed on the one hand to stand for more analytical variables, and on the other to organize distributions. Hence the theory is particularly suitable for comparative analysis of empirically different systems both over time and ecologically.

Linkage variables between these larger problems of choice and the political ones are also operationalized. We employ the notion of an inverse relationship between information and coercion and by the use of these variables indicate when a government reaches a "political ceiling" beyond which it can no longer maintain order or expand choice. The normative and structural aspects set up concrete situations which the structural theory must solve. Such solutions are attempted in the form of projected constitutional instruments. For the predicaments of modernizing societies, a "development constitu-tion" is projected. For those which obtain in industrial societies, an "equity constitution" is described. These "constitutions" are based on the need for coercion in relation to development in the former societies and the need for high information in the latter. They represent possible structural arrangements which derive from the analysis of the model relationships.

Perhaps the most controversial aspect of my present work is that it specifies a normative conclusion to the issues discussed. Pursuing the implications of the model in normative terms, leads me toward a radical equilibrium theory in which the structural conclusions are shown to work best in the context of a liberal socialist ethic.

My over-riding interest is how to link the problem of choice with an analytical theory which is integrated with operational variables, both structural and behavioural. In turn, the normative implications need discussion so as to show clearly how political objectives can be reinforced and clarified in a context of systems theory.

These, then, are my more recent concerns. If the recent structural studies hold up in field work, as I hope they will, my next concern will be with the behavioural dimension of choice. That will require a rethinking of the entire approach. Behavioural analysis is a field with many pitfalls for the relatively uninitiated. There is also a vast literature to be read. All this gives one pause. Few can claim connection to Minerva in the social sciences. We are perhaps more like petulant Dianas, with large feet.

BIBLIOGRAPHY

Apter, D. E. 1972 *Ghana in Transition* (Princeton: Princeton University Press). This is a new and revised edition.
—— 1971 *Choice and the Politics of Allocation* (New Haven: Yale University Press).
—— 1968 *Some Conceptual Approaches to the Study of Modernization* (Englewood Cliffs, N.J.: Prentice-Hall).
—— 1965 *The Politics of Modernization* (Chicago: University of Chicago Press).
Sachs, I. (n.d.) "Marx and the Foundation of Socio-Economic Prevision", in *Marx and Contemporary Scientific Thought* (The Hague: Mouton).

2

The Old Anarchism and the New*

Anarchism as a doctrine has a peculiar fascination for scholars. It both repels and attracts. It attracts because it embodies rage—the particular rage people have when they see man as an obstacle to his own humaneness. It is the ultimate statement of how outrageous the human condition can be. But it is precisely because man does not live by rage alone, but must master it by discovering proximate means to solving the ordinary problems of daily life, that anarchism repels. It seems a romantic luxury at best—a cry of pain for the future, just as nostalgia is for the past, and, like nostalgia, this cannot fail to be attractive.

Perhaps because of this, anarchism is not a mere reflection of anger but also a contributing source. It is thus more than a lightning rod for the anger that exists. Anarchism is associated with unreason and bombs, violence and irresponsibility. The ancestral cry of the anarchist in the 19th century is that "the only good bourgeois is a dead one". On this score the doctrine remains unregenerate. But its attack is not limited to capitalism. The anarchist rejection of socialism and Marx because of their centralist contradictions is equally complete. Hence anarchism assigns itself a position of extreme vulnerability. Moreover, none of the major social doctrines can absorb anarchism because, where it is most fundamental, it is anti-political—that is, it does not really offer political solutions. Although the language of today's anarchism is more psychologically sophisticated it remains a primitive doctrine which wants to convert a structural condition of hate into a sentiment of love, and by the same token transform rage into peace.

Some theorists of anarchism such as Kropotkin stressed the need for rationality and theory. Others, perhaps more persuasive because of their own personal vitalism, urged the importance of violence, as did Bakunin. The virtue of anarchism as a doctrine is that it employs a socialist critique of capitalism and a liberal critique of socialism. Because of this its doctrines remain important even when they lead

* Reprinted by permission of Macmillan (London and Basingstoke) from *Anarchism*, edited by David E. Apter and James Joll.

11

it in the direction of terrorism and agitation, much of it of the hit-and-run variety. This critique is one cause for its revival which comes as a surprise because anarchism had appeared to have run its course in the early part of the 20th century. It was quaint, its leaders slightly comical, and relegated to a shelf of antique doctrine which included Annie Besant and the Theosophist movement and the burned out engineers of Technocracy, Inc.

Clearly, anarchism has turned out to be like other antiques, capable of renewed significance in the social and aesthetic lives of many people. It has darkened with time. Some of its power is black. The black flag belongs now to black people as well as others. (In this respect anarchism is reaching out to people other than the bourgeois radicals who were its most ardent followers in the past.) In India the effects of Ruskin's doctrines on Gandhi and in Japan the more direct acquaintance with the writings of early anarchists also helped to give anarchism a more international flavour, and a universality lacking in its earlier period when confined to Western Europe, Russia and the U.S.A. Anarchism today is a form of liberalism which rejects capitalism; as a doctrine of individualism divorced from the classic western form it has relevance despite the flamboyance and gesticulations of some of its practitioners. The latter should not dissuade us from recognizing that the ground covered by anarchism is as a normative antithesis to contemporary capitalism and socialism. Anarchism in this normative sense can be separated from its organizational characteristics and seen to stand on its own. Indeed, in the nature of the case organization could never be a strong point of anarchists. As a moral phenomenon, no matter how much it waxes and wanes it has constant roots in the fundamentally offending character of organization *qua* organization.

In this commentary, and it can be no more than that, I will consider aspects of anarchism as a normative force. First, compared with socialism or liberalism it can be seen as a discontinuous phenomenon. There has been no consistent accumulation of ideas and theories. This discontinuous quality of anarchism, however, is as we have suggested, likely to be confusing. Anarchism may appear to be dead when it is dormant and exceptionally fresh when it springs to life. Secondly, as a doctrine it differs from others in so far as it is concerned with meaning more as rejection but projects no specific structural solution. Moreover, because anarchism leaves meaning "open" its receptivity to violence or to use the contemporary language, of each man "doing his thing" makes happenings into a substitute solution for programmes. This aspect is particularly important with respect to contemporary youth subcultures where the ambiguity of meaning is greatest to start out with. As part of a subculture which has become both more structurally important and powerful as time has gone on, anarchism has recently been able to enlarge its significance without any increase in organizational power as such. It is a piggy-bank normative doctrine able to join on, as it were, to quite diverse groups. Indeed such normative power is almost inverse in significance to its degree of organization. But it is by joining particular subcultures, with all the special conditions these encounter, that contemporary anarchism takes on a peculiarly psychological dimension which in the past it lacked.

Before going on to a discussion of these points, let us try to review some of the main characteristics of anarchism as a doctrine both in its older and newer forms. We seek that common core of belief which forms the substance of its own debate.

RATIONALITY AND CREATIVITY

The primitive core of anarchism is not so very different from Christianity. That is, it rests on the notion that man has a need, not just a preference, to love. Love in its generic sense is the central principle from which two other needs derive. One is rationality. The other is emotionality. Religious and political doctrines tend to come down on one side or the other of these and make one serve the other. Emotionality may use rationality but it restricts its appropriateness. Rationality may recognize the importance of emotionality but it tries to channel it into approved directions, destroying its spontaneousness

For anarchists the appropriate balance between the two is creativity. Creativity emerges both from rational and emotional processes. The language used must reflect the blend. The pure doctrine may be said to originate in love which in turn is expressed in emotionality and rationality which in turn must be integrated in creativity. Since emotionality derives from action and rationality from reflection, maximizing creativity is a balance of action and reflection which in turn enlarges man's capacity for love.

If contemporary anarchists are less rational they are also more psychological. They combine the radical critique of society by Marx with the insights of Freud. What the early anarchists particularly objected to was Darwinism, preferring mutual aid to mutual struggle.[1] Today's attack on capitalism is not only because of the injustices of capitalism but also includes a strong desire to create a new symbolic aesthetic designed to break through the many layers of human consciousness which organized life restricts and stunts. While it is true that all radicalism tried to deal with these matters, it is particularly the contemporary form of anarchism which gives a high priority to the psychosexual and symbolic aspects. Hence the significance of the work of Erich Fromm, Wilhelm Reich, Herbert Marcuse, Paul Goodman, R. D. Laing and others who have had a sudden (and in many cases belated) prosperity among more radical students in particular.

THE ROLE OF THEORY IN ANARCHISM

Having tried to suggest some differences between the new emphases in anarchism and the old we can now suggest some differences between ideologies and social movements which have had a continuous organized existence for a long time and those which have not. In the first instance we encounter the problems of orthodoxy and of the hardening of the doctrinal arteries. To some extent it becomes a matter of retranslation and language whether or not change is to be welcomed or fought. Debate centres about how much doctrine should each inheriting group absorb and in turn pass on as values or norms. How much that is embedded in the old structural forms of party and organization should be reaffirmed in orthodoxy lest the pristine quality or originating ideology of the movement be destroyed? These concerns are irrelevant with ideologies which come and go like rashes or epidemics. Orthodoxy is not at issue. As a result the ideology when it has subsided becomes difficult to recapture. The singular quality of origin which gave it significance is lost. But such doctrines, when they do appear, capture the quintessence of relevance. They define the hypocrisies of society. Their proponents lance the swollen, more fatuous phrases on which all orthodoxies depend. It is precisely the lack of continuity of movements like anarchism which gives them exceptional moral power. They are released from the burdens of past error. Orthodoxy is not at issue with anarchism but substance, the substantiality of the doctrine. As a matter of sheer continuity the new anarchism can have little in common with the old except in language.

This leads to another point. Anarchism stresses the role of theory far less than socialism for example. It is also less intellectual. The central and institutionalized values of socialist doctrine are theoretically complex and ideologically elaborate. Within the ideologic of anarchism there is sufficient attraction to old concepts so that it is possible to discover a fresh interpretation. Not requiring a rejection of the revolutionary past this allows a look towards a radically different future. And that itself is a source of creativity. This is quite different from conflicts between various forms of Marxism which are more a function of theory *qua* theory.

What do we mean then when we say that anarchism has come

back, but in a new form? For one thing those who raise the black flag are probably less serious than in the past and much less so than socialists requiring theory and organization. For the latter, party must be everything or there will be nothing. The memory of Marx's attitude towards the classic figures like Bakunin and Kropotkin is perhaps in point. But the latter were concerned with total change. In contrast there has been no call today for an organized anarchistic movement such as a revival of the first international for example. Contemporary radicals read anarchism along with Tarot cards. Thus if it has a resonance of its own it is also difficult to take too seriously. It is instead redolent of experiments in the simple life.

With such emphases anarchism can never have a permanent reputation. Whatever its prosperity at any moment, its origin lies in some important and continuing inadequacy of existing systems, qua system and extends as well to the standardized solutions. We say system because it is not the event that causes anarchism but an interpretation of it which says that present arrangements are responsible and not chance or some temporary considerations. The ingredients which make up the system whether real or concrete, whether theory or practice, *need* to produce the inadequacy. This is as true of a system of theory as of a system in practice. Both are irredeemable because their important conditions depend on organizational means.

For this reason, even when a system is generally perceived as bad, anarchism is bound to appeal to a minority. For one thing people are afraid of changes which they cannot predict, which is the reason why theory remains so important for radicals other than anarchists! Theories are a part of revolution. They are a means. By reducing the ambiguity of change the translated and convenient ideological expressions make projective sense about change and point in a desired direction. Anarchist "theories" do this only slightly at best and in a relatively utopian manner. That is to say few offer detailed empirical analysis. What a contrast between say Bakunin and Marx for whom radicalism was less a matter of disgruntlement than prediction.

If anarchism is not very concerned with theory *per se*, anarchists commonly assume that human affairs constitute a naturalistic order which *needs* to be rendered "uncontrived". Spontaneity and even a certain randomness can be seen to go together. Theory in the view of anarchists should not be an intellectual contrivance because this will reduce freedom and clutter the will with tempering injunctions. The contrast is complete. For Lenin or Mao, theory is all important. It represents the basis for a new system, i.e. a different structural order based on particular norms, which endows behaviour with an element of puritanism. Theory for them is important because it enables doctrine and action to go hand in hand.

How can one explain this continuous preference by anarchists for spontaneous association? Behind the appearance of anti-intellectualism there lies a presumptive belief in an ultimate rationality as the common and unifying property of all men if unfettered by an inappropriate system, a rationality which, moreover, will temper relationships of people whose lives are based upon intimate and localized associations.

Such views are, of course, not too different from traditions of evangelical radicalism based on personal vision, the denunciation of injustice and the regeneration of self as a continued approach to social betterment. To convert the group it is necessary to begin with the self. With such views it is not surprising that anarchists tended to be strong and independent characters.

Anarchism contrasts most sharply with socialism in the particular substance of ideas and attitudes about organization; the fear that a political infrastructure will assert itself above the primacy of the individual. But if it emphasizes the tyranny of the collectivity, anarchism lacks a clear picture of what kind of social community is necessary to replace what we have. Anarchists may be closest to socialists in their common critique of capitalist society, but they are diametrically opposed in the matter of solutions.

HAPPENINGS NOT PROGRAMMES

We said that anarchism lacks doctrinal continuity. It has no younger generation which arises explicitly out of the older one, as does Marxism or liberalism. In what sense does it have a new relevance if few are informed by its doctrines and live under its banner? In one sense the answer is metaphorical. Students who proclaim communes, wave the black flag, and strike out against organization are anarchic or have anarchic tendencies. That is, in the contemporary social and moral gesticulation of the youth subcultures of many societies we find the equivalent to earlier anarchism.

Today's anarchists in this respect are different from their earlier counterparts in ideas about the collectivity. They themselves are organized differently. They are younger. If they can join with various militant bodies in the attack on capitalist society they also feel free to collide with them. With their highly individualized styles they conflict with other anarchists. They are Rorschach radicals. One needs conflicts to obtain clues to the next concern. Each conflict in the context of youth is part theatre, most particularly the theatre of the absurd, in which public happenings are staged in order to demonstrate the falseness, the emptiness and the perfunctory quality of the symbols of society, law, school, family, and church, i.e. of the stable institutions of the middle aged.

Since today's anarchism is more a part of a youth culture than in the past, anarchism is a contributing source of normative conflict. Youth, not the whole of it, but the counter-culture, serves as the main carrier of anarchist ideas. Anarchism today depends on the power and position of youth as a counter-culture. In this it is very different from the past when anarchism was more inter-generational.

This is perhaps another reason why anarchism remains so anti-theoretical. The simplicity of anarchism is in part a basis of its generational appeal. Youth today is bored with the doctrinal complexity of alternative and competing ideologies. The early figures associated with anarchist movements in England, France, Switzerland, Russia, Germany, and the United States recognized that the guide to action was a theory. This was as true of Proudhon's mutualist doctrines as it was of Tolstoy's primitive Christianity. Even the pamphlets and memorials of Bakunin and Kropotkin showed a concern to spell out the conditions necessary for an improved and different social condition. Theory was a part of life as an enduring radical preoccupation. But youth today reads very little such literature.

Anarchism as a youth counter-culture is a genuinely different structural phenomenon than in the past. The more so since although generational time shrinks, the period of youthfulness expands. In the days of the old anarchists, one went from childhood to manhood very quickly—overnight as it were. Today what we call youth refers to an extended period of role search, the trying on of different identities. Anarchism challenges this. It downgrades the roles and the identities offered by society. In a very real way it denies what youth in general is for. That is, if youth can be defined as the period of role search between childhood and working adulthood, then the new anarchism is an attack on youth. The attack takes such an attractive form because more and more members of the youth subculture find themselves repelled by the roles and identities which society provides. The result is that anarchism as a counter-culture provides a double basis for rebellion, first against society as it is, and second, against the youth subculture as a preparatory period. Its relevance depends on how youth feels as a whole about societies' roles, i.e. whether they are reluctant to be recruited to them when society ordains that they should. Whether they basically do not reject such roles. Whether they reject them as a system. Anarchism does not mean mere rebellion, i.e. an unwillingness to make a commitment in the face of pressure to select roles and conform, a kind of rebellion associated with a more generalized irresponsibility and a desire for a longer period of exemption. Anarchism means the rejection of the roles themselves. Youth represents a period of exemption granted to youth by society in order to provide a longer period of role search. Anarchism annihilates the roles. It is a doctrine of role rejection.

ROLELESSNESS

A youth culture is part and parcel of the need for more time before accepting society's roles, of sorting them out, and trying, with many false starts, to adopt an appropriate set. This is essentially a method of socializing individuals into the structure of existing social roles. Anarchism as a counter-culture may reject those roles but can it create new and alternative ones as could be done by making more central those activities which had been peripheral in the past? For example, law students can change the role of lawyers from those of practitioners of the art of mediation into investigators of social abuse. Teachers may be redefined outside the specific institutional setting of schools. Socialism and related doctrines do just this. Their proponents look for a redefinition of roles according to their varied ideas of how the structure of society should be altered.

Here anarchism is not very helpful. Since it seeks not alternative roles but their obliteration, this may, when pushed to extremes, end in the obliteration of self instead of its liberation. Rolelessness is the social equivalent of randomness. A random universe cannot define freedom. When the self is obliterated as a social person, the result is withdrawal from action rather than intensified action, or violence for the sake of violence. One sees the pathological aspect in the use of drugs, the emergence of what perhaps can best be called the cult of solipsism, and the alternation of extreme passivity with extreme violence and anxiety.

True the anti-role is not rolelessness. It is a role, too, and one directly involved with other roles. Perhaps we need to distinguish between the "anti-role" which produces a fierce and continuous controversy over the terms of group action and sheer rolelessness. Moreover, there are "advantages" to "anti-roles" as distinct from "rolelessness'. The anti-role sets itself against socially validated roles. But it has a place in history. The history may not be very edifying. But that does not matter, even if history in this sense replaces economics as the dismal science with "system" its contemporary voice.

The anti-roles generate the rebirth of innocence. In order to be innocent (and pure) it is necessary to take an anti-role. Each person then "does his thing" but dares not have a theory about it. (Theory would be a source of weakness not of strength.) The contemporary anarchists most commonly accused of anti-intellectualism are in this sense being misunderstood. Contemporary critics fail to recognize that innocence is itself the goal, the source of redemption, the means and the end. The search for directness and simplicity is precisely what is wanted as the ultimate answer to complexity and com-promise.

This brings us to the key question. The relationship between innocence and violence. If our assumptions are correct, violence, because it becomes a total non-answer (which is no answer) is the key to innocence. Here the modern anarchists can relate the theatre of the absurd to the existential quality of death. To prove innocence and protect it is to smash society and turn against confounding theoretical constructions. Out of the first, the smashing of society, the hope is that something new will emerge since from the violence itself will come a more purified image of man. This is where anarchism is perhaps closest to its traditional form. But today, in so far as such views are primarily the preoccupation of youth subculture and most particularly that part which denies itself roles and identity, then violence has quite a different cause than in the traditional anarchist movement, namely violence is both a function and a cause of identity smashing. If this is true, then for today's youth culture anarchism acts first on itself. It smashes its own identity. But the resulting innocence is behaviourally not supportable without violence. This contrasts with the old anarchism where violence was a tactic or a weapon. In short, when anarchism is the property of a youth subculture, violence is a psychological necessity.

IN SEARCH OF LIBERATION

If this is the case then what are we to make of anarchism in its present form? At its best, it has its liberating side. It represents a form of social criticism against capitalism as a system and socialism as a form of bureacratic tyranny. At the worst extreme, it liberates individuals from society only in order to help them destroy themselves as individuals. But what about the larger intermediate group attracted to the doctrines of anarchism? Here the history of doctrine provides its own answers. Future anarchism like the past will prove to be episodic, providing those engaged in role searching with the chance to create some new roles which are partly inside the system and partly not (particularly in the arts). That at least is for the more gifted.

For others, perhaps, it will mean a search for some patterned irregularity in their lives, particularly in the alteration of those roles embodied in the sacred social institutions of family, church, school and court. Anarchists may modify the family through communes or other types of association, create new holy days, chants and festivals, alter the quality and the form of education, and redefine both grievances and their redress. In this respect the most important contribution which the new anarchists can make is indirect. Anarchism if it can be anything is likely to be a social doctrine for more personalized living, a recipe for the homespun, and not a political solution for the world's problems. It is more a matter of lifestyle than explicit revolution. But perhaps there is nothing more revolutionary than that.

From a doctrinal standpoint we have said that anarchism represents the most libertarian of socialist ideologies. It begins in the view that men as individuals are, given half a chance, better than the societies in which they live. But to change society is not enough. Individuals need to see in their own salvation a new way to live together. A kind of rational ecclesiasticism pervades traditional anarchist thought.

If it is necessary to break through the shell of society by means of violence, then anarchism has on the whole accepted the principle of violent means. In some of its earlier varieties, at least, it embodied a devotion to discipline and asceticism which at times took narrow forms. Violence might be necessary to free the human spirit from its containment within an unsatisfactory social environment. But once this freedom has been attained it was up to the individual, indeed his obligation, to direct it into constructive and socially useful channels. Whatever it was, anarchism was not a doctrine for the lazy. Quite the contrary, it made exceptional demands on its adherents.

Too many demands, one might argue. This has perhaps been one of the causes of its unevenness. Anarchism is in perpetual danger, not least because of the hammer blows of Marxism and the new organized left. It remains a doctrine of the absurd. Even today when its resonance is stronger than ever before its proponents, from Kropotkin to Malatesta seem *bouffe*. Witness Malatesta, "I am an anarchist because it seems to me that anarchy would correspond better than any other way of social life, to my desire for the good of all, to my aspirations towards a society which reconciles the liberty of everyone with co-operation and love among men, and not because anarchism is a scientific truth and a natural law. It is enough for me that it should not contradict any known law of nature to consider it possible and to struggle to win the support needed to achieve it."[2] One can hear the snorts of derision from the Marxists. For it is a fundamental point, whether or not a revolution is based upon a scientific understanding of certain developmental laws, or the more uncertain reliance on an attitude of mind and a sense of solidarity. For the Marxist it is the first which makes revolution necessary. For the anarchist, it is the second which makes revolution desirable.

For all that, both Marxism and anarchism have been "right" in the special sense that the weaknesses and ills of each have become the accurate prediction of the other. Marxists see the absurd in anarchism, its lack of a programme, the vagueness of its grand design. Anarchists see the implications of statism in Marxism, and the magnified control granted by the apparatus of industrial power. They find bureaucracy and control under socialism no more appetizing than under capitalism.

Perhaps, however, as issues are raised and morality speaks from impromptu pulpits in the socialist societies as well as in capitalist, anarchism is a language useful for identifying the more grotesque anomalies of these systems. It is a doctrine for the young in their anti-roles instead of being nursed along in dark and obscure places by the immigrant Italian printers in Buenos Aires or New York who carried the faded memories of their anarchist days carefully wrapped in the old newspapers of their minds. They had no hope, only regrets. Old anarchists have a better sense of tragedy than young ones.

Today's anarchism is fresh because its innocence grows out of the degenerate sophistication of the past, like the flower on the dungheap. Indeed that is precisely how it began, with "flower children" and "happenings". It is as if a new entrance to the corridor of the human mind had been suddenly exposed and an important part of a whole generation dashed down it expecting it to lead to unexpected but exciting outcomes. Today's anarchism randomizing the universe and hoping that by keeping it unpredictable, it will be possible to generate freedom, is a far cry from the rationalistic anarchism of the 19th century. It is no wonder that the elders of society shake their heads in disbelief. What they see and fear are the wonders of indiscipline, the medicines of hallucination, the physicalism which produces an erogenous solidarity, alternating periods of self withdrawal and intense social living, the privacy of total self preoccupation with the giving and sharing of the commune.

Certainly one message is clear. That is the growing importance of the fringe or the margin of society for the whole. For the first time, the margin of the society has the capacity to define the morality of the whole. What begins in society's moral rejection of some becomes the moral rejection of society itself. Anarchism is an important doctrine for this and it remains on the whole imbued with the moral. It also lacks humour, although it may embody sweetness. It has already shown great power to define caricature and assault. And it is not an accident that its first contemporary arena of action has been the universities for it is here that human promise seems to be sliced and packaged more systematically than in any other institution, and done with a more incredible piety. The universities are the instruments with the greatest singular significance in highly industrial societies because they create knowledge, define validity, establish priorities, and screen individuals accordingly. They thus represent all the inherited wisdom of the past which can then be used as a form of authority for the present. In this sense the central significance of the university as an arbiter of ideas and roles makes it the natural focus of attack. Moreover, precisely because the university provides the place of congregation, creates the groups and its facilities, much of the contemporary anarchist activity takes place in the university setting. Ex-students and "non-students" live around the university creating youth subcultures. But the focus is shifting. Groups of anarchists as well as individuals have become wanderers. They may be found in Nepal as well as on the left bank. They ask for little. They are willing to pay with their health. Violence and self-destruction are forms of existentially necessary penance. Every man is his own Christ.

REFERENCES

1   See P. Kropotkin, *Memoirs of a Revolutionist* (New York: Doubleday, Anchor Books, 1962), p. 299.
2   See Errico Malatesta, *Life and Ideas*, V. Richards, ed. (London: Freedom Press, 1965), p. 25.

3

Radicalization and Embourgeoisement: Hypotheses for a Comparative Study of History*

Comparative studies are moving into a stage where the technology of research can be fitted together with the more abstract components of research design and applied to case materials. When such a fit is more secure it will be possible to treat many cases and classes of events diachronically and synchronically. This represents a change from an earlier period when individual monographic studies were essential for the gathering of materials on exotic cultures and social systems in order to show how the parts of each made up a functioning system. Today, the research techniques and analytical constructs developed in industrial societies can not only be utilized by modernizing societies but can also be employed by historians for comparative purposes. Although the use of history, particularly in developmental analysis, has been a commonplace since Karl Marx, and Max Weber brought analytical historical comparisons to the status of a high art, most historians remain wary of sweeping historical generalizations and of the efforts of contemporary social science to be methodologically novel.

Whatever the view taken by historians, history as a form of data has no precinctual preserve or sanctuary. If social scientists make bad use of it, the problem is to improve their abilities; this is a matter of enlarging not only their detailed empirical knowledge, but their concepts as well. It may indeed be necessary to treat history explicitly as a testing ground for analytically derived propositions and, even in a rough-and-ready fashion, to plunder events in order to do hindsight analysis. Such analysis, if well done, should help to interpret known events differently. If it also allows us "metaphorical" projections from past to future in which discretely different events become analogues, so much the better.

* Reprinted from *The Journal of Interdisciplinary History*, 1 (Winter 1971), by permission of *The Journal of Interdisciplinary History* and The M.I.T. Press, Cambridge, Massachusetts.

To do this will often violate the texture and detail of the concrete historical occasion. But, since history is subject to continuous revision, such violations can only be regarded as minor transgressions. Moreover, they can be remedied. What is needed is a set of defining characteristics or structural boundaries which have an analytical durability of their own and by means of which "properties" of events can be revealed in their interrelationship. An appropriate set would serve as a framework for handling widely differing cases in space and time. We want to avoid the historical fallacy of taking the event for the universal, and instead see the universal in the event.

There is nothing in this suggestion which needs to affront the historians' canons of exactness and validity. An emphasis on analytical rather than concrete structure implies that historians, in deciding what information should be recorded, often assume that facts are like books in the library—the more you have, the better. The result is that historians become more like librarians and have a similar custodial view. Assumptions of causality, expressed as time-sequence, tend to generate epiphenomenal evidence in vast quantities with the danger that much of it is not evidence at all but mere pedantry. To put it another way, evidence changes in significance according to the theory employed, and in order to use historical facts one needs also to know the precise nature of the concepts being applied. One seeks, then, a method of working backward and forward between facts and theories, events and analytical structures. To find an underlying set of boundaries or principles is as important to the task as the discovery of a new set of facts. The latter can serve as a test of the former, and the former can suggest the relevance of the latter.

If the views just expressed are commonplace enough in the social sciences, they still have the capacity to infuriate some historians. Nor is this reaction limited to historians. Claude Levi-Strauss, for example, can make some historically minded sociologists, like George Homans, very unhappy with his presumptuous notion that there is a kind of linguistic template which underlies our thinking (which historians, like others, share with the savage mind) and which has a deeper level of "reality" than all of the events men can scrounge from oblivion. Of course it is true that ideas must square with the facts. That is why history is so important. But historians have been long on facts and short on ideas. Where are the contemporary versions of Frederic William Maitland or Paul Vinogradoff, Friedrich Meinecke or Ernst Troeltsch, Max Weber or Marc Bloch? Why is it that a Georges Lefebvre stands out so clearly? It is not only because of his facts, but because, as a Marxist of sorts, he at least has a general conception of analytical order to impose upon the chaos of historical events.

Here we represent a point of view opposite from the usual norms by which historians write history. We want to deal first with constructs which are related to each other. At a most general level we find three such boundary-setting notions. One is normative. It defines the cultural and ideological characteristics of meaning, i.e. the principles and priorities by which men live. A second is structural. It involves the roles (functionally defined and institutionalized positions in a social system) arranged in alternative sets of relationships. The third is behavioural. It deals with the perceptions and motivations of members of a community. The normative, the structural, and the behavioural constitute a framework for the analysis of choice. Choice is the single general problem common to all people at all times. Relationships among norms, structures, and behaviours are rarely in a good "fit" or balance. Norms change dialectically. Structures alter as the functions of roles vary. Behaviours change when perceptions differ and motives vary. Not only do the changing relationships of these three variables constitute a system; the first two, norms and structures, form the boundaries within which choice occurs, while the third, behaviour, indicates which of the choices will be selected. Any combination of these can be used as a method of determining hypotheses. In the essay which follows we shall deal primarily with norms and structures, indicating how they create particular systems of choice defined as political systems, and suggesting how these categories can be utilized in empirical work.

In order to keep our comments brief we have been gratuitously assertive in both the statement of the point of view and the description of the model. But a certain cantankerousness in expression should not be confused with bad humour. We want to be able to use history, work with historians, and engage them in an analytical dialogue. Otherwise they are in danger of becoming merely a research arm of the social scientist whenever he feels nostalgia for a backward glance. In turn social scientists are likely to lose all perspective and understanding of what it is they propose to analyse.

Since this paper will not attempt to handle technical matters, the cases as discussed will not serve as an ideal advertisement for our point of view. Our purpose is to illustrate through time and space a number of political systems on an impressionistic basis. We will not discuss the general design of the categories, for these have been articulated elsewhere in the form of a structural theory of politics.[1] Briefly, what is involved is an attempt to describe certain characteristics of political system change based on the normative and structural categories suggested above. We use four types of systems: *mobiliza-*

tion, the object of which is the realization of potentiality; *bureaucratic*, the object of which is the maintenance of control; *theocratic*, which is concerned with maintaining belief; and *reconciliation*, which is a system of bargaining.[2] The types themselves form two continuous variables: the degree of instrumentalization of political norms and the degree of hierarchy.

Each political system is conceived of as a combination of potentiality, control, belief, and bargaining. These we can regard as political universals. The particular combination they take in any concrete case will allow us to describe such a system as *predominantly* a mobilization system or a reconciliation system or whatever the case may be, depending on whether the distribution of political norms is predominatly consummatory or instrumental or the structure of authority is hierarchical or pyramidal.

In addition to defining these political system types analytically, we shall use certain stratification and representation categories to articulate those forces in a society with which governments must deal and which project a political system in one direction or another. These stratification categories are based on two criteria, the permeability of the boundaries, or mobility, and germaneness, or functionality. They are (1) segmentary, i.e. having a fixed membership which is highly solidaristic and includes caste and ethnic groupings with norms that are primordial and based on race, tribe, or religion; (2) fused, i.e. possessing well-defined boundaries, limited mobility, and normative ideologies that locate class interest; (3) differentiated, with weakly articulated boundaries expressive of competitive interests; and (4) functional status, with high mobility according to germane qualifications, and with norms of professional expertise.

These different stratification categories provide a base for elites whose participation in decision-making can be evaluated independently of the pattern of stratification. These elites create information that is transmitted to government and participate in coercive efforts, both in varying degrees and on behalf of or in collaboration with government. The functional criteria on which we rank elites are as follows: (1) goal specification, or the degree to which elites share in the organization and definition of political objectives; (2) central control, or the degree to which elites co-ordinate or coerce the system; and (3) institutional mediation, or the degree to which the elites perform both ideological and organizational brokerage functions aimed at minimizing structural and normative incongruities. These represent a minimal generalized set under which elite political activity can be subsumed.

This brings us to two hypotheses that can be profitably examined in the light of these categories. One is that the greater the degree of

modernization in a system, the greater the tendency toward *embourgeoisement*—while the greater the degree of industrialization, the
greater the tendency toward *radicalization*. The second is that the
greater the degree of *coercion* in a system, the less *information* there
is available to a government. These two hypotheses can be evaluated
in an impressionistic and limited way by reference to some empirical
cases. To operationalize them in the form of a theory would require
the quantification of each of the stratification and representation
variables (probably in the form of rankings of qualitative variables).

Of the four contemporary cases that we shall now introduce to
illustrate the assumptions from this theoretical base, two are industrial and two modernizing (one representing late-stage modernization
at the threshold of industrialization, and one early-stage modernization). Each represents different political approaches: in the industrial
societies, socialist and non-socialist; in the modernizing societies,
a variety of political systems. These illustrative cases—the United
States, the U.S.S.R., Argentina, and Ghana—are offered here as no
more than interpretative "glosses", to be followed by an even more
speculative effort to interpret and generalize their theoretical
implications.

THE UNITED STATES: AN INDUSTRIAL
RECONCILIATION SYSTEM

In our view, the United States confronts the emergence of a
meritocracy. This poses a central normative problem of highly industrial societies, namely, excessive instrumentalism. Riesman describes
this condition in the United States as follows:

> [The] scientific and rationalist temper of our meritocracy may undermine
> the morale of even those within its protection; it has no religious basis.
> Is America's romance with practicality and efficiency enough to sustain
> it? Men serving a system with no goal other than its own further
> advance have no transcendent aims. They are vulnerable to an inner and
> outer attack that criticizes them for sustaining a self-perpetuating
> structure, rather than helping to cure the diseases of society.[3]

Although aspects of the condition can be found unevenly distributed
in all industrialized societies, what Riesman describes is, above all,
an American problem. Representing the "developmental problem"
at the highest industrial level, it is likely to get rapidly worse. There
will be increasing conflict between competitive groupings within the
utilitarian sector of industrial society at the structural level, with
growing anti-utilitarianism generated by an equalitarian (equal
opportunity) ideological system at the normative. In rich capitalist

countries like the United States, and increasingly rich socialist ones,[4] well trained, well educated groups of functionally capable elites who are professionally powerful in their own societies but normatively estranged will trigger events leading to political system change. However, our present interest focuses on the United States and the problems particular to it.

In America, organizational power is the key to the political system. Features of this "organizational explosion" are temporariness of position, lack of inherited status stability, non-cumulative advantage, and continuous organizational competition. But along with such competitiveness goes bureaucracy. Bureaucracy is an attempt to impose stability on a society in continual competitive flux. Under these conditions, two types of conflicts can be identified. One is between organization-like interest groups. The other may be described as creativity versus bureaucracy—the most creative, technically advanced, and functionally useful individuals attempt to maximize their power and reduce the restrictiveness of the bureaucrats. The bureaucracy seeks to maintain stability, continuity, memory, and so on by enlarging its control over the powerful status elites. The more creative groups seek to free themselves from being "locked in" by the bureaucracy.

As a consequence of the "knowledge" and "organization" explosions of post-industrial America, small business men, insurance brokers, and managers, who during an earlier fused class industrial period were extremely important, are increasingly downgraded, making way for the more competitive status elites, bureaucratic or creative. They are becoming a "functionally disinherited" group. Of course, their downwardly mobile position in no way approaches in tragic implications that of the functionally superfluous ("poor whites", Negroes, Mexican-Americans, Indians) who have become the marginals of American society. For such groups, segmentary caste/ethnic factors become increasingly relevant as sources of identity and organizational power. Thus, the functionally superfluous use ideologies emphasizing primordial discrimination to legitimize and maximize their significance. Examples are "Black Power", the Third World Liberation Front, and other "nativistic" movements. It is as though the contents of the great "melting pot" had crystallized and shattered, with each fragment now trying to rework the entire contents according to its own image.

Apart from the unique plight of its functionally superfluous, the United States shares systems problems of other industrial societies. We shall summarize these problems briefly as they relate to the current situation in America before proceeding to more particular considerations of their origins.

The American pattern of industrialization has created a universalized differentiated pattern of stratification. In outline it consists of a residual segmentary caste and fused class section composed of the downwardly mobile and/or the functionally superfluous. At the top of the functional stratification hierarchy are the most creative and the most successful professionals. In the middle, increasingly bureaucratized and in varying degrees mobile, are the solidly established range of bureaucratically organized roles—administrator, technician, teacher, corporate executive, civil servant. Between these two levels are some who, although qualified, are reluctant to be part of the bureaucracy, and others who, although educationally qualified, fail to reach the top of the hierarchy—perhaps for lack of genuine excellence or creativity, repugnance for the system, or various combinations of both. These form a potential revolutionary core articulating new values. High standards of excellence combined with normative estrangement and doubts about the value of functional relevance are reflected in anger and hostility toward the meritocracy system. These we can call "bourgeois radicals". They are mainly intellectuals and students (and now including some Negro and Third World militants) who have a tendency to romanticize the functionally superfluous and to try to mobilize them for change by calls for militant action. The functionally superfluous remain largely indifferent, however, except insofar as they are interested in the upward mobility of "embourgeoisement". Many lean toward traditionalism and conservatism, and a few show a capacity for joy in immediate emotional or sensual expression, including religious ecstasy. More common is an apparent incapacity for planning far into the future and a consequent lack of responsiveness to available educational opportunities. Where they break through these boundaries, they often find themselves thwarted because they lack necessary language skills or because the temperament necessary for survival in ghettos is not easily adapted to learning in disciplined courses or training programmes. Frustrated, alienated, and potentially destructive, the functionally superfluous marginals may or may not become temporary adherents to radical causes, but they are not likely to contribute to a sustained radical mobilization effort. For these and other reasons, radicalism from above and embourgeoisement from below can make common and temporary coalitions, but not common cause. In addition, in the context of a democratic reconciliation system like the American, there is increasing competition for access at the elite level among segmentary, fused, differentiated, and functional status groups. Such competition takes the form of elite efforts to participate in goal specification, central control, and institutional mediations. This has several effects. It makes authoritative decision-making extremely difficult, and accountability perfunctory and unpredictable. In addition, since high levels of information do not result in a corresponding capacity for government to make use of such information in effective decision-making, many basic problems remain unresolved. This predicament is one of the most dangerous in the United States today. In an earlier time, a certain enlightened rationality (despite the gaudy atmosphere of populist politics) provided better scope for individual leadership. Now that all is organized, bureaucratic, *and competitive*, it is somehow less rational. (It is perhaps the non-rationality produced by competitive rationalities.) Also a certain innocence is gone from American life and with it the bland hope of progress. In the past, competitive coalitions operated under a condition of marginal gains so that a proximate utilitarianism worked as an integrative force. Today the emphasis is on marginal losses and protections, with negative or malintegrative consequences.

One reason for this is sheer structural complexity. But another is normative, a decline in legitimizing consummatory values, i.e. those embodying ultimate normative ends. How did these values decline? Is there an end to the process? Probably not. Such changes are long-term and slow in coming. Perhaps it was the assassination of President Kennedy—certainly a dramatic turning-point—or the war in Vietnam that helped make visible a crisis of role and priority.[5] American society has undergone a change from a reconciliation system with many strong theocratic elements to a reconciliation system without them, leaving a diversity of "populist" groupings morally defenceless, confused, and with a weakened sense of solidarity.

What were some of these original theocratic elements? The conditions of our origins and the formation of the society, as Lipset shows in *The First New Nation*, were associated with a deistic optimism (a belief in the perfectibility of man), moral inspiration, and superb resources and opportunities—including a highly educated leadership, a resourceful population, and great and easily available natural resources.[6] The various communities depended upon a kind of enlightened Protestantism, which, although containing its own bigotry (as manifested in attacks on Catholics and other immigrant populations during the nineteenth century), implied a pattern of reserved but appropriate behaviour, embodied in the normative principles of Unitarianism, Congregationalism, and Presbyterianism for the fused class elites, while ruder forms of a similar ethic prevailed for the "lower classes"—Lutherans, Methodists, and the like.

When Catholicism spread, it combined normative religious conflict with class conflict. This is why "allegiance", rather than religious doctrine *per se*, became the point of the dialectic between Protestants and Catholics in the United States. Protestants attacked Catholics not only because of the question of papal supremacy and loyalty but also because they were aliens of a different ethnic background. Catholics, it was said, placed the Pope first, the President second. They were Irish or Italian or Polish first, American second.

If the religious dimension posed a normative problem, the absorption of immigrants was an extremely important structural one. This was particularly the case for those groups—Irish, Poles, Portuguese, Germans and Jews[7]—which were forced to amalgamate in ghettos and accommodate the different caste/ethnic population. These not only inhabited the urban areas but gradually spread to adjacent rural communities. They not only helped to develop suburban and intermediate communities, but also shifted the basic rural quality of American life away from the ideal. These groups created a new environment. Their problems were different from those of the marginal groups, which are by no means limited to blacks. But the latter, the only large group which could not own property because they themselves were property, represent the most important marginal group in the country. In cities they were ostracized outwardly because of colour and alienated inwardly because they were not geared to the pace of industry, its mechanisms, or its depersonalization. In the cities they were forced into lowly jobs (when they could get employment) and sank to the bottom of the fused class strata.[8] In the country, they remained bound to the land as sharecroppers or domestics even when they were freed. Their plight—along with that of the rest of the rural poor—was ignored as the nation became increasingly industrialized.

Such changes resulted in the downgrading of sectarian deistic or Protestant beliefs, the progressive secularization of the schools and the upgrading of a general "promised-land-chosen-people" form of nationalist ideology—the general term for it being "Americanism". Precisely because it was devoid of specific content, it conveyed a certain buoyancy, a pattern of belief acceptable to all—Catholic, Protestant, and Jew, and even the black.

The rise of "Americanism" coincided with rapid industrialization and collective mobility. None of the immigrant groups remained permanently a part of one working class in the sense of a focused class proletariat. Until World War I, few competing solidaristic ideologies made their appearance, such as socialist movements. The development of trade unions with radical ideologies such as the I.W.W. never occurred but rather a highly instrumentalistic preference manifested itself in effective bargaining. Class crystallization never occurred.[9] Fused class confrontations—polarization of large numbers of proletarians and of small numbers of owners—were to some extent prevented at the top by anti-trust laws and to a larger extent by the fact that the post-Civil War rural landowning class was small and politically powerful only in the West, the "rural proletariat" consisting of Negroes and other "imported" caste/ethnic groups. Instead, a middle class—which was commercial, semi-urban, and distributive—grew rapidly as a consequence of industrial development.

Yet sufficient fused class identification existed to promote the organization of trade unions. This organization was often accompanied by violence. If search for greater equity accorded well with ideologies of "Americanism", the issue of specific populist claims to access could be fought out in the name of specific demands in a framework of collective bargaining. The principle to be fought for and won was the basic right to organize. (Characteristically, Negro and other agricultural workers remained outside the battle.)

In other words, development in the form of industrial expansion of the system was accompanied by claims to access based on functional significance in terms of work essential to industry. Widened choice of occupation seemed to certify the existing nationalist consummatory values embodied in "Americanism". The "chosen-people" ideology gave way to the more visible testimonials of success in the form of growing productivity and an increasingly higher standard of living. Moreover, greater participation by various groups—interest, populist, and professional—not only created information, but also indicated the priorities for pay-off necessary in order to keep the system balanced. During the Depression, when the numbers of the functionally superfluous grew alarmingly and pay-off was at a low, fused class polarization reached its high, this time including rural conflict between landowners and farm workers in the West. However, immediately after the Depression, particularly from the Roosevelt period onward, it was the growing professional elite, using the rationale of Keynesianism (or economism of some sort), that was able to influence interest rates and to introduce deficit financing as well as other mechanisms of monetary policy, including controversial farm subsidies.

Thus, what revolutionary potential existed during the post-Depression 1930s was rapidly eliminated as differentiated class opportunities began to expand. Unions became bureaucratized, with their elites given a larger share in goal specification, institutional mediation, and eventually central control. Meanwhile, the rapid expansion of interest groups enabled differentiated class groupings to manipulate Congress and force action on special consumer, producer, ethnic, urban, or rural claims. Populist rewards could be made on the basis of general welfare considerations, the size of the voting population, and the degree of party organization. As a system, it was fluid, clumsy, and vulgar and had fearful "ups" and "downs"; but, on the whole, it worked.

The situation today renders the old solutions more difficult. During the period of the absorption of immigrants and the embourgeoisement of the working class, Negroes (as well as all agricultural workers' were left out. The "black bourgeoisie" that did develop was residual, a fused class rather than an industrial proletarian class. Those who felt their exclusion most keenly are now organizing in much the same fashion as did the trade unions, but in doing so they are faced with the meritocracy problem.[10] It is therefore more difficult for Negroes and other Third World ethnic groups to accept the original trade union pattern. Increasingly their situation is a common predicament shared with all of those who are at the bottom of the functional hierarchy, including those who drop down from the "old" fused middle class and the lower echelons of the new differentiated (or multi-bonded) class, i.e. those strategic marginals who lack solidaristic class affiliations, skill, and knowledge.

Furthermore, because of its high degree of voluntarism, multiple access of widening elites to decision-making, and very high accountability, the American system had traditionally managed to stimulate new information and apply it in decision-making with little need for coercion. Now there is an information glut on the one hand and an organizational failure on the other. The visible "products" of superiority—industrial products—have gradually come to represent the consummatory values of the society. "Americanism" has lost its normative content: the New Jerusalem has become a New Babylon.

One response to the crisis has been a revival of primordial United States utopianism. An appeal to ideological nationalism in a holy crusade against Communism has animated the radical right with its nostalgic view of rural or suburban middle-fused-class America—its white clapboard churches, its Rotarian clubs, its Carnegie libraries, and its doctors and lawyers as intellectuals rather than scientists and writers. At the same time, right-wing nationalists elevate the importance of industrial functionalism and applied technology (as opposed to creative scientific achievement). The response of the radical left has been a similar revival of old ideologies, such as militant Marxism, and newer ones such as Maoism, and even a revived and modified anarchism.

In spite of this revival and continued attempts to find new ideologies, the United States system has exceptional latitude in the sense that its degree of payoff will sustain it for a long time to come. Moreover, the great virtue of a democratic form of the reconciliation system, despite its obvious defects, is that, except under very difficult circumstances, it has the capacity for using conflict as a perpetual source of normative rejuvenation. Militant "marginals" such as Negroes who demand "Black Power", intellectual activists, and students give voice to demands that are essentially populist in that they are directed to the satisfaction of pluralistic public needs.

No matter how much these spokesmen for the marginals (who cannot or will not speak for themselves) claim to be "against the system", they are precisely the ones who in the final sense are for it. They force the society to review the significance of its norms and to modify its values, just as they force liberals and others to recognize that their own well-meaning tolerance and promotion of marginal goals from a safe distance may simply serve as a way of rationalizing an unacceptable *status quo*.

THE CASE OF ARGENTINA:
RECONCILIATION AND THE FAILURE TO INDUSTRIALIZE

Argentina, which was regarded in 1930 as one of the world's industrial countries, is now considered one of the "less-developed". In a sense, it has beome "de-industrialized"—a unique achievement, to say the least. Whereas Poland and Yugoslavia are just over the "industrialization" line, Argentina is now just under it.

Like the United States, Argentina is an immigrant new world community. In sharp contrast to the United States, however, it was never Protestant: its colonial antecedents were Spanish, not English, and it never created a theocratic New Jerusalem. The bureaucratic system created by the Spaniards was persistent, perhaps because it was periodically reformed (as when the Rio de la Plata area was freed from restrictions on trade administered from the Vice-Royalty of Peru, and Buenos Aires became the seat of a new Vice-Royalty).

Certain superficial parallels with the United States exist. Argentina became independent in 1818 under the leadership of José de San Martin, a national hero comparable to George Washington. Its first centralized constitution was unacceptable to the rural *caudillos* despite early urbanization. In 1869 the first census in Argentina already showed a population of 1,800,000 inhabitants. Here the similarities end. Of this population, one-tenth lived in the city of Buenos Aires and one-third in the city and province of Buenos Aires. Four-fifths of the people lived in huts of twigs, cane, or straw, with earth floors, and at least 78 per cent were illiterate.[11]

Argentina's system had become instrumentalized despite a romanticized nationalist ideology. The content of this ideology was individualistic and escapist—as if the prevailing belief system in the United States had been based upon the "cowboy" ethic rather than upon more puritanical beliefs. Colonial consummatory values, associated with the primary stages of Spanish colonialism, combined Catholic beliefs, endowed with the reforming zeal of the Inquisition, and a highly organized system of mercantilist exploitation of gold and silver. These values, representing the Crown, never prevailed in Argentina. The decline of Catholic consummatory values and the mercantilistic system that stultified other Latin American countries coincided with the rise of Argentina and the growth there of commercial settlement. In Argentina the corrupt colonial system was quickly superseded by a growing urban fused class, a type of bourgeoisie intermediate between native Indians (and the rural Spaniards who replaced them) and the bureaucracy of the Crown. This new class produced a system change well before the formal recognition of independence.

Hence Argentina's war of liberation was not waged to create a new society (an important objective of the American revolution), but merely to relieve the nation of colonial abuses. Immediately after independence, conflict broke out between rural Spanish *haciendados* and *gauchos*, identified with romantic nationalism, on the one hand, and the urban *portenos*, identified with commercial enterprise, on the other. This conflict reflected basic differences over access to government—populist and interest, rural and urban, agricultural and business.

In a certain sense, the issues of independence were settled before the campaign began, while the unsolved problems existing at independence remain to this day.[12] In our terms, Argentina went through a period of bureaucratic colonialism that lacked the originating significance of the more militant early colonial period (such as that which obtained in Peru). In 1810, the date of the Revolution, there was created a reconciliation system without any prior theocratic elements, which depended upon the instrumental pay-off of the system for its viability. (This lasted intermittently from 1810 to 1928, and from 1853 to 1930.) On the whole, the system was successful; but it was troubled by periods of instability in which access alternated between the rural populists and the commercial interests of the *portenos*.[13]

Coalitions at the rural caste level were sustained in patron–client relationships. What consummatory values there were were embodied in these primordial attachments of rural caste relations; and in Buenos Aires, just as in the United States, fused class conflicts between the working poor and the wealthier commercial bourgeoisie heralded the beginnings of class conflict.

The fact that the United States in 1852 became a "model" for Argentina's political system points up the underlying differences between the two countries. After the fall of Juan Rosas' military regime in 1852, an attempt was made to create an American-style democratic reconciliation system.[14] Conflicts within the various caste and fused class groupings were such that coalitions which cut across rural–urban and unitary–federal lines were possible. The ideal of a commercial society—which demonstrated a high degree of civic virtue, was anti-*gaucho* in its inspiration, and was augmented by European immigration—has been most closely associated with Domingo F. Sarmiento. But the coalitions were frangible; competition between elites for access often broke down in provincial rebellion. Fraud and corruption emphasized the more immediate and short-term advantages of public office, and the shift to a more coercive alternative was the result. Growing coercion was a prelude to local secrecy and led ultimately to rebellions, resulting in a shift to a more bureaucratic system-type under General Julio Roca, who was a hero of the Indian wars. A period of military rule followed.

Thus we see two major patterns in this case. The first is a continuous record of political system change between two predominant types, bureaucratic and reconciliation, neither of which ever quite succeeded; each one, however, altered the access of various groups to representation and decision-making. High information alternated with periods of high coercion, resulting sometimes in system-change within the same regime, and sometimes in shifts between regime types. At the same time, immigration from many areas, similar to that of the eastern seaboard of the United States, brought in increasing numbers of Germans, Italians, Poles, and Eastern European Jews, most of whom remained in Buenos Aires, but many of whom went into the rural areas. A commercial market resulted, leading the way to industrialization.

Argentina modernized as the population grew. The immigrant population consisted mainly of those accustomed to urban living and occupations. A reservoir of skill and talent, especially in trades, was readily available. The problem was lack of opportunity. There was little conflict between fused class groups, and it tended to be vitiated by the openness of the commercial middle class. Enlarged, too, was a differentiated multi-bonded group that lived in the suburbs of Buenos Aires—well educated and increasingly professional (especially engineers and lawyers). This period (1916–30) was most clearly identified with the Hipólito Irigoyen/Marcelo Alvear regimes. Argentina became an entrepreneurial paradise, with easy access to the functional elite. The ruling Radical Party was in reality a mechanism for organized plunder, and, while creating opportunities for industrialization, it also allowed fantastic waste and misallocation of resources.

Since 1930, which marked the beginning of the revolution which threw the Irigoyen government out of office, Argentina has been in search of a political system with consummatory values appropriate to development.[15] Some leaders, like Juan Perón (1946–55), have favoured a mixture of fascist and radical ideas under a pseudo-technocratic elite in which elements of populism and primordial loyalties could be used to create new stratification groupings around a disciplined fused working class, controlling (in the sense of keeping in check) a largely irresponsible class of foreign-dominated expatriate industrialists. This mixture of corporatist ideas, xenophobia, and populism comprises a somewhat familiar synthesis of primordial and corporate consummatory values.

Curiously enough, the Perón government failed to act upon these principles. Its first efforts to create a mobilization system lacked conviction. Its ideology, although elaborate lacked the zealot's reforming eye. The newly mobilized groups became bargaining levers in the hands of Perón, rather than the nucleus of a new society. After some initial economic success, the regime was held together by increasing pay-offs on the one hand and increasing coercion on the other. The latter resulted in intensified efforts to overthrow the regime.

Perón represented the first major effort to link a structural group—a "class"—to a bureaucratic-technocratic elite, giving both exceptional representation by allowing them access to the functions of the elite while excluding others. Trade unions participated in goal specification and, increasingly, in central control. But Perón failed to create a universalizing mobilization system and instead presided over a bureaucratic polity in which embourgeoisement increased but industrialization did not. He extended embourgeoisement by incorporating the working class into the process, increasing its significance as an interest group, and giving broader access to elites. Although the essentially derivative character of the society and the economy did not change, the demands upon his government increased. The response was pay-off, not mobilization.

The next meaningful political shift after Perón was to a reconciliation system under President Arturo Frondizi. It failed in its attempt to control short-term coalitions composed of increasingly competitive differentiated class groupings. However, it gave "technocrats" and other professionals and intellectuals greater access to government. Centralized planning was attempted in order to rectify and stabilize the economy, but its failure polarized functionally significant groups, such as interest groups, and the intellectuals and professionals.

The critical long-term normative problem of Argentina is that its consummatory "space" or normative vacuum has never been filled. Those who would fill this space include nostalgic *peronistas* who have transformed Perón's doctrines into a limited but varied mythology relating student radicals, *fidelistas*, Trotskyites, and militants of all kinds. In the middle are the Catholic technocrats who see in Roman Catholicism a new civic culture attuned to the needs of industrial society.

These last represent the norms of the present predominantly bureaucratic systems first of General Juan Onganía and currently of Roberto Marcelo Levingston. However, the degree of embourgeoisement and industrialization that exists today in Argentina is precisely what prevents any kind of effective use of either information or disciplined coercion. As a result, the symptoms of competitive normative withdrawal, similar to some of those currently plaguing the United States, are common. The coercive propensities of the regime restrict the flow of information and innovation. The flight of *intellectual capital* alone is very significant, and there is much random political violence. At the same time, the rate of pay-off (for all except rural marginals or recent urban marginals, as in the United States) is sufficiently high to prevent radicalization. "Pay-off" provides a maximum coalitional base and prevents the crystallization of cleavages likely to lead to populist revolutions from below (as contrasted with Cuba, for example). Although it allows a very modest net gain in industrialization and per capita income, there will be periodic unrest and populist violence led by revolutionary "bourgeois radicals" among the intellectuals, primarily from the differentiated class sector of society. Since these represent "privileged marginals", however, they are as vulnerable as they are radical. If Argentina has successfully avoided the meritocracy problem of the United States by failing to realize full industrial potentiality, it lacks the latter's capacity as a democracy to rejuvenate consummatory values through normative conflict.

Whereas the United States is vulnerable to its own success, Argentina is hardened to its own failure. Uncertainty, short-term rationality, and political system-change—all cause the people to harbour a deep distrust of political solutions.

THE CASE OF THE U.S.S.R.:
FROM MOBILIZATION TO BUREAUCRACY

Our analysis here will be limited to four regimes, which can be labelled Tsarism, Leninism, Stalinism, and Khrushchevism. Normatively they represent a mixture of Great Russian millennialism with the more theocratic aspects of Marxism.[16]

It Tsarism is regarded as a mixed bureaucratic-theocratic system in which religion was important to the legitimacy of the state, then the greater the degree of secularization, the more residual was legitimacy itself and the greater the problem of control. In opposition to Tsarism, however, the Soviet Union began not as a bureaucratic-theocratic system but as a mobilization system. As the consummatory values it embodied broke down, it became ritualized and dogmatized, and increasingly faced a similar control problem because of the theocratic vision which was embodied within its bureaucratic framework. Systemic pulls in these opposite directions generated further coercion and a resulting decline in information. In effect, the political effect of Stalinism was to narrow the forms of information to economic information and loyalty, while maximizing control, a condition more possible in the early stages of industrialization than later. Since the government of an industrialized society needs a high level of information in order to prevent the curtailment of industrialization, there must be a wider sharing in elite representation and access. This was the situation under Khrushchev, who took the first steps to recognize the systemic "pull" away from a predominantly bureaucratic system to that of a reconciliation system—a course also being pursued in Yugoslavia, Hungary, and Czechoslovakia, and to a lesser extent in Poland.

A characteristic of the Soviet pattern on the innovative side is that it foresaw more clearly than most revolutionary situations the central role of intellectuals. The legitimizing value of potentiality as an ideology had more diverse sources than the purely Marxian. The revolutionary temper in Russia was articulated by the intelligentsia: gentry like Alexander Herzen, bourgeois radicals like Lenin and Leon Trotsky, and the Polish–Jewish Marxists, such as Rosa Luxemburg. Moreover, intellectuals drew much of their support from theorists and writers outside the Russian tradition, some earlier than Marx himself (François Emile Babeuf and Claude Henri de Saint Simon), as well as from later Marxists, Karl Kautsky, Eduard Bernstein, and other revisionists. Enlightenment, intellectuality, a theocratic vision, and a visible despotism characterized the socialist elite that fought Tsarism, producing an original dialectic between primordial religiosity and visionary enlightenment, or pure belief and chiliastic rationalism.

One organizational result of such diversity was orthodox Leninism, which disciplined and narrowed the priorities of internal controversy by means of a "revolutionary bureaucracy". After the chaos of the civil war, this buraucracy became a dominant structural characteristic of the Soviet system. The immediate post-revolutionary period was, however, one of continuous experimentation, and even the specific shape of the regime was an open question, especially for the intellectuals. Government was the property of a small disciplined band of intellectuals which included professionals like the economist Grigoriy Sokolnikov, military intellectuals like Vladimir Antonov-Ovseenko, and those interested in educational reform and cultural experimentation, like A. V. Lunacharsky. The promise of the revolution was in reality a challenge to the intellectuals' creativity at both the theoretical and the tactical level, and the intellectuals sought to rely on the party as a captive weapon for innovation.

The use of the party as an instrument of Marxist doctrine meant the triumph of reason and materialism as instruments of social progress. War, revolution, famine, and economic paralysis, and years of exile, imprisonment, studying, and writing had created the revolutionary consciousness through which the despairing public could be manipulated. The resulting political system was both a bureaucratic and a mobilization system. Throughout the period exceptional access was granted to military leaders, whose exploits saved the revolution and whose presence was necessary because of the isolated and vulnerable position of the U.S.S.R. With the help of the Red Army, the Red Guards, the secret police, and the militia, a mobilization system was organized to transform the entire system of social stratification. The aim was to create a new society in which exploitation would be ended and a more humane, equalitarian condition would be realized: the theocratic goal of applied Marxism.

These three pulls, the mobilization, bureaucratic, and theocratic, have been visible throughout the life of the Soviet Union. As industrialization has proceeded, two types of bureaucratic elites have formed, each with enormous access to government in terms of sharing in goal specification and central control. First, the engineering planner or technocrat assumed an exceptional role because, as the revolution came to an end, the task of restoring some semblance of normal economic life was a first priority. The measures taken by this group, while having the appearance of planned strategy through centralized fiscal action, were mainly improvisations to meet emergencies, especially during the periods of military Communism and the New Economic Policy (N.E.P.).

The second group, the intellectuals, ran the government, which was to be the instrument of those grand architects of potentiality, Trotsky, Nikolai Bukharin, and Lev Kamenev (to name only a few who originally provided the meaning and direction of the revolution and were to become its victims). Whereas the economic technocrats were functionally critical for development, and the military technocrats were essential for survival against outside intervention, the non-technocratic intellectuals had a different function. They were the chief recipients of information, which they translated into alternative solutions to immediate problems. Their assets for this role were a cultivated sense of history and a philosophy that embodied consummatory values capable of being integrated with the instrumental ones put forward by the technocrats. Although they did not hesitate to use coercion, in general they were opposed to it as a regular feature of decision-making.

Moreover, they had the support of the general public—populist support of a kind rarely extended to intellectuals. Perhaps in the end such support was also a snare, for leaders can easily become the prisoners of their own mass public: an organized bureaucratic system was essential to secure freedom of action in decision-making. This bureaucracy took shape not within the Red Army, but within the party. The party was the link to the people, whose representative access was accepted in principle only to be rejected in practice. Populist elites came to share minimally in the information side of government and maximally in the coercive side. Those who represented the information side gradually lost significance and found their access reduced. As this happened, the need for coercion became more and more apparent. Uprisings occurred, beginning as early as 1921 at Kronstadt; fears of subversion grew.

In the party, Stalin tried to create a mobilization system that combined primordial consummatory values and Marxian universalistic ones. The doctrine of socialism in one country was not merely a tactic of practical politics brought about by the failure to materialize of the German revolution. It also served to narrow the millennial appeal of Communism and, by mixing it with nationalistic routines and downgrading nationalist and ethnic groupings to the category of living museums, to parochialize it. But within the mobilization system was a bureaucracy organized so ruthlessly that the intellectuals in control of it eventually became the instruments of their own downfall.[17]

To prevent the mobilization objectives of the regime from being undermined, the coercive factor was raised to unbelievable heights. As a result, a peculiar inversion process began to occur, with individuals sustaining a belief in consummatory values because failure to do so was too dangerous. But the losses in information under Stalinism were tremendous. Although the possibilities for a system change were postponed (through the continuous deification of Stalin, the intensification of indoctrination about his omniscience, and so on), change, in our terms, actually took place within the shell of the mobilization system. This became visible even before World War II. The mobilization system had disappeared, and the bureaucratic system had taken over. The functionality of the managers and technicians, although uncertainly accepted as a criterion for leadership, became increasingly entrenched. Meanwhile, the intellectuals who had been the architects of the mobilization system had all been killed, and the military bureaucrats severely restricted, especially after the war. Instrumentalism reigned supreme. Hierarchy was the political order of the day.

The decline in consummatory values was immediately apparent in the new post-war generation of intellectuals (the so-called gilded generation), particularly those who represented the best-educated children of the bureaucrats and technocrats who had sustained Stalin's bureaucracy (including Stalin's daughter). Poetry became a weapon of revolt by highlighting the search for consummatory meaning. Young intellectuals demanded equity in the political sphere and freedom as an absolute value. But even the instrumentalistic were dissatisfied, and many of them clamoured for structural reform in the form of decentralization, greater competitive access, and economic representation. The technocrats' demand for more autonomy on the structural level indicated a direction of structural change toward a reconciliation system through a "managerial" revolution. Their emphasis on greater efficiency (required if crucial information is to be produced, and decision-making made more effective) and the intellectuals' efforts to create new consummatory values in the historically more liberal context of Marxism point to a need for a more democratic system of equity and greater governmental accountability.

What the Soviet case illustrates is the tendency toward a system-change in which the growing functional access of technocrats is supported by an increase of need for information to sustain the expanding industrial system that fathers creative and scientific ideas and technology. Needed, too, is a drastic reduction in coercion or its threat. But in the Soviet Union coercion can be reduced only with the rise of new consummatory values, those which invoke some of the *original technocratic* vision of the early revolutionaries and liberal Marxism. Otherwise the entire political structure is likely to lose its legitimacy. The technocratic tendency exerts a bureaucratic-reconciliation "pull", resulting in conflicts over which of the elites should rule, how representative the system should be, and which kinds of access should be made more freely available. Meanwhile, the intellectuals (symbolized by Andrei D. Sinyavsky, Yuli M. Daniel, Pavel M. Litvinov, and others) apply pressure for change in the direction of a theocratic-reconciliation system. The question is how these two could be brought into meaningful resolution, if, in fact, it were possible to do so.

Any effort to realize these tendencies concretely requires basic reform at the political level, particularly the establishment of high accountability, high participation, and high access. The government has dealt very harshly with the freethinking intellectuals, clearly recognizing the normative threat they imply.[18] Also, because of the highly coercive character of the government (and the corresponding subservience of the elites), information is lacking at the populist level, so that no one knows how much loyalty there is to the system as presently constituted, especially after the belief in Stalinist invincibility and omnipotence was shattered in 1956 at the Twentieth Congress by Khrushchev's speech. More likely than basic political reform is a growing acceptance by the government of decentralization on instrumental grounds, with representation extended to interest groups, particularly the most functional, while interest group information becomes more freely available.

The new Soviet technocrat may also be an intellectual with an increasing interest in a more open and experimental cultural environment for art, literature, science, and criticism. Moreover, as the need for new information rises, it is possible that the intellectuals will become more instrumentalistic and the technocrats more consummatory in their outlook (while the main enemy remains the party hacks).[19] How long such a process will take is by no means clear. Nor is it a purely domestic affair. Certainly influences are at work that began in Yugoslavia and reached their sharpest form in Czechoslovakia (long the most bureaucratic of the Soviet bloc societies). Each is experimenting with changes that involve broadening the structure of accountability, providing more populist representation, whether through the workplace or the party, and, as a consequence, increasing the access of elites. These structural reforms may carry with them consummatory values embodying norms of freedom, privacy, and the protection of the individual through law. It is extremely important to note that the claims being made for basic structural reform emphasize not revolution but, quite the contrary, stricter observance of the law by the government, which in practical terms means restrictions on its coercive powers. Nor is it without significance that the case in which these demands for reform were strongest was Czechoslovakia, the *most industrialized* of all the countries in the Soviet bloc. The spearhead of such normative demands is composed mainly of scientists and students, whose presence is a testimonial to the functional needs of the industrial society.

The functional tendency toward pluralistic groupings, the growing competition between elites for participation, and the widening of access to decision-making as a result of decentralization of leadership in enterprises, combined with the ritualization of originating norms, imposed severe strains on the present system—strains most evident in the recent suppression in Czechoslovakia. The U.S.S.R. has lost its mobilization characteristics and is pulled between the bureaucratic system, which is its predominant political tendency, and a reconciliation system made more compelling by the existing lacuna in consummatory values.

The present Soviet leaders do not know how to deal with such political system "drift". They are frightened by the tendencies manifested in their neighbours. They could not tolerate the Czech's move toward the reconciliation pattern with its structural decentralization and potential for the development of pyramidal authority, justified both on instrumental grounds and on the basis of a revival of Marxian consummatory values in a liberal form. However, they must (at least temporarily) tolerate the fact that the mixture of theocratic and mobilization tendencies that formed the once-powerful moral impetus and background for Soviet legitimacy has been taken over by China. Thus, the consummatory values of modern militant Marxism are Maoist, while the structural patterns (although hierarchical) have become *decentralized*, to permit populist participation on many issues. The question is whether a political "ceiling" has been reached in the Soviet Union. It remains to be seen whether the present bureaucratic system can do other than contribute to a political systems change.

Although both may have reached a political ceiling, the difference between the changes taking place in the post-industrial Soviet Union and the post-industrial United States are vast. In this sense a "convergence" theory is misleading. In the one case, the decline in consummatory values creates the crisis—a crisis of meaning. In the other, the reaffirmation of consummatory values creates a crisis of structure. The one is a condition of high information and semi-paralysis, the other a condition of growing information and increasing structural ambiguity. What has happened, of course, is that the U.S.S.R. has changed political systems types according to its stage of development. It used a mobilization system to initiate industrialization, moved into a bureaucratic period of consolidation, and now, as a highly industrialized nation, is pulled increasingly toward a reconciliation system. In both cases it is difficult to know where the processes will end. But it is easy to see the "dialectic" that could be possible between them. In this larger sense, East is attractive to West and West to East in consummatory terms. Their intellectuals want some of what we have. Our intellectuals want some of what they have. And, in both cases, it is the intellectuals, particularly the younger ones, who create the bridge.

THE CASE OF GHANA: SYSTEMS CHANGE IN A SMALL SPACE

Ghana represents an early-stage modernizing society that has gone through a series of political system-changes rather rapidly since achieving independence in 1957. At independence there was a reconciliation system based mainly on the British pattern of parliamentary government that had evolved on a constituency basis and a local government pattern under the aegis of the colonial authorities. The Nkrumah government, itself democratically elected, had created in the Convention People's Party an effective electoral instrument and a national movement prior to independence, and its success was the main factor in the final devolution of authority.

The first political system-change occurred in 1961 when the party was elevated to a central and coercive role, in which goal specification became minimal, central control extremely important, and institutional mediation a primary objective. Elite access was increasingly restricted to party officials, supporters, and selected foreign advisers. The system became a predominantly mobilization type, in which functional auxiliaries of the party served as the new representative elites, with considerable access, displacing the representatives of the constituencies (the parliamentarians).

As this process occurred, the structure of accountability was basically altered, consent groups like the Supreme Court and Parliament were reduced in significance, and three groups—technocrats, bureaucrats, and party officials—were in effective competition for access to decision-making, with the latter increasingly playing a coercive role and the first two an informational one. Particular groupings in the caste/ethnic sector were excluded from participation, and attacks were made on their leadership, especially among groups whose ethnicity and chieftaincy formed a natural basis for opposition. Non-universalistic or competitive consummatory values (for example, those of religiously based political parties such as the Muslim Association Party) were attacked and restricted in political significance.

Consummatory values were manipulated in the form of the doctrine of Nkrumahism, which incorporated certain traditionalistic ideological characteristics, in particular communalism. The resulting emphasis on *African* socialism was combined with a more explicit form of neo-Marxism, African *socialism*. The goal was a new moral community organized around mixed private and public enterprise, a high degree of centralized planning, and a universalizing African mission in the form of pan-Africanism; it would be run by a "vanguard" party similar to a communist party, with its own ideological institute.

Particular attempts were made to insure that this mobilization system would take on a certain permanence, given its domestic task of rapid development and its foreign or pan-African role of mounting an African revolution. On the normative side, both these objectives were made part of the same process and embodied in a larger vision of black liberation throughout the world. Kwame Nkrumah was the personification of this, and he became the symbol of the revolution itself.

Structurally, there was little effort to alter the existing arrangements, and the stratification system remained much as it had always been, with a large caste/ethnic tribal system, on which a small fused class of merchants and a miniscule group of miners and industrial workers had been superimposed. Because of increased development, urbanization, and education, there was a rapid growth in the differentiated class of civil servants, educators, schoolteachers, and politicians—all products of embourgeoisement. This group engaged in competitive coalitions that vitiated attempts at structural reform. By increasing the number of unofficial points at which elite access could occur, they simply expanded opportunities for corruption. Hence, Ghana represented a dual tendency—the desire to establish a mobilization system in the first flush of independence, and the residual tendency to sustain by various means the reconciliation aspects of the society.[20]

The effects of both tendencies were resolved in favour of a bureaucratic system in the form of a "neo-mercantilist" presidential monarchy. Capricious rule, increasingly sustained by the police, signified a general increase in coercion by means of preventive detention and other similar ordinances. This increase led to losses of information at the populist centre. As coercion increased, the consummatory values of the system declined rapidly and instrumentalism took the form of opportunism, regulated by hierarchical authority under Nkrumah's police. As information declined, each of the projects designed to increase support and loyalty at the populist level began to backfire. Criticism came from all sides. The left radicals were concerned about Nkrumah's lack of revolutionary expertise. The market women, the youth, and the slum dwellers resented the corruption in high places and the rise in prices necessitated by developmental reform and pan-Africanism. Tribally based antagonism went "underground" along with a highly sophisticated opposition elite that had been banned from any access to government. As uncertainty grew, coercion did as well, until it was impossible to know who was for and who against the government.[21]

Although there had been three types of systems since independence —reconciliation, mobilization, and bureaucratic—a change in regime did not occur until 1966, when the army, together with certain police groups, revolted. Although the army was still being used by the government as an instrument of coercion, it had become alarmed that its access to decision-making was being restricted. A new bureaucratic system, with instrumentalistic objectives (including economic reform), was established under a military police force that in turn gave access to an elite composed of academics, lawyers, and senior civil servants. Nkrumah escaped to Guinée, and a political committee was established to draft a constitution leading to the formation of a new reconciliation system.

Residual caste/ethnic groups emerged in the form of chieftaincy elites advocating a non-party state and of differentiated class intellectuals advocating a parliamentary system with restricted access to the more important former followers of Nkrumah. Some parallels can be found between this situation and the one in Argentina after the downfall of Perón—namely, residual support for the fallen leader (such support, however, has been much more evident in the Argentine case than in Ghana[22]).

Groups that were singularly represented in the Nkrumah period, such as the young fused class lower bourgeoisie, tend to be excluded from elite access, while the functional status elite (professionals, bureaucrats, technocrats, and educators) is overrepresented. This situation was altered after the general election of 1969, which was held under a new, reconciliation type of constitution.

AN EVALUATION

Each of the four illustrations represents a different problematic emphasis derived from the application of the same set of categories to each case. The American case shows the effects of its own instrumental success, and, as the example of the most advanced industrial system, the problems of the meritocracy. Competition for access in functional terms favours the growth of status elites in an increasingly open and equalitarian system just as the driving force, its utilitarianism, begins to be spent. The problem is to create a new set of consummatory values and eliminate the worst excesses of the reconciliation system.

In the Soviet case, the issue is different. Here the need for structural reform and the revival of previously held consummatory values combine to push the society toward a reconciliation system which itself has a "revolutionary" potentiality.

In both cases it is the youthful intellectuals who are the main sources of dynamism in the system.[23] In both cases, too, they demand sweeping reform leading to the revitalization and realization of consummatory values.

The industrial illustrations also show the critical influence of the theocratic element. In the American case, this element was evident in the incorporation of deistic and Protestant notions of equity into a universalized system of law. In the Soviet Union a theocratic nirvana was to be realized through the transformation of the society as presently constituted. Despite the concrete differences between the ideologies, however, both could regard themselves as instruments of a higher synthesis of moral aims expressed in recognizable achievement. A consummatory-instrumental synthesis will have profound motivational consequences because it is capable of generating a certain behavioural dynamism which is lacking in both early- and late-stage modernizing systems. In the latter case, Ghana, the decline in consummatory values came about because of the unsuccessful attempt to translate primordial ethnic values (nationalist) into a contemporary socialist belief system. In the former, Argentina, the instrumental accomplishments of the regime were vitiated by failures, corruption, and short-term gain, and political system-change continues to alternate between bureaucratic and reconciliation types. In Ghana, the government reached its political ceiling relatively quickly and became immobilized, instrumentalized, and vulnerable.

Each situation contains coercion—information, a paradox that characterizes its present "systems problems". In the United States the problem is how to create new forms of meaning without increasing coercion or improperly utilizing freely available information on issues of equity. In the Soviet Union, it is how to increase information without creating structural changes which will cause the present hierarchy to dissolve into open chaos, and to realize its consummatory values through greater "democratization". In Argentina, it is how to create consummatory values capable of allowing effective decision-making for more than short-term gains, or, conversely, how to establish an effective coercive system with the capacity to universalize itself in a mobilization system which can carry the society into major industrialization. In Ghana, the problem facing the Prime Minister, Kofi A. Busia, will be to establish an adequate mixture of bureaucratic controls within the new reconciliation system in order to effect a working balance between coercion and information which is also appropriate to resources and planning.

COMPARATIVE IMPLICATIONS

The Reconciliation System. Modernizing reconciliation systems like the one being established in Ghana, or those that have prevailed in India or Malaysia, are likely to be extremely unstable in the primary stages of modernization because of the survival of many traditional practices. Nigeria is a good illustration of this. Overlapping ethnic, fused class, and differentiated class relationships provide the basis of competing coalitions so that interest representation predominates; central control is weak and bureaucratic; goal specification of the developmental variety is manipulated by politicians with only marginal participation by technocrats; and institutional mediation is based on corruption, mobility, and pay-off. Under such circumstances popular representation militates against developmental planning. Uneven access to power accentuates inequality and social discrimination. So many Latin American countries fall into this category that the number of bureaucratic responses in the form of military regimes is not surprising.

In the next stage of modernization, with the growth of differentiated class and its intermediary status clusters between fused class structures, central control tends to become more organized around a bureaucracy; goal specification is shared by competing class and status groupings, while institutional integration is sustained through multiple and overlapping institutional groupings. The pattern is likely to lead to organized plunder, with repeated interventions by the military. The combination of political and economic stagnation, popular representation in voting, and functional representation through the bureaucracy, army, and developmental agencies creates conflict between popular and functional principles of representation.

Reconciliation systems are not, of course, necessarily democratic in the Western sense of the term. Caste-ethnic, fused class, and differentiated class relationships can be linked to familial and personalistic ties. Such overlapping role-sets can combine within a single community elements of caste opportunism and class threats to the political system (as in *campesino* movements). With the development of multi-bonded class and status relationships, the structure of representative government can be used as an umbrella to protect familial and caste interests from the newer differentiated class groupings. Moreover, if such conflict gets out of hand, this can constitute a formidable management problem for the differentiated class elites so that they are likely to favour military intervention leading to a new constitutional framework.[24] Such efforts are usually accompanied by strong elite mediation at the weak points of social relationships and roles (patron–client, owner–worker) on the basis of interest representation. This also provides exceptional opportunities for corruption and strengthens the tendency to plunder the system, leading to a crisis of control.

The liberal solution, that of sharing power by means of voluntary associations, committees, and local governments, as well as general participation in assemblies and councils throughout the structure of pyramidal authority, is likely to intensify the conflict between popular and interest claims to representation. Moreover, since the elites, in the exercise of their functions, emphasize distribution rather than development, they help to exaggerate a "plunder" psychology. There is little emphasis on managed savings and effective planning. Representational access in terms of any one organized interest— whether based on class or function—occurs at the expense of the others in a kind of zero-sum situation.

The reconciliation system in industrialized countries is, as the American case shows, in a "crisis of meaning". Class conflicts have given way to status coalitions, each supporting popular representation and interest representation in competition with functional representation. Central control has become a function of conflict between bureaucrats, technocrats, and politicians. Goal specification is a tug-of-war between interest and functional representation. Institutional mediation replaces popular representation. Here lie many of the familiar problems confronting democratic societies, including the inadequacy of representative mechanisms and restricted access.

In any case, representation is much the same as in the modernizing society, except that either a party, a bureaucracy, or a military group is responsible for both central control and goal specification, while institutional mediation is more and more a significant function of specialized elites, arbitrators, specialists, conflict resolution experts, etc. In other words, industrial reconciliation systems tend to be "tolerant" of the social system and to allow institutional mediation to replace long-term planning, while functional access becomes increasingly prominent.

Modernizing Mobilization Systems. Characteristic cases of modernizing mobilization systems would include Guinée, Ghana, and Mali immediately after their independence. The stratification relations of modernizing systems are of both the segmentary and the fused class types. In other words, one finds a typical traditional caste/colonial or an expatriate caste stratification system coexisting with a "middle class" conscious of its position and performing modern tasks.[25] A mobilization system tries to eliminate the colonial caste, and to integrate class and remaining traditional caste relations around new political clusters—a political "class" of the fused type that embodies the community, such as the Parti Démocratique de Guinée, the Union Soudanaise, or the Convention Peoples Party—while manipulating populism as a substitute for popular representation.

Party organization creates representative clusters and attempts to define participation in functional terms: a *socialization* function (youth movements), a *production* function (trade unions and corporations), a *rural innovation* function (co-operatives and farmers' associations), and an *ideological* function (ideological institutes). Interest representation is likely to be suspect and regarded as "neo-colonialist" or capitalist. Attempts to alter caste relationships are made by changing the principles of representation and by modifying sources of mobility—both politically, through a "single party", and by bureaucratic co-optation. Central control is likely to be in the hands of a party-government coalition in which the key posts in each are occupied by the same individuals. Goal specification is in terms of planning based on a combination of ideological and technical goals in which technocrats, engineers, economists, statisticians, and the like play a large part, normally in some conflict with political leaders. Institutional integration is based on increasing bureaucratization, again with a high ideological component. The two main types of conflict in modernizing mobilization systems are between government-sponsored elites and the remnants of traditional elites, and between ideological specialists in the party and civil servants and technocrats. Here we find representation on the basis of function ideologically linked with relevant groupings in the society. Counter-elites are excluded, but even these may not necessarily be restricted in terms of social mobility within the system.

The main differences between traditional and modern forms of mobilization systems are that (1) populism is used to support functional representation in the modern forms; and (2) populism requires a consultative base, while functional representation requires a special access to functional elites. Populist and functional elites contend with each other for power, and access to central control and goal specification is restricted to those concerned with development or maintenance of support. The institutional integration function is restricted to programmatic ideology, with organizations modified according to the degree to which they fit the ideological pattern.[26]

In general, we can say that, even where there is a minimum of popular representation, growing competition between populist and functional elites for access to central control and goal specification produces considerable accountability. Even the functional elites seek to expand their competitive access by broadening their recruitment base in society. The tendency is to move downward through the restratification of the public into corporate functional groupings relevant to development and systems-maintenance. Not class, but *corporate* grouping is characteristic; hence a kind of "corporate representation" in primary stage modernizing mobilization systems is seen as the means of reconciling populism with functional expertise.

The above solution is rarely achieved, however, because of "embourgeoisement", which breaks up the stratification pattern into too many complex coalitional multiples for restratification along corporate-functional lines. Moreover, even segmentary caste/ethnic elements prove difficult to eradicate, as do fused class type groupings. The middle class of the differentiated type, growing as modernization proceeds, makes demands based on wider needs. Thus, central control needs to be even more tightly organized in a military or para-military type of formation. The result is government in conflict with elites. Goal specification comes to rely more heavily on systems-maintenance than on development, and institutional integration tends to combine ideological orthodoxy and coercion.

Government-monopolized central control is allocated on an appointive basis to administrators, and goal specification is toward a future objective. An elite of ideological specialists is required both to create such goals and to ensure their status as consummatory values. Institutional integration is handled by administrative magistrates or tribunals dedicated to the preservation of ideological uniformity. The functions of an elite are performed within a narrow circle, closely associated with government and hostile to other groupings, particularly other caste groupings in the system. When there is weakness or failure in the performance of any of the elite functions, government is likely to apply coercion. Hence, "embourgeoisement" creates the conditions for mobilization and also prevents the mobilization system from working.[27] Under such paradoxical conditions, popular representation, in the form of a party elite, would collide with the governmental functionaries or technocrats over its increasingly restricted access to elite functions.

The Industrializing Mobilization Systems. During industrialization, the problem of the decline of consummatory values in favour of instrumental ones tends to be associated with a structural pattern of differentiation in which class conflict gives way to a multi-bonded class, with coalitions and groups forming on the basis of functional significance. Party leaders and technocratic elites are likely to compete for central control, as in the modernizing case; but party leaders and bureaucrats are likely to handle goal specification by means of consultative instruments, while institutional mediation is similarly dealt with by party leaders and plant managers.

The industrial system injects new and mutually opposing elements into the picture: on the one hand, the need for decentralization of command units (as the complexity of the system grows) and, on the other, the increasing bureaucratization occasioned by efforts to retain command over a decentralized decision system. Representation is thus likely to be functional on the basis of the productive system and consultative on the basis of the hierarchy. We can call the resulting sub-type *consultative* (as distinct from popular) representation, as exemplified in China by the direct contact between cadres and the masses.[28] But even in China the emerging stratification pattern creates an interesting problem, namely, the phenomenon of "embourgeoisement", which breaks up society into competitive status groupings, making it difficult to treat the population in terms of any given class or corporate interest rather than as a representative of elaborately distributed needs.

Breaking up the fused class pattern into a differentiated multi-bonded class emphasizes competitive claims to popular representation under the guise of the "Nader effect". If new technocratic elites crucial to the development process were to gain supremacy over the party elite, central control would be shared by administrators, civil servants, and managers. Goal specification would be decentralized, with a corresponding depoliticization of many aspects of social life. Institutional mediation would be provided by the shared and overlapping organizational pluralism associated not only with production and distribution, but also with local government. At this point consultative representation may be transformed into popular representation. If that should occur, then the political system could become democratic.

The industrializing mobilization system is of great importance because it seems to produce a contradiction between political and economic needs. In highly industrialized societies. the multi-bonded pattern of class spreads throughout the system. It becomes virtually meaningless to speak of classes in the Marxist or Weberian sense.[29] The new types of status groupings, each with special claims to representation and power, are competitive in terms of the elites' function and their type of claim to representation. Most important is the role of the new technocrats, whose functional value is based upon knowledge or innovation. They are opposed by the bureaucrats, whose claim is based upon continuity and efficiency, and by the politicians, whose claim is based on instrumental or consummatory values of a populist variety.

This conflict arises because of the role of information. The modernizing society has a model to follow and a goal—industrialization. It can afford to be imitative. The main difference between modernization and industrialization is that the latter creates a revolution in innovation and technique. In industrial systems it is necessary to reconcile representation of interests and function with new knowledge (innovation). Each of these types of representation involves a form of information that government requires during industrialization. Hence, the effect of high industrialization is to diversify need as a basis of information, setting up the following causal chain: The need for information results in more diverse representation on the basis of complex interests and emphasizing instrumental values. As consummatory values decline and the need for information grows, the mobilizing industrial system will move toward a reconciliation system.

The Theocratic System. While the concrete and modern systemic pulls are among mobilization, bureaucratic, and reconciliation systems, leading to combinations of the three types, the theocratic appears to be merely a historical or traditional remnant. But it would be wrong to infer from this that the theocratic system is obsolete in analytical terms. On the contrary, it will be noticed that each "successful" concrete system begins with a theocratic base. This is one of the great contrasts between Argentina (and, indeed, other Latin American countries) and the United States.

Two aspects of the theocratic system should be noted immediately. The first is its utopian quality. Efforts to work out ideally integrated ethical systems are designed to result in a voluntaristic structure with minimum need for hierarchy. In religious terms, the kingdom of God is also the kingdom of man with explicitly religious values employed. If hierarchy is necessary in this life (as in the Catholic Church), it is only to promote the possibility of its termination in a higher existence. Non-religious theocratic forms, however, in which creating the political kingdom is a more immediate human endeavour, try to abolish all forms of inequality between men, allowing them to concentrate on shared values and common enterprises. This was the central principle of many experiments in utopian communities, whether religious, like the Menonites, or political, like the Owenites. Each theocratic system depends entirely on the integrative characteristics of ethical beliefs. These beliefs, whether "utopian" in the pejorative sense, as Marx used the term, or theoretically attainable as the ultimate vision of the "classless society"—the theocratic element in Marx's system and the source of its ethical imperatives— lie behind most formulations of political theory in the sense that they define consummatory values. Hence, the first importance of the theocratic system is that it is a system which seeks to satisfy the needs of equity.

The second aspect of the theocratic system follows from the first: namely, the lack of hierarchy. If equity combines with allocation so that hierarchy is unnecessary, then human beings can live in perfect harmony (order); such a goal implies the solution of all allocation problems. To achieve this requires a perfect distributive system on the structural side. The norms of such utopias become the validating myth for real systems, even those in which the presence of even the most extreme hierarchy serves to resolve the allocative crisis and therefore promote the more ideal and voluntaristic community. In some mobilization systems, particularly contemporary socialist ones, the rationale for extreme action is a future state of extreme egalitarianism, with hierarchy being combined with explicit consummatory values in order to eliminate all other forms of hierarchy, economic and social in particular. The theory is that once perfect equity has been established, the political hierarchy becomes increasingly residual and eventually disappears.

The importance of the theocratic system, then, does not lie in its concrete possibilities as a type. Rather, its importance is as an originating source for political mythologies that purport to define equity and order in terms of development. As such, it serves as a validating instrument for rule, or a basis of revealed legitimizing values. Each theocratic system defines a set of ethical "givens" deemed appropriate to the way human beings are supposed to live together; these serve as principles on which appeals for legitimacy can be made. In the American case, the theocratic elements were explicitly deistic and rationalistic; the individual expression of want, governed by the appreciation of virtue, created a "civic culture" which itself was egalitarian and anti-hierarchical, indeed, anti-governmental.[30] Where such theocratic elements are entirely lacking, so is the legitimacy of government itself, which then must maintain itself by either coercion or pay-off.

It is precisely the growing irrelevance of its theocratic presuppositions that creates the American predicament. Since coercion cannot easily be applied because of the fractionalized power and emphasis on the instrumental pay-off inherent in the pyramidal system of authority, there is a normative space that needs somehow to be filled. This is what produces the crisis in meaning. But while this crisis is less severe in the Soviet Union at the normative level, it is easier to resolve because their problem is structural. To terminate the hierarchical pattern of authority is to open up the government to populist demands for access which cannot be predicted or, once expressed, controlled. Their crisis is one of ignorance compensated for by coercion. Since professional and interest information is more easily dealt with, it is not surprising that theocratic radicalism is relevant in the American case, while liberal reformism, a neo-utilitarianism, is more common in socialist countries.

E

CONCLUSION

Historians emphasize "time", which becomes meaningful because it implies that certain sequences are more important than others. We give these sequences names, the cogency of which contribute to our understanding of similar events. For example, in this essay we have treated time analytically, referring less to cultural periods or epic phenomena than to alterations in political system types. The types are not concrete. They are analytical and point the way to typological tendencies, several of which will always obtain in any real situation. Looked at in this manner, political change is a progression of conditions from one type to another. Each type is not only the beginning but also the end of a process. To summarize the process we delineated two global and opposite tendencies, embourgeoisement and radicalization. The importance of each lies in the different patterns of authority and sets of priority implied. Radicalization points out the inequities of a system as a system. Proponents gather these inequities into ideological bundles in a convincing manner in order to show not only that a particular concrete system will no longer work, but that as a type it cannot be made to work. Radicalization, then, is a catalogue of moral consequences to be embodied in a new political system type. Embourgeoisement is the opposite. It is concerned with how largesse is distributed. That there can be violence and bitterness over the issue would not disguise the matter. For the proponents of embourgeoisement the workaday world is an instrumental not a moral one. Individuals are preoccupied with problems of place and function, reward and satisfaction. The problem is that, if these are in the last analysis the objects of revolution, no revolution can withstand success.

Of course, none of this is new to historians who have been dealing with such matters for generations and in much the same terms. But it is perhaps because of this that the tendency to see alternatives in sequence differs from the more contemporary methods of social scientists who see the same things in terms of simultaneities. Increasingly, embourgeoisement and radicalization occur more or less simultaneously in the same society with the one depending on the other rather than winning. This is true whether we are dealing with capitalist or socialist industrial societies and is increasingly the case with modernizing ones. The classic sequence—revolution, innovation, consolidation, embourgeoisement, radicalization, revolution— no longer obtains. This is the way we are accustomed to think about political history, and in some ways it is very misleading to do so. What emerges instead from this brief attempt at a historical overview is perhaps a not very surprising "behavioural" departure. We see in the search for fresh meaning the radicalization process at work. This involves the psychologizing of rationality. The definition of rationality as objective and publicly validated by agreed standards of germaneness (cause and effect) becomes a subjective experience. The symbolization of this experience is diverse, and its explanation must be deciphered by those who know how. Expression of such rationality can be found in happenings, in experiments with body and mind. This occurs because embourgeoisement, the pursuit of the instrumental, can also be seen by an individual as embodied in himself. Such embodiment is capable of generating such self-hatred that radical man includes himself among the enemy. That indeed is the meaning of the term alienation. Yet it is precisely the need to translate radicalization from a moral to a concrete phenomenon, to establish programs for increased opportunity, growth, and development, that creates embourgeoisement. Programmatic radicals are its chief architects and instruments.

This suggests a behavioural rather than a normative dialectic of history. If no one is interested in the grand Hegelian manner, there is perhaps a need to be concerned with the growing complexity of roles and institutions and the effect of these on human personality. History shows us that in this sense time itself is shrinking. Changes of magnitude occur long before individuals are emotionally prepared for them. More and more, it would seem necessary for the historian to do what the rest of us in the social sciences are doing, namely to learn to follow analytical theory through whatever fields and methods it takes us and to apply the appropriate ones to the large questions as well as the small. When there is a quickened motion of time, then explanation needs to be seen as cause and projection as prediction. And that is a matter of comparative method and theories of structures and behaviour.

This paper was prepared under the auspices of the Politics of Modernization in Latin America Project of the Institute of International Studies. The author also wishes to acknowledge the support of All Souls College, Oxford, where, as a Visiting Fellow, 1967–68, he prepared the first draft of the manuscript, and the Guggenheim Foundation for a Fellowship during that same year.

REFERENCES

1   See D. E. Apter, *Choice and the Politics of Allocation* (New Haven, 1971).
2   I have discussed these systems extensively in other writings. See in particular *The Politics of Modernization* (Chicago, 1965) and *Some Conceptual Approaches to the Study of Modernization* (Englewood Cliffs, 1968). For a more elaborate form, see *Choice and the Politics of Allocation*.

3   David Riesman, "Notes on Meritocracy", *Daedalus*, XCVI (1967). p. 898.

4   For example, in Rumania, Hungary, and Czechoslovakia.

5   Jeffrey Butler has argued that the Boer War was such a turning-point for England as an imperial system, although it took two wars and much internal struggle before the implications of the changes really worked their way out (personal communication).

6   Seymour Martin Lipset, *The First New Nation: The United States in Histori-cal and Comparative Perspective* (New York, 1963), *passim*.

7   See Louis Wirth's classic study, *The Ghetto* (Chicago, 1928).

8   Where Negro communities were established within large cities—Harlem, for example—some patterns of embourgeoisement emerged that probably (as in the case of modernizing nations) contributed to their ghetto status.

9   During the fused class period, ethnic conflict expressed itself by pejorative terms, such as "wop", "bohunk", "mick", "dutchman", "kike", and "nig-ger" (mainly working-class terms). Class conflict was not the major issue at this time.

10 Educational opportunities are increasingly available to Negroes, starting with the Southern Negro colleges and Howard University and culminating in current large-scale attempts on the part of major universities to bring Negroes into the intellectual main-stream of the post-industrial society—at the least to provide them with technical skills, at the most to prepare them for professional roles as part of the functional status elite. Recent Supreme Court decisions have done much to eliminate educational and employ-ment barriers based on race. In fact, since the Negro's entry into functional elites has preceded his acceptance into labour unions, one may conclude that he is tending to make the functional leap from agrarian to post-indus-trial society without passing through the industrial period.

  That the leap is proving difficult for many is signified by the current efforts on the part of black and other ethnic militants to change the structure of higher education to accommodate their special needs. Organized militants, determined to avoid embourgeoisement or worse, are literally storming the strongholds of the industrial meritocracy just as organized labour moved against factories in the 1930s. The post-individual meritocracy, which has proved a boon to some Negroes as individuals (because it has eliminated the colour barrier), has also proved a curse to this group (as well as other caste/ethnic groups) collectively because they are unprepared or unmotivated to meet the educational hurdles it puts in their way. In terms of the white mid-dle-class culture, they are "culturally deprived". Their own culture, rooted in slavery and/or agrarianism, infected with the poison of a long-standing racial inferiority complex, has tended to stress physical over intellectual activity, the immediate and concrete over the abstract and long-range (with fundamentalist religion the long-range comfort for immediate suffering), and "shorthand" dialect over standard English. Indeed, as Grier and Cobbs point out in *Black Rage*, the Negro tends to use the patois deliberately and to play down his intellectual prowess because both destroy his solidarity with his equals—other blacks—while placing him in competition with whites whom he believes subconsciously to be his inherent superiors. (William Grier and Price Cobbs, *Black Rage* [New York, 1968], especially pp. 142–43.) These cultural traits constitute internal barriers to academic progress which are as serious as or even more serious than colour. Black bourgeois radicals—caught between the need to preserve their sociological roots and their knowledge that higher education is the key to salvation in the meritocracy—challenge the latter in a way that suggests the nature of future systems-change.

11 Cited in George Pendle, *Argentina* (London, 1963; 3rd ed.), p. 51. For a thorough analysis of Argentine developments see Carlos F. Diaz Alejandro, *Essays on the Economic History of the Argentine Republic* (New Haven, 1970).

12 Indeed, there are Argentines who seriously suggest that the great defeat suffered by Argentina occurred when the people of Buenos Aires successfully fought off British invasion and occupation of the city. Even the brief period of British administration resulted in considerable economic reform.

13 An example of such alternation was the sequence in which the personalized regime of Bernadino Rivadavia in Buenos Aires, characterized by its concern with commerce and utilitarianism under a "unitarian" constitution was followed by the regime of the more romantic, aristocratic, landowning "federale", Juan Manuel Ortiz de Rosas, who established the first of the "bureaucratic systems" (in the sense of an instrumental and hierarchical system based on military rule).

14 The constitution established in 1852, patterned after the American, lasted until 1949.

15 See Juan Perón, *Tres Revoluciones Militares* (Buenos Aires, 1963), pp. 10–86.

16 This is not to compound the historically simplistic argument that, since Greek (*cf.* Russian) orthodoxy and communism are evangelically similar, they are the same or even serve the same political purposes, and that Stalin was a more efficient version of the Tsar.

17 In his massive biography of Trotsky, Deutscher shows clearly how this was done. See Isaac Deutscher, *The Prophet Armed* (London, 1954); *The Prophet Unarmed* (London, 1959); *The Prophet Outcast* (London, 1963), *passim*.

18 The intellectuals may be able to become public heroes and populist leaders To discredit them, they are sometimes put in lunatic asylums.

19 See, for example, the comment by Albert Parry in *The New Class Divided* (New York, 1966), p. 303: "In its lower and higher echelons the professional elite is far more interconnected than it may appear to the naked eye. Pressures from the lower echelons do reach upper ones, even in a totalitarian society. There is no such socio-political vacuum below the Kremlin heights as some Western Sovietologists sometimes briefly and erroneously describe and contemptuously dismiss. Nor is there such a foolproof control of the Party-decreed rigid structure of, say, the Academy of Sciences or sundry professional technical societies as some Western experts hopelessly concede to the Kremlin.

"There is no such airtight compartmentalization of Soviet science and technology, no such inner Iron Curtains between one field of research and another, as some Western observers claim to see as one more tool of Party control over the professional elite. The experience of Siberia's Science City in collecting and integrating so many divergent institutes and laboratories in one place; the role of computers in cutting across disciplines, in bringing together physicists, biologists, economists, linguists in common projects— all this is sufficient proof that Russia's science and engineering cannot be so readily or lastingly thwarted by the Party hierarchs from free and easy cross-fertilization and thus from one more step to independence and political influence."

20 See Geoffrey Bing, *Reap the Whirlwind* (London, 1968), *passim*.

21 See David E. Apter, *Ghana in Transition* (New York, 1963), pp. 325–73.

22   See the discussion in "Nkhrumah, Charisma, and the Coup", *Daedalus*, XCVII (1968), 757–792.

23   One of the most articulate statements in this regard was made recently in Poland by a young economist, Antoni Zambrowski, who was expelled from the staff of Warsaw University. He considered the "bureaucratic deformation of revolutionary power [after the October Revolution] as a transitory phase, peculiar to the period of construction socialism—a disease . . . [which] can be diagnosed and effectively cured by applying Marxist theory. It arises from the political superstructure and not from the foundations. This is why social revolution is not now inevitable. The problem is to repair socialism, not to bring it about by a violent agitation of the present state." What he advocates is the "democratization of public life" and the establishment of democratic freedoms and personal liberties that were "restricted and choked" under Stalin. See the discussion in *The Times* (London), March 27, 1968.

24   See José Nun, "America Latina: La crisis hegemonica y el golpe militar", *Desarrollo Economico*, VI (July–December 1966), pp. 22–23.

25   Obviously, I would reject the view that there is no class in Africa.

26   See Aristide R. Zolberg, *Creating Political Order* (Chicago, 1966), pp. 93–127.

27   *Ibid.*, p. 127.

28   J. K. Townsend, *Political Participation in Communist China* (Berkeley, 1967), *passim.*

29   Nor does the concept of "false consciousness" prove very useful.

30   See Gabriel A. Almond and Sidney Verba, *The Civic Culture: Political Attitudes and Democracy in Five Nations* (Princeton, 1963), pp. 473–87.

4

Political Studies and the Search for a Framework*

Marxism, Weberism, Parsonism, operationalism, empiricism, "integrationism", "conflictism", all are words capable of inflicting wounds, leaving scar tissue, and serving as ideologies in the debates over what social science is, what it should be and what might constitute its terms of relevance. That there are general principles to which proponents of all these points of view might subscribe means that there is a common arena of discourse no matter how diverse the approaches. Few scholars would take serious issue with Duverger's dictum that "to seek facts and record observations without any systematization is not scientific".[1] They could also agree with alacrity to the opposite proposition that any systematization which does not seek facts or record observations is unscientific. But between these two propositions, both of which have that improving piety which a common discourse requires, lie all the real questions.

If this is a common problem in the social sciences generally it is acute in politics as a discipline. The field is not noted for its coherence. Its importance as a field lies in the question it asks. The questions themselves to some extent contain answers. This is true whether we concern ourselves with such large matters as war and revolution, change and stability, the role of parties and leaders, the generation and decline of ideologies, or a more narrowly conceived concern with the workings of specific instrumentalities and their variations in time, place, manner, and cultural context. To develop a suitable general framework for these and other questions political scientists have sought procedural guides. In that search they have tended to extremes. Some like myself have preferred global forms of systematization leading towards deductive propositions. Verification and disproof become substantially logical rather than empirical. Others regard such a recourse to abstraction as a methodological anachronism. For them, the solid accumulation of the facts in the basis of

* Reprinted by permission of Cambridge University Press from *African Perspectives*, edited by C. H. Allen and R. W. Johnson (1970).

precise observations must precede more general statements with more precise correlational methods of proof.

Of course there is nothing new in this, but in so far as work in the social sciences involves teaching and research, as well as competition for time, money, and other resources, the principles and techniques embodied in both approaches are often elevated to the status of ideologies. It is true that conflict between them is as old as science itself, but these matters have now become more complicated due to the introduction of new mathematical techniques. Machines which enable the handling of large numbers of variables quickly have not only sharpened the divergence in approach but at times have taken on "sinister" implications.[2]

If we put such matters in the context of developing societies the question is how the orderly expansion of human potential may be rendered compatible with the more suitable requirements of ordinary life. The political analyst has turned his full attention to patterns of development in society—where individual and collective opportunities expand or shrink. He sees the world exploding in every sense of the word—new choices, new involvements, new people. Events can be read as codes to be broken, inkblots to be deciphered, or creative whorls projected in history or time as on some giant canvas. Indeed that is perhaps where the high drama is. But it is here that the framework is sadly lacking. What remains underdeveloped is the state of our thinking about it. Lacking is the step-by-step development of ideas, which, systematically arrived at, give more mastery by relating the large problems of development and political systems change to the small ones.

One question which arises is how systematic is it necessary to be? Here is one venue for the debate. Is classification a sufficient definition of "systematic"? Do we need to deal with such a low level of abstraction that data become a vulgate? Does a system need to contain a theory, or is it a theory? As methods improve and specialization or professionalism develops, answers to such questions will be essential if we are to reduce the enormous mountain of human problems to manageable size. Not only is there no common agreement on such matters, but when one goes into the real world of Africa and Latin America, or Asia for that matter, one tends to lack the terms of reference which might serve as a guide. This is one reason why perhaps the most powerful general theory, despite all the recent work, remains Marxian. The historic Marx, the flesh and blood fellow who took himself with his carbuncles each day to the British Museum and pored over the statistics of capitalist exploitation, made such analytical concerns explicit when examining the contemporary society of his day, not only in its development, but its science too. Indeed, so concerned was he with the framework of analysis that it is tempting to rephrase his views in a contemporary context. In this sense alone there is little doubt about his continuing relevance. Perhaps a contemporary Marx might look with a certain degree of bemused contempt at some of the narrow scholasticisms produced—by those claiming to follow his tradition. These would offend him as certainly they did in his own lifetime.[3] I prefer to think that he would not any longer entertain capitalism as his main object of inquiry or his particular interest, because capitalism could be seen today not as *the* system to be observed but as a variant, although a critical and originating one, of the more general phenomenon of industrialization. Indeed, I incline to the view that neither capitalism nor socialism as such would provide the focal points for analysis (nor ownership, property, or surplus value) but that his strategic variables would more likely be industrialization, modernization, allocation, development and equity.

If one accepts Marx as a guide in the sense I suggest then he provides us, in addition to a subject focus, with certain philosophical admonishments. His concern with historical materialism as a philosophy, applies, if anything, to a more intense degree than in his day. It is a necessary way to link empirical variables to a larger analytical paradigm. If he would deplore what has happened to philosophical inquiry in this century, it is safe to assume that he would also have been sufficiently influenced by current methodological trends to enlarge his original emphasis on dialectical method to include a more self-conscious concern with problems of verification, experimental design, proof, etc. Doubtless he would not stop until he had fitted such concerns into the broad framework of his original mode of thinking—the philosophy which closets "action" with "thought" in a concrete social setting. Nor, I suspect, would he continue to regard "ideas" as pure "superstructure". Even a brief backward glance at the impact of his own ideas would force him to change his views about that—about the creative force of ideas on the material world.

But Marx was not only a theoretician and a philosopher. We might ask in a more political vein, where would he see his revolution, his Paris Commune, his July uprising? In a Russian October? This conjecture is more difficult to resolve today. No doubt he would find many counterparts, many prototypical rebellions, movements, indeed revolutions, and also many betrayals and failures. Lost innocence would only spur him on—not to replace nineteenth-century evolutionism with contemporary utilitarianism but, I prefer to think, to the view that as any system develops it acquires certain revolutionary propensities. Each successful society creates its own marginals to be plundered or repressed, not necesarily by design or plan but even residually in its pursuit of a particular course of action or object, so that every society creates its inequities along with its achievements. That is its paradox, its dialectic and continuing predicament. Revolution as a criterion of history is no longer the "lynching party" of historical progress, but a court of last appeal to be rendered as a public judgement when both the innovative capacity of a society and the responsibility of its leaders have been exhausted. Such a view requires that models be abstract, not concrete; not the Paris Commune, but a type of revolutionary condition.

Of course, applied to Marx, such an analytical emphasis would have the effect of separating his revolutionary bite from its bark. He could not pin his hopes on particular events or regimes. On the other hand with such a view he would not be disappointed by human failings. (The U.S.S.R. might offend him most perhaps, even more than some capitalist countries, because it transformed his ideas into a ritual and made them a cloak for political inequality and brutality.) He would still pay attention to societies in their concreteness; only his selection of illustration for his theory would no doubt be less dictated by the moment than by theory itself. He would no doubt be deeply concerned with societies at the outermost point of the industrial process, such as the United States and the U.S.S.R., because these show a continuous explosion in technique and ideas, technology and application. But today he would need to take greater interest in an opposite concern, which for him remained marginal, i.e. modernizing societies where the shape and form of political life is still plastic—not yet hardened into a rigid mould. Perhaps here he would see opportunities to apply the lessons painfully learned from the history of advanced industrial countries, capitalist and socialist, to avoid repeating their worst consequences—the economic inequality of the West and the political inequality of the East.

So Marx might stand Marxism on its head. He was always and above all else a revolutionary theorist. Of course, he was so complex and subtle a thinker that to put words in his mouth in this fashion is presumptuous to the extreme. But there is a lesson to be learned in it. To take a point of view and locate a direction of change requires the articulation of a "large" theory showing logical links between variables and the establishment of some as independent. The point is that Marx did this more clearly and explicitly than any other "global" theorist. To this degree, whether right or wrong in his points, he remains a taskmaker of general theory. No one has done the omnibus job better than he.

What then are the valid criteria of research originally embodied in Marx's design? They include, first of all, the identification of an ongoing process, a transforming agent, a kind of manifold—not mystical, but complex—with defining characteristics which lend themselves to empirical study. For him it was capitalism; for us it is development. Secondly, he employed abstract modes of thought rather than purely descriptive ones. His abstractions were proximate to data, and linked quantitative and qualitative variables, and established hypotheses. In the context of today's problems these criteria raise formidable questions of research design, including sequence, the movement back and forth between analysis and research, codification and exploration, as well as various tests of validity—logical, statistical, mathematical.[4] Finally, he saw politics in its moral dimensions. Marx in his widest theoretical relevance provides that link between the moral and the political which gives him contemporary freshness. Indeed, we can argue that more than one Marx was the purveyor of his theories. Freud, when he tried his hand at historical biography developed a theory of the two Moses—one an Egyptian and the other a Midianite—who as time went on became fused into a single semi-mythical figure. We can entertain the idea of a double Marx.[5] Marx the First was the neo-Hegelian who invested the theory of alienation with a material context. Normative Marx was preoccupied with the estrangement of man from his meaning. Marx the Second was the field commander of the doctrine of revolutionary truth, who created a theory of material evolution according to laws of history. Perhaps too there is Marx the Third, the synthesis, the Phoenix, who by combining both in the work of contemporary scholars is a continual source of inspiration.[6]

But if Marx the Phoenix is with us it is because of the framework rather than the formal commitments to the theory as writ or dogma. The two different analytical emphases, normative and structural, need to be examined in their relation to each other if the unfolding pattern of history is to be laid bare. The second Marx took the centre of the stage because all the main stuff of the theory was to be objectivized and universalized in structural terms. The earlier Marx (the one which he subsequently strove to bury) emerges today as equally important. Marx the Phoenix is not the one or the other, but both. He provides the formal basis of a variety of neo-Marxian paradigms. The dialectic of norms constitutes one boundary of analysis in Mannheim, Marcuse and others. Marx the Second leads into the functional analysis of structure.

Most of all, what has happened today in the works of young scholars is that they have translated the Marxian notion of structural dialectics into development. Once this is done a wholly different political theory has been created. For it is an obvious point, although rarely made, that Marx, for all his qualities as a field commander of revolutionary truth, working, as Sir Isaiah Berlin would have it, through ineluctable laws, nevertheless had no political theory.[7] That may seem an odd thing to say about the most political of all theorists and the one with the most political consequence of all. But the dialectic is not a political theory, only a statement of conflict within the socio-economic structure. It fails as a mechanism of objectification. In this sense, political life is only a manner of response, a residual reflex, powerful empirically but possessing little theoretical substance. This is why, even in his theory, contradiction ends at the same point as that at which empirical politics begins. Marxism as a political theory is aesthetically perfect but totally empty as a concept. It is a powerful and ingenious idea but one that does not work—or, more importantly, one that does not need to. And generations of social scientists have been tinkering with the results, in the whole or in part, in a hostile manner or constructively, ever since. Indeed, it is because it does not work that one can say that there is still room for political theory.

But if the theory Marx established was not entirely correct—and if he claimed truth, he did not claim to be a seer—he makes it clear that a political theory requires more than a simple statement of mechanisms. Rather, what is required is a linking up of various levels of analysis in the context of a dynamic process. First there is the larger picture which defines a logical structure. Second there is the analytical content of the relationship which the logical structure reflects. Third there is the descriptive itemization of the substance or experience to which the relationships refer. Finally there is the specification of real events as a pattern of meaning—or to put it another way—as a concrete theory.

An analysis of Marxism can help us prevent repeating the mistakes and flaws embodied in it, especially the leap to faith within the context of the theory itself. To be hortatory in a probabilistic universe is to obliterate likely combinations of variables while to accept the multifunctional and multivariate relations of variables is to impose a modesty upon the future which we prefer.

Having described some of the standards and obligations involved in a Marxian approach it might be helpful to see how other theorists in the field of politics deal with such matters. If the outlines of proper procedure have been known and explicit for so long, why should it be necessary to refer to them? There is now more empirical and operational "science" in the discipline than ever before. To define an empirical problem as quickly as possible and in the most workmanlike manner is indeed the current style. But this rush to the professional task may disguise an unwillingness to face up to the broader implications. This is the reason why so many young scholars feel it necesssary to "begin at the beginning" and make as explicit as possible the ingredients of their theory. They must do this if they do not wish to beg the larger and equally professional issue of political moment.

But there is another reason. To cite Marx is to emphasize what might be called the basic intellectual poverty of political science as a discipline. The problems of political science are, of course, perennial and not resolvable in any final sense. But if we want to clarify our expectations of the likely and the possible in the future then clearly contemporary theory fails us. This is particularly true if we consider predictability the supreme scientific test. So far, what modern social science shows is that its predictions are likely to be trivial or so general that they can be put down to good fortune when true.

How ready is political science for a general framework? That is the question. And is it possible to have a general framework capable of handling the diversity of questions political scientists ask? As I see it, political science has reached the stage where it has rejected institutionalism and is moving into a phase of descriptive functionalism (the sort more or less abandoned by anthropologists some years ago and by sociologists more recently) just at a time when the technology of quantitative research is expanding rapidly. This produces a serious problem: inadequate conceptualization with adequate techniques. Hence the theoretical work that is going on is too general and the technological research too particular—applicable only to micro-units.

If this is an accurate diagnosis of the problem, then without a framework we are working at cross purposes—and this after many years of effort, talk, conferences, reports, and papers. Political science it would seem, having at last arrived at the stage of intellectual development achieved by anthropology in the 1930s (with Radcliffe Brown) and sociology in the 1940s (with Talcott Parsons), has lost most of its intellectual forebears (Plato, Aristotle, Machiavelli), and having hitched itself for a time to the star of historical sociologists like Weber and Durkheim, is increasingly concerned with latter-day psychology. The result is that it is "analytically systematic" which is only a slight improvement over the earlier condition of "organized description". The transition from one to the other is marked not only with much ambiguity in purposes and wide design, but also the splitting up and fragmenting of the core concepts to be employed.

These comments are not intended to belittle the achievements of political science, which have been too easily underestimated. In my view, what advances of the past decade or so there have been, while not standing as any sort of triumph, represent the necessary antecedents to a more formal basis for a theory, a more organized approach to field work and monographic studies, and the application of particular comparative methods in research. Why political analysis has lagged behind some other fields in this aspect of the social sciences will not detain us. (To answer this question would require an evaluation of the entire structure of political science. This is an enterprise as unappetizing as it is unworthy, and we have had enough such digestive displays.) No other discipline has been prey to more soul-searching and approach-mongering. The main defence of its condition should go without saying; the subject matter is so formidable it cannot easily be stuffed into tidy disciplinary schemes.

What then represents progress? A few of the issues so intensely joined in combat some years ago appear to have been resolved. Confusion remains, of course, but it is of a rather different sort. We no longer make techniques of research into ideologies of reform. It is not necessary any longer to define the boundaries of the field in terms of precedents, lore or institutions. Indeed, it has become gratuitous to prescribe in any narrow sense what falls properly within the field or without. The contemporary political scientist draws on theories from any useful source, regardless of discipline, with little fear of the dread question which not so long ago embalmed the profession: "but is this political science?" The danger of badly using "alien' concepts remains a practical difficulty, just as bad research has always been a problem. But the only way to resolve the latter is to make it better. To do so requires examination of the structure of theories themselves and the styles of thought which underlie them— an obligation which is increasingly well accepted in fresh confrontations with methods and technique. We are no longer prisoners of our descriptive categories. We do not employ specific mechanisms of rule as a context for remedial ideas or specific reforms. The stage is set for an analytical round. The recent literature is witness to the need.

Yet to draw a new design using the old rules of perspective is a far more difficult task than criticizing the results of previous work. How far can such rules be altered? It is in some ways a haunting question. A few years ago the problem was narrow orthodoxy. Today it is randomness and purposelessness. Having sniffed at the salt air of intellectual freedom, paid our respects to the monuments and mummies on the shore, boarded our ship and widened our eyes to the open tides of discovery, we also discover, upon looking down at the shallow water beneath us, that our travels have not taken us very far. Political science is less a discipline than a subject matter, widened in coverage, to be sure, but a subject-matter for all that. Having made this discovery, many of us have rushed to don life jackets with the word "typology" stencilled on (donated through the generous auspices of the various shipwreck and lighthouse societies known as philanthropic agencies) in the hope that altogether they will keep us afloat. We now have typologies galore with which we hope to get on with our travels, if not with greater speed, at least with more peace of mind. But we are labouring under an illusion. Descriptive typologies have so far been capable mainly of producing simplistic theories in complicated language which have the opposite effect from which they are intended. Life-saving typologies may keep us afloat, but they are most inconvenient for swimming (either with the tide or against it), and our very immobility is an uncomfortable reminder that the ship may founder without sinking.

Nor will the situation change much in future years as long as we show such small interest in the relation between analytical thinking about problems and the models which we can apply to the problems themselves. If we are to move toward a more positive science of politics, then what is required is a conscious sensitivity to the alternative sets of rules which confine, articulate, and identify levels of relationships, modes of meaning, and forms of comprehension. These concerns force our attention not only to matters of technique, but also, in a quite opposite direction, to philosophical antecedents and assumption just as they did in Marx's day, or earlier for that matter. Without due regard for both, politics will remain as it now is, a subject matter rather than a discipline.

And why should it not remain so? Simply because its present state undermines our original purposes and the seriousness of the enterprise. It is one thing to separate ourselves from metaphysical speculations with justifiable relief when they have become philosophically empty, but not when we are then bereft of a wider integrity—an integrity which cannot be redeemed by recourse to the "history of political ideas". Unpersuaded by the positive and linguistic philosophers (whose attempts at clarification are so thorough that they would paralyse research entirely as long as it continues to employ language), we have also come to regard our own traditional intellectual substructure with suspicion. Perhaps this is one reason for the poverty of ideas in the field today. We shy away from our philosophical and historical antecedents as if they contained a poisonous vapour. After all, we do not want to give the impression that we are more alchemists than scientists, or that deep in our hearts we prefer pointed hats to white coats. Instead, we are inclined to elevate technique as a self-validating goal.

Today's political scientists are not in a position to resolve these conflicts. Rather, they becloud them, replacing one orthodoxy with another. Meanwhile our general concepts remain obscure and their logical coherence and relation to data unexplored. Only recently have we begun to discover what other social science disciplines have known for some time, that there is a need to establish general concepts capable of generating *a priori* theories, the empirical referents of which allow valid inference and verification. Our task becomes clearer if we recognize that each such theory can define a slice of reality, that each slice of reality contains its own meaning and experience, and that the theories themselves are arbitrary. Perhaps one needs to accept the view that although theory is not a God, God is a theory.

The need for relevant and cohesive theory is especially evident in the field of political science, and above all in comparative studies, where the emphasis at the moment is turned towards techniques and practices of research, field work of all kinds, data processing by machine methods, and the application of tests of significance, variation and validity. With all these areas expanding rapidly both in quality and efficiency there is a growing danger that manipulation of data will become a substitute for necessary logical work. To throw descriptive typologies into the breech when they lack a good analytical substructure is to compound the difficulty. To mistake descriptive categories for formal analytical ones is to produce anachronistic results. Indeed, this is one of the reasons why (reasons of pure complexity aside) there are so few comparative theories, and even fewer genuinely comparative studies.[8]

We promised not to explain our present predicament, but rather describe it. And we have suggested earlier, analytical categories are too general where they are theoretical, and too descriptive where they are not. They do not help very much in the comparative study of the particular and the concrete. Nor can they combine in powerful logical systems. For example, most comparative categories fail to combine operationally with empirical cases and in concrete illustrations. Nor do they identify marginal cases by means of which comparison can test hypotheses. Global comparisons on the other hand lead to an illusion of completeness, as if process is a description of history and vice versa. If our inheritance of acquired comparative categories leaves much to be desired, the new ones are not much better. We find ourselves arriving at the predicament described by Franz Steiner as:

> working with the broad concepts and categories which were developed in the comparative period. But we now use them for the close scrutiny to which the expert, when in the field, subjects his own data. In this use the categories are found unsatisfactory. They are then redefined, and by this process they become so narrow as to lose all significance outside the individual analytical study to which they are tailored.[9]

Do the various neo-Marxists offer a solution? Probably not, although it is too soon to tell. Their approach has the virtue of preventing abstraction for its own sake. For a neo-Marxist nothing could be further from the truth than to assume that the ladder of abstraction leads to some final hierarchy of ideas. It is necessary to move "down" as well as "up", so that measurement, further description, and the incorporation of new variables is possible. The problem at each stage is to be sure of the independent variables being employed, and the questions to be answered.

Needed for this "upwards and downwards" procedure are better "intermediate" analytical categories. A neo-Marxist theory if it is to work, requires systematic, moderately detailed comparison of many concrete societies and their governments. How governments respond to the problems of development and what happens when they reach a "ceiling" beyond which they are limited in their capacity to act might be one concern. Indeed, translated into analytical terms, various "political systems" types can represent hypotheses about how such applications of power will occur, with each containing its special form of creativity, and each its political "ceiling".

Such hypotheses can constitute one useful point of departure for neo-Marxist theory when the general problem is to relate politics to development to see how each affects the other. This at least turns us away from the unilinear pattern of the relationship assumed by Marx. He was very misleading on this score.[10] On the other hand, the relations to be established cannot be chance or random. We need, then, a different scheme of highly generalised continuous variables.

We suggested at the outset that development, because it is not entirely dissimilar to the Marxian use of capitalism as an empirical process of a highly generalized character, is one place to begin. The difficulty with the Marxist theory is precisely that its findings deal primarily with capitalism (and a certain period), leaving socialism more or less derivative. Today the study of industrialization (including both private and public forms of enterprise) turns attention to organization, communication and ideology with modernization as derivative. For our purposes, then, the relevant and crucial process is industrialization, the particular application of that process in non-industrial societies we call modernization, and these define a problematic focus for a general political theory. Such an approach emphasizes two things. One is the dynamic quality of industrial society and its resulting hegemonic impulse leading to imperialism or external control. The other is the derivative and vulnerable character of modernizing societies which become more vulnerable as they modernize further. These concerns were perhaps better related in the first two Marxes than any of the Phoenixes in flight today.

F

REFERENCES

1   See Maurice Duverger, *Introduction to the social sciences* (London, 1964), p. 233.
2   To some, it sometimes seems as if student, scholar, research worker, all, are in danger of being chewed up with data, the only remnants of human preservation left behind and with little profit to the people on whom all these neologisms are inflicted.
3   Perhaps he would find more disturbing his position as the Bodhisattva of the militants, the Guatama of the radical rationalists; and the object of an iconography, both pictorial and ideographic, offensive to his peculiar mixture of intellectual arrogance, social modesty, and personal honesty.
4   For this I have preferred to use a combination of functional and dialectical analyses. Where Marx took Hegel's dialectic away, I restore it, and where he uses it, I have removed it and instead employed a concept of need on the basis of which functions are derived.
5   See Sigmund Freud, *Moses and Monotheism* (New York, 1939), pp. 50–51.
6   See the theory of the two Marxes in Robert Tucker, *Philosophy and Myth in Karl Marx* (Cambridge, 1961), pp. 165–76.
7   See Isaiah Berlin, *Karl Marx* (New York, 1939), pp. 8–13.
8   Usually, and despite lip-service comparison, we are plunged into the specialized mysteries of the subject or research. If, after a prolonged submersion, there is any life left in us, we are permitted to bound upward, gasping for air. Specialization is necessary, of course, but what is it really all about? If we are not to be inundated by detailed studies of the unique, we need a method of comparison capable of utilizing such work and relating the comparative and the more specialized area, cultural, or historical materials.
9   See Franz Steiner, *Taboo* (Harmondsworth, 1967), pp. 17–18.
10   See Marx's letter to P. V. Annenkov, 28 December 1846 in which an evolutionary position is clearly stated in *Marx–Engels, Selected Correspondence* (Moscow, n.d.), pp. 39–51.

5

Government*

The study of government has followed several main lines of inquiry. These include both an examination of the source and distribution of authority and the classification of types of government (such as presidential systems and monarchies), as well as analysis of levels of government (including such units as national societies, clubs, churches, and trade unions). Although a thorough review is impossible here, we can examine the main themes which unite these various approaches and evaluate their theoretical status.

At the most general level, government consists of a group of individuals sharing a defined responsibility for exercising power. At this level the definition applies to cases where government is sovereign, as well as to cases where it is not. Sovereign government, the most important type, consists of a group of individuals sharing a defined responsibility for the maintenance and adaptation of a national autonomous community, on behalf of which it exercises a practical monopoly of coercive powers. If by "a defined responsibility" we mean its legitimacy (the sanctified right to exercise power on behalf of others by means of decision making), then the characteristics of sovereign government are as follows: a government is a group of individuals exercising legitimate authority, and protecting and adapting the community by making and carrying out decisions.

These characteristics impose certain limits of variation upon government. One limit is efficacy, i.e. the capacity of a government to cater to community needs. A second refers to the internal structure of a given type of government, i.e. its form. Changes in form which occur when one type of government is transformed into another are ordinarily related to the efficacy, or performance, of a particular government. Hence, the limit upon government is observable when for any reason (inability to make decisions, failures to comply with widely distributed but central values) it can no longer function. If this is not merely a matter which can be remedied by

* Reprinted with permission of the publisher from *The International Encyclopedia of the Social Sciences*, David L. Sills, editor. Volume 6, pp. 214–30. Copyright (c) 1968 by Crowell Collier and Macmillan, Inc.

changing the incumbents of political office, i.e. if the political roles and supporting offices are no longer acceptable, then the withdrawal of legitimacy denotes that the system of government is no longer regarded as appropriate by the public; its limits have been breached. At that point, change from one type of government to another is likely.

The most common distinctions that have been made between types of governments include the following: is the government competitive or monopolistic? democratic or totalitarian? pluralistic or monistic? presidential or monarchical? Of course, these well-known categories overlap considerably. For example, it is possible to have a totalitarian presidential system. As is the case with all dichotomous variables, these distinctions force the observer to put a particular government in one category or the other, even when it demonstrates characteristics of both. Such distinctions are based on two criteria: the organization of government and the degree of control it exercises over the community. These criteria combine the moral, or normative, dimension of politics with the dimensions relating to governmental structure and political behaviour. These three analytically distinct elements, i.e. the normative, structural, and behavioural aspects of government, will now be separately examined.

Normative aspects of government deal with such abstract questions as justice, equity, equality. Through these, men define their lasting values, their ideas of right and wrong. Normative theory represents, therefore, certain speculations about those aims and activities of government which embody the central values and ultimate ends of a political community; it defines political legitimacy.

In contrast, structural principles are those which deal with the arrangements and instruments involved in governmental decision making. Of course, they are related to normative issues in so far as the form of a government is seen as a means of attaining the ends of society. Preoccupation with the structural dimension leads directly to the analysis of alternative forms of government, with normative considerations employed in order to evaluate those most suitable for realizing the goals of the community by means of governmental decision making. In the past, structural analysis has been mainly concerned with the distribution of political power, describing various types of government in terms of how widely power is shared by the members of a political community.

Classical writers were particularly interested in normative issues and structuralists have been preoccupied with governmental forms. Both groups, to the extent that they considered it at all, assumed behaviour to be a condition of conflict. For both, a propensity to conflict is regarded as the normal political expression of human nature, much as economists assumed that man has a natural propensity "to truck, barter, and exchange". Hobbes, for example, put this assumption very sharply as "the war of all against all". Such assumptions led both Plato and Hobbes to seek authoritarian governments as the best means of regulating the condition of conflict. Other theorists have seen a division of powers as the best method to control conflict.

Certain combinations of normative and structural approaches have been called institutionalist theories. Institutionalists, such as Carl Friedrich (1937), Harold Laski (1925; 1935), and Herman Finer (1932), concerned themselves with the normative and structural relations between law, constitutional forms, and governmental procedures in wide historical, religious, and economic contexts. Their considerations included an interest in practical reform as well as theory, and they consciously built on the formulations of Ostrogorskii (1902), Bryce (1921), Graham Wallas (1908), and others.

Emphasis on the behavioural dimension originated largely in the 1920s, with the "Chicago school" and, in particular, with Harold Lasswell, who sought to introduce behavioural explanations into political affairs. This is most explicit in his pioneering work *Psychopathology and Politics* (1930). However, until recently, few theorists followed this lead. It is, therefore, not surprising that the study of socialization processes, motivation, and political culture has been handled mainly by political sociologists.

Analysis today is characterized by the refinement of structural theories of government into a system, i.e., a set of interrelated elements which can be integrated with behavioural theories. The resulting analysis has taken many different forms and has made some advances, but it is particularly weak in its treatment of normative theory.

THEORIES OF GOVERNMENT

Historically, most theories of government have fallen into one or the other of two main analytical sets: mechananistic and organic.

Mechanistic theories. The first set reflects the view that society is composed of competing and interacting interests (both individual and group), that these generate conflict, and that it is the job of government to ameliorate or resolve such conflict. Government is thus a device for finding ways to relax tension in the political system. These theories, relying heavily on the free exchange of information, see government as a point in a flow of activity which is initiated by the political community. Since government has a decision-making apparatus, which responds to tension points in the system, the appropriate actions will be forthcoming. Behavioural tensions represent "inputs", or stimuli affecting political leaders, who by responding to them generate decisions, or "outputs" (see Figure 1).

INPUTS   OUTPUTS

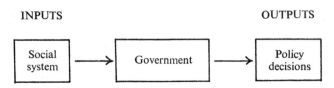

Figure 1.   Government as a dependent variable

In Figure 1, assume that the social system is a national society. Government responds to a variety of societally generated inputs, including customs and beliefs (normative characteristics), classes and interests (structural characteristics), and preferences and perceptions (behavioural characteristics). Democratic theories of government are based on this model. This is why they have been particularly concerned with the establishment of a useful set of intervening structural variables between the social system and government itself. Hence the preoccupation with the analysis of political parties, electoral systems, and the like, which are seen as devices for improving the relationship between the social system and government in order to raise the quality and appropriateness of policy decisions and increase the efficacy of government.

It is the liberal democratic approach which accepts this view, with government cast in the role of mediator and judge in conflicts between contending parties. The principles of structural organization are embodied in law, which serves as a framework for all other forms of organization. Normative consensus centres around the maintenance of the legal framework itself. Government strengthens consensus by ensuring the widest realization of norms already held. Such liberal theories are contained in the ideas of Diderot and d' Alembert, Holbach and Helvétius, Condillac and Locke, Rousseau and Hume, It is a tradition which includes Voltaire's innocent rationalism and Bentham's equitable utilitarianism. What these thinkers had in common was an emphasis on individual knowledge and shared reason, a position which elevates the individual to the centre of the political stage. Rationality is a norm, and it requires a framework in which free ideas and competitive views can be put forward.

The Western democratic governments reflect variants of this model, but it was also accepted, at least in principle, in other areas.

For example, the constitutions of many of the new Afro-Asian nations were drawn with this general approach in mind, even where the actual practice of government is wholly different from its normative and structural theory.

To sum up, the normative assumption underlying the model is that a social system is composed of individuals or groups with an equal right to be represented. Structurally, it is assumed that a government must reflect proper representation; the behavioural assumption is that competitive conflict between the members of the social system renders representative forms necessary. The model therefore displays the following characteristics: the unit of which the social system is composed is the individual; the ends of the individual are maximized; the structure of government is organized in such a way that a plurality of ends is maximized; the decisions of government, by maximizing a plurality of ends, maintain balance or harmony in the social system; and the principle of legitimacy is equity. The concern of political theorists following this tradition is with the improvement of devices that government can use to maximize a plurality of ends. Certain structural procedures have, therefore, become endowed with the quality of norms. Moreover, underlying this view is an assumption, rather mechanistic, that government is a contrivance. It does not grow organically. It must be established, with each structural principle becoming endowed with a predictable consequence. Government is, first, a kind of social physics, with particular devices having predictable results.

Organic theories. The classical view is different (as are many contemporary ones). For example, both Plato and Aristotle related government to the evolution of human society from lower to higher forms. Therefore, government was essentially an educational body, embodying a set of ideals and perfecting rationality, thereby directing the state toward a new golden age. Moreover, this conception of government has had as durable a tradition as the liberal democratic one. Although such views were widely accepted in medieval Europe (Gierke 1881), it was Hegel who gave the conception its most powerful rationale and Marx who brought it into popular currency. Marx accepted nineteenth-century notions of progress but saw in the evolution of man's higher purposes a relationship between change in the material world and the unfolding human consciousness. Government is an instrument of this relationship. As such, it has its own cycle. It becomes an instrument of revolutionary action, of insurrection, which, if successful, represents the most dynamic class. It comes to power as the instrument which must transform revolutionary impetus into practical accomplishment. Having accomplished this, it will in turn be rendered anachronistic and vulnerable until the final stage, when government is itself no longer necessary.

Nor was Marx alone in accepting an organismic conception of government. More liberal-minded proponents include Thomas Hill Green, who saw government as an instrument of morality. Herder, a philosophical romantic, also shared the view that government was a transitional phenomenon by means of which an "aristo-democracy" would educate the public and develop a sufficient level of political consciousness to render government superfluous. "The ultimate aim of aristo-democracy, Herder saw in the disappearance of the State as an administrative 'machine' of government, and its replacement by an 'organic' way of ordering social life, in which active cooperation would render all forms of subordination obsolete and superflous" (Barnard 1965, p. 77). Similar views were expressed by Fichte, Schelling, and Bosanquet. Today this approach is particularly attractive in developing areas, where government is seen as the instrument of an evolutionary ideal.

The organic evolutionary concept remains an alternative to the liberal democratic one. It implies a role for government, which directs society toward higher ends. Evolutionary in conception, this tradition is often enriched by ecclesiastic and theocratic ideals. It stresses the role of the community over and against the role of the individual. Although modern organic conceptions elevate man to a central position, they emphasize that the community is the instrument of his perfection; such views are endemic in revolutionary governments, which see themselves as the instruments of social transformation. Where the role of government is so central, we can say that it becomes the independent variable (Figure 2).

INPUTS   OUTPUTS

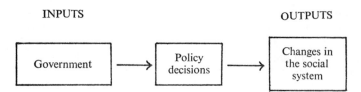

Figure 2.   Government as an independent variable

Government is the instrument by means of which change is produced in the social system. The purposes and objects of such change (normative characteristics) are defined by government. The organization of government (structural characteristics) will depend on the best means to accomplish these purposes. The activities of government will include whatever symbolic manipulation through education, communications media, etc., is necessary to affect both the content and manner of policy decision making pursuant to changes in the social system.

In the first model (Figure 1) government is the dependent variable and social system or community is the independent variable. Power is seen to inhere in the public, which creates the inputs of stimuli to which government must cater (Easton 1957; 1965). In the second model (Figure 2) government is the independent variable and social system the dependent one. Such systems tend to be centralized in the form of their authority. They tend to elevate the goals of the government into norms and make them sacred and ethical precepts, through which legitimacy is defined. Governments resembling the first model tend to be competitive, pluralistic, and democratic; those resembling the second tend to be monopolistic, monistic, and totalitarian. Normatively, the first are more secular than the second. Structurally, they are less hierarchically organized. Behaviourally, they rely heavily on internalized norms and self-control, rather than on external authority. As opposing paradigms, these two generalized types, in their various concrete formulations, are perpetually vulnerable to each other. Indeed, one can see over time that they form a permanent dialogue of conflict. They represent two fundamentally different approaches to government.

POLITICAL NORMS AND FORMS OF AUTHORITY

We can now begin to explore some of the implications of that dialogue of conflict. One way of describing it is in terms of the difference between sacred and secular norms. This difference is important because it draws our attention to the normative basis of a government and, therefore, to its legitimacy. Normative conflict generally takes place between sacred and secular beliefs.

Sacred political norms. Governments based on sacred norms cover a wide range of cases, ancient and modern, including ancient China and many of the early Semitic kingdoms. Consider the following description: "The Egyptian of historic times did not have our doubts and difficulties. To him the kingship was not merely part, but the kernel of the static order of the world, an order that was divine just as much as the kingship was divine. . . . From the earliest historic times, therefore, the dominant element in the Egyptian conception of kingship was that the king was a god—not merely godlike, but very god" (Fairman 1958, p. 75). Or take the case of ancient Greece. There the principles of patrilineal authority and ascribed status were linked to an ancestral and religious source, not only for kings but for every citizen (Hignett 1952, p. 63). Ascribed status applied particularly to priests and to the distinction between nobles and commoners. Hence, political norms represented an explicit validation of the structure of authority.

Sacredness does not apply only to theocratic or primitive societies. It applies as well to many modern states. The sacred qualities of Marxism-Leninism in the Soviet Union are today enshrined in an elaborate philosophical system. Many of its sacred attributes were cruelly visible in the various purges and trials of the 1930s. It appears, even today, in the controversies over the political role of literature and the arts. Clearer still is the case of modern China. Mao's prescriptive sayings assume such a sacred characteristic as to define the basis of political legitimacy. Many new nations share this characteristic (although to a lesser degree), particularly in cases where an attempt is made to ritualize the authority of a charismatic or highly personalistic leader by endowing his words and teachings with special insight.

No government is entirely free from sacred qualities, whether these be elaborate and ideological or be token symbols, such as a flag, or a constitutional document. These aspects of government may be merely ceremonial, or what Bagehot called the "dignified part", or they may represent high drama in which the solidarity and unity of a community may be expressed.

It is possible to distinguish three main varieties of sacred attachments, which, even if they overlap, are analytically separable. Ranking them in ascending order of sacredness, they are (1) primordial attachments to or beliefs about race, language, and nationality (a typical expression of primordial attachment is nationalism); (2) philosophical attachments (the most generalized moral and philosophical ideal in which a total synthesis is expressed relating man to his environment and specifying the way of the future is to be found today in socialism); and (3) religious attachments (this refers to religious beliefs in which the origin of the society, moral purpose, and a particular pattern of transcendental beliefs are associated in a universal religious doctrine, such as Christianity).

In practice all three of these may be blended. Modern populist and totalitarian regimes, as in Nazi Germany, mixed primordial attachments of race and theological attachments of religion. In the Soviet Union during World War II, the symbols of government were more and more primordial, i.e. nationalist, and less and less philosophical, i.e. Marxist.

Secular political norms. Secular norms rely on a framework of rules rather than on some higher purposes of state. The most common cases of secular systems are those in which the sacred elements have declined through institutionalization. They do not disappear, but they become so completely a part of the accepted pattern of right and wrong that it is not necessary to do more than refer to them on ritual occasions. Thus, ceremony rather than the substance of belief is characteristic of these systems.

By tacit agreement secular systems reserve the "higher" goals to the individual, and these goals inhere in his body of private beliefs. If governments should violate these norms, they run the risk of overstepping their limits of variation and of being eliminated.

We can now cut across the sacred–secular normative distinction with a structural variable, the pattern of centralized or decentralized authority. Once again we must employ a caveat and remind ourselves that it is always difficult to use dichotomous variables to divide concrete cases. What is in theory decentralized may be quite the opposite in practice. Or highly centralized systems may show informal patterns of consultation and accountability to various groups in the community. Indeed, at any given time even the most highly centralized system may act on certain issues in a highly decentralized manner. Moreover, centralized government includes monarchical and bureaucratic systems, represented by ancient empires, that can combine monarchy with decentralized administration. This configuration includes different types of government: systems where the hierarchy is based on a king who is a father of his people, with authority deriving from a totemic ancestor, as in many tribal governments, or systems where authority lodges in a patrimonial figure and the relationship between ruler and ruled is that of patron and client.

Centralized authority. Let us ignore all these variations in form and say boldly that centralized power begins from the top and is applied downward through a specific delegation of authority. A military organization or a bureaucracy represents a clear-cut "command" case, with autocratic and totalitarian governments defined as those which employ this system of hierarchy. Government may then be represented by a single figure, a king or dictator, or by an oligarchy or junta (Friedrich & Brzezinski 1956). Such highly centralized systems show the following characteristics: concentrated power is subject to few checks: power inheres at the top; subordinate authority is derivative; and there is strong reliance on the personality of a particular leader.

Decentralized authority. Decentralized authority represents an opposite conception of power: power is generated by the public through the aggregation of their political wants, is expressed through various groups, and is regulated by an abstract system of rules. (Its usual normative expressions include the acceptance of the principle of majority rule, protection of rights, and representation.) This is what we mean by a democratic government. It is characterized by checks and balances, parliamentary control over the executive, and some form of election as the method of political recruitment to sensitive positions. Of course, such practices do not exhaust the forms of decentralization. Decentralization may be functional, based on the allocation of the economic power in society among various groupings, such as guilds, protective associations, professional associations, and other interest groups.

The distinctions between sacred and secular and between centralized and decentralized types of government can form the basis of a more general model by means of which to analyse government.

TABLE 1. THE DERIVATION OF POLITICAL TYPOLOGIES

| | | Concentration of Power | |
		Centralized	Decentralized
Predominant Political Norms	Sacred	A	C
	Secular	B	D

Table 1 pinpoints the four combinations that will be examined in detail. To summarize the possibilities, the highly centralized and sacred system, *A*, represents modern populist totalitarian governments. The centralized and secular system, *B*, represents many autocratic forms of government. The sacred and decentralized system, *C*, includes many early forms of theocratic society, from the feudalism of the High Middle Ages in Europe to religious or theocratic governments in America, such as the Puritan colonies of New England. And modern democratic governments fall into the secular and decentralized category, *D*.

SACRED AND CENTRALIZED GOVERNMENTS

The modern sacred-centralized type of system is likely to be associated with the establishment of a new political system. Government is the independent variable and is associated with a new moral framework. Such conditions commonly apply after a major revolution or in territories that have recently gained independence.

Communist governments. The distinguishing feature of the sacred–centralized communist government is the high degree of centralization encompassing the total community. The sacred object of government is to transform the material conditions of life and the consciousness of the people at the same time. The evolution of the community becomes a moral goal, to be sought under the leadership of a militant vanguard—the Communist party—serving as the spearhead of government. In the classic, Leninist form of the communist regime, no competitive sources of power can be tolerated. In recent times, however, a slight trend toward secularization and decentralization can be seen in the Soviet Union (Brzezinski 1962).

Historically, the Soviet Union is an interesting case of external beliefs influencing internal social groups to revolt against a highly autocratic monarchy, a weak parliament (the Duma was only founded in 1905), and a centralized bureaucracy liberally sprinkled with foreign, particularly German, immigrants (Pipes 1954). Not only was the revolutionary instrument based on a small but dynamic working-class movement; Marxism itself was largely restricted to Russian middle-class intellectuals. It was essentially an alien doctrine (transformed by Lenin to meet Russian conditions) leading to a revolutionary organization which later became the centralizing mechanism of state power. When the religious beliefs of the Greek Orthodox church were replaced by the secular ideology of Marxism–Leninism, the goals of political development became sacred and formed the new basis of the legitimacy of government. Of course, a wide discrepancy existed between the theory and practice of government. Power was in fact centralized in the hands of the first secretary of the Politburo of the Central Committee of the Communist party, while constitutionally the Soviet Union was a federal system with an elected "supreme organ of state power", the Supreme Soviet, which had, in theory, the exclusive right of legislation.

This system formed the model of state organization for all other communist systems until relatively recently. Since the death of Stalin, however, two interesting features may be noted. The sacred quality of Marxist–Leninist ideology has declined, particularly as younger generations find it less significant as a doctrine than as a ritual; and a trend toward decentralization has begun. A struggle is on between the communist political leaders and the technical specialists, economists, scientists, and the like. Moreover, as "polycentricism" on an international level becomes more accepted, the necessity for a more "liberal" approach to Marxism–Leninism reduces its orthodoxy. Alternative structural experiments are increasingly common, such as those in Hungary, Yugoslavia, and Poland, in which "cultural" decentralization (in the case of Hungary and Poland) and economic decentralization (in the case of Yugoslavia) represent experiments in greater freedom. [see also Laqueur & Labedz 1962.]

The communist examples are of particular relevance because they have become attractive models to governments of developing areas bent on following the Soviet pattern of rapid industrialization (Ulam 1960).

Fascist governments. Fascist governments were more secular in their orientations. The developmental or evolutionary sacred ideology around which communist governments try to organize their societies embodies certain universalized moral aims. In contrast, the sacred attachments of fascist governments showed greater attraction to primordial sentiments, including race and nationality. Although there are structural similarities between communist and fascist governments, particularly with respect to the roles of a powerful totalitarian political leader and a weak set of parliamentary institutions, one important difference should be pointed out. In the communist case, government is monolithic, emphasizing the evolution of the entire community. Fascist governments, in contrast, tolerated certain corporate groupings.

Three fascist governments are of interest here: Germany, Italy, and Spain. All were highly centralized, but they varied considerably with respect to the sacredness and secularity of political norms.

The strongest attachment to sacred primordial political norms was exhibited in Nazi Germany. The supremacy of one race and the liberating effects of war and conflict were embodied in the revived Nordic myths ("Odinism") and blended into a set of nationalist political norms. Structurally, although the government was highly centralized under a personal dictatorship, four main groupings were given exceptional attention: army and secret police, large-scale industrial enterprise, labour organized into fronts and battalions, and military scientists and technicians. The Nazi case also shows that even under a highly centralized form of government, economic control can be kept separate from ownership, with private industry continuing to operate under government regulations. Unlike the situation in communist systems, in Nazi Germany a market system of economic allocation coexisted with government-organized fiscal and credit manipulations. Each corporate group obtained special conditions of privilege.

Italian fascism showed less commitment to primordial political norms than Nazism, as well as a somewhat less centralized governmental structure. The norms themselves were composed of ambiguous combinations of primordial sentiments, appeals to historical precedent, and claims to philosophical universality. Primordial claims were mixed with the corporate organization of the state, under the inspiration of the collegia of the late Roman Empire. The "corporation" was thus associated with the great period of

Italian imperial and cultural achievement and became the legitimizing basis of the regime.

A second claim to universality, which was of minor importance during the period of Italian fascism, may yet prove to be highly significant. This is the view that the proper way to organize the state is in corporate groupings functional to development and industrialization. In arguing the case of corporate government, it was pointed out that fascism as a form of government, although totalitarian, emphasized the role of the corporation as both the point of reconciliation between state and individual and the instrument of individual expression (see Barker 1942, pp. 328–66). This possibility remains as an important structural device, midway between highly centralized and decentralized systems.

Both the German and Italian systems contained important normative ambiguities, which they attempted to resolve in the apotheosis of violence. This was most apparent in their total repudiation of democratic, decentralized forms of government (which were regarded as catering to human weakness). Italian and German fascism both represented an authentic totalitarian populism (a modern form of tribalism), in which medieval ideas of corporation, organic concepts of the community, and primordial sentiments were intertwined within a highly centralized system of administrative government.

The Spanish case has been less ideological and less centralized. Despite the exceptional power of Generalissimo Franco and the concentration of authority in the national cabinet, the Falange, as a political party, plays a lesser role in government than the National Socialist party did in Germany, or the Fascist party in Italy (Payne 1961). One reason is that within six years of Franco's accession to power, Italy and Germany were defeated. Their systems no longer served as models of successful dictatorship. Even more important is the Catholic tradition, to which the right wing of the Falange and significant proportions of the population generally subscribe.

More decentralized than the others, and therefore more autocratic than totalitarian, the Spanish system remains an extension of an old and established bureaucratic system which traces its roots to the imperial Spanish tradition, the Inquisition, and a centralized monarchy. Even today the Spanish government tries to preserve a vague commitment to monarchy as a traditional form of legitimacy. This allows the government to revive memories of Spanish grandeur, treating communism, secularism, and socialism much as Philip II and Archbishop Carranza of Toledo treated Protestantism, Islam, and Judaism (Davies 1937). This fervour would indicate the presence of sacred political norms, derived from Catholicism and more or less indifferent to the structure of authority. Many of the same norms served equally well in Perón's Argentina, and the more socialist forms of Catholic corporatism are sometimes embodied in modern and decentralized socialist or democratic governments, for example, in Chile.

SECULAR AND CENTRALIZED GOVERNMENTS

The most pronounced characteristics of a secular–centralized system of government are autonomous power in the hands of a president or monarch (or perhaps a presidential monarch); a single political party, whether in the form of an elite (a communist party) or a populist mass party with an elite centre (most nationalist parties) a truncated or largely ritualistic parliament, which does not have a real veto power over the executive; and an elections system which does not allow effective competition between candidates for political office.

Such centralized systems show several characteristic problems common to all forms of centralized government with the exception of institutionalized monarchies. The most important of these are, first, succession to high public office (which is usually accompanied by severe struggles for power) and, second, the institutionalization of disagreement.

The normative content of both the communist and fascist forms of government gives direction and shape to the entire society. Historically, however, there have been many cases where the normative content is relatively low (or largely ceremonial and ritualized), while power remains centralized. These include most nineteenth-century monarchical forms of government. Indeed, precisely because their sacred characteristics were emptied of content (while retained in form) they were unable to survive as types and were either transformed or removed. In France the monarchical form, attempted periodically during the nineteenth century, had been effectively destroyed by the French Revolution. Only Bonapartism had any genuine normative success. In Britain the secularization process began with the transformation of the monarchy or, symbolically, with the beheading of Charles I. The Act of Settlement of 1701, whereby the sovereign occupies the throne under a parliamentary title, established parliamentary supremacy, although it took many generations before the full implications were worked out (Dicey 1885). Real structural changes in the form of decentralization were embodied in the widening of parliamentary control over the executive and in popular representation from 1832 onward (Gash 1953). If the record of historical cases of secular–centralized government is any guide, then one useful proposition can be stated as follows: as sacred political norms become secularized through ritualization, government must decentralize, since its legitimacy disappears.

Examples of secular–centralized governments include czarist Russia (although there were important theocratic elements incorporated in the role of the czar), and Bismarck's Germany. More recent cases are colonial administrative governments in British and French Africa, south Asia, the Netherlands, the East Indies, and the Belgian Congo.

Many of the new nations have gone from one form of highly centralized system, under colonialism, to another, in the form of one-party government, but with a change in the quality of political norms. The norms often become endowed with intense attachment to primordial loyalties associated with race and nation and, to a lesser degree, with some aspects of socialism and public ownership, all wrapped up in a particular ideological message, such as Nasserism in Egypt, Nkrumahism in Ghana, or "Communocracy" in Guinea.

SACRED AND DECENTRALIZED GOVERNMENTS

Where new constitutional governments have been most successful, they have evolved a shared set of political norms deriving from a previous period when such norms were explicitly sacred, either in an ecclesiastical form, as in the case of the Puritan commonwealths, or in a more directly political form. This suggests the following proposition: decentralized–secular governments are most stable and effective when they have developed out of an earlier centralized–sacred or decentralized–sacred form, with norms of self-control becoming behaviourally widespread. Modern democratic government emerged when the decentralization of authority and secularization of political norms proceeded more or less simultaneously with a corresponding increase in the standard of individual civic obligation (Almond & Verba 1963).

The origins of Western democratic governments derive from a synthesis of generally agreed religious values, which is associated with a generalized Christian ethic. The theocratic origins of democratic government are not to be taken lightly. Even the American experience assumed a unified set of Christian (mainly variants of deistic and Protestant) theological precepts. Law was based on the prior conception of agreed principles of political propriety. The formation of these principles can be found in many different theologically articulated forms, including the religious wars between Catholics and Protestants and between various Protestant groups

G

as well. Nor was the body of precept within the Catholic church much more unified. Certainly the conflicts over conciliarism and the role of the church councils, not to speak of the nationalization of the church itself within each country, all testify to the explicitly political consequences of religion. These issues were so important to politics that much of the process of secularization can itself be traced to the search for some mutually agreeable and satisfactory common denominator of precept in order to render politics more secular.

In the United States this was most clearly recognized in the works of Brooks and Henry Adams, both of whom saw the modern economic state, with its emphasis on instrumental values, economic exchange, and corporate finance, as destroying the implicit basis of the original Christian values. Nowhere is this more explicit than in Henry Adams' essay on Mont-Saint-Michel (1904; see also Brooks Adams 1898). Such views, which tended to idealize the classical and medieval civilizations, were romantic expressions of this religious ideal. But in addition to energy, there was doctrine and creed. The church militant was not always composed of simple stuff. Even in Catholic Spain during the "golden century", the conquistadors, who combined the adoration of the Virgin with great greed in plundering the New World and founding an empire, were vastly different in their political aims from the various religious orders, Jesuit, Benedictine, and Dominican, and these in turn had their constitutionalists, such as Juan de Mariana, Francisco Suárez, and Bellarmine (Lewis 1954).

The secularization of political norms can be seen as occurring in three historic steps. The first was nationalization of the church. By this means the political universalism of the church, symbolized in the term "Holy Roman Empire", was restricted, and various national churches arose.

The second step was the extension of that process to government. It was symbolized in the expression "divine right of kings", whereby authority was traced to the Deity through the principle of royal inheritance and kinship. This established the idea of a sovereign government as a legitimate unit with rights to protect itself against external sacerdotal power.

The third step was the growth of Protestantism, associated first with the unfolding of Christian principles through equity and with the radicalization of instrumental values. The transition was particularly significant because Protestantism emerged as a particular religious ideology with a mutually reinforcing synthesis between sacred values and instrumental objects germane to industrialization. In this sense, Protestantism was the mode of transition from the more explicitly religious form of government to a more secular one, which merely reflected religious values. This is why the roots of modern Western constitutional ideas are so deeply embedded in the Protestant ideal of the community.

In a sense, the secularization of religion emerged as a result of the utter loneliness of Protestantism, which in Calvin's doctrine excluded even the church from participation in individual salvation. Weber makes the point that this is the singular difference between Catholic and Protestant doctrine, and the result was an emphasis on an individualism held in check by the concept of a calling embodying good works and sobriety. Rationality was reflected in a political community of individuals. Thus, self-control became the founding ethic of representative government, in conjunction with the economic doctrine of capitalism. Catholic doctrine, in sharp contrast, "punishing the heretic but indulgent to the sinner", retained a conception of the organic community that, although not necessarily antagonistic to decentralized government, did not support its basis in individualism and the doctrine of individual representation (Weber 1904–05: McNeil 1954).

The consequences of Protestantism and Dutch, British, and American capitalism helped to create the conditions of secularization, with a greater degree of emphasis on legal and constitutional political devices. Weber quotes John Wesley: "I fear wherever riches have increased, the esence of religion has decreased in the same proportion" (Weber 1904–05, p. 175 in the 1958 edition). This view is central to modern secular democratic government, where law has replaced religion as the foundation of the community. Thus, secularization in political terms is important in the West because, as a process containing a constitutional element the object of which is to establish a framework of government responsive to change, it leads to an explicit acceptance of the idea of the sovereignty of the people. Secularization paid particular attention to the accumulation of wealth as a duty, which favoured rapid economic growth. The process is its own problem, however. Secular and decentralized government has wrestled with the question of how to retain the idea of obligation and responsibility in the face of continuous radical secularization.

It should not be assumed that there is a linear progression from centralized to decentralized or from sacred to secular systems. The opposite occurred (and in a peaceful manner) in Weimar Germany. Legitimacy was withdrawn from the constitutional government when the voters freely chose the Nazi party. This implies that the norms of a secular and decentralized system were relatively weak and insufficiently institutionalized. It also means that such a system can operate only when self-control and nonpolitical restraints on behaviour predominate.

SECULAR AND DECENTRALIZED GOVERNMENTS

As secularization occurred in Western societies, theological obligations were changed into codes of civic responsibility. Law replaced religion as the basis of political norms. With the rising prosperity of Europe, there developed a general belief that free, democratic governments with maximum political participation for all would provide a beneficial political condition. Indeed, struggles during the nineteenth century were over the speed and thoroughness with which constitutional democracy would incorporate the entire membership of a system rather than over structural principles of government.

A view of government analogous to the approach of classical economics was widely accepted. The community is composed of voters, who are like consumers, and their choice is tantamount to consumer sovereignty. The election system represents the market, in which voters choose their representatives on the basis of stated preferences. Government, consisting of parliament and cabinet as well as administrative cadres, is similar to the productive unit and manufactures decisions, which the public evaluates through the electoral mechanism. The courts are present to ensure that the rules of the system are not violated.

The principles on which the system works include a high level of information, rationality as an attribute of voting and decision making, and equal representation (Downs 1957; Easton 1966). Such principles underlie the American form of presidential government and the utilitarian systems advocated by John Stuart Mill and the Benthamites in England. Advocates of this form emphasize the improvement of information, the uses of education in order to reach rationality (only the informed voter can be rational), and, in particular, the improvement of electoral systems in order to achieve the maximum reproduction of public wants in a representative chamber. Hence, for example, one of the problems considered most important is whether proportional representation is preferable to simple plurality voting or some combination of weighted balloting or lists.

Important questions also arise about the role of political parties in government. How do parties, acting as agents by which public desires are transformed into government cognizance, facilitate the political process? In this respect political parties are designed to emphasize certain publicly held priorities and make them explicit, so that as the problems confronting government become more complex and individuals cannot make their views known on all of them, politicians stand for some symposium of priorities and on this basis are accepted or rejected by the voters.

The principle of majority rule implies in effect that the rightness of a doctrine is measured by the degree of support it obtains and that support creates power. Hence, majority rule is a principle of power which credits the rationality of the majority and elevates reason, plus numbers, over abstract morality. It is because of this that instrumentalities begin to take on their own moral proprieties.

Not all democratic polities accepted this highly individualistic form of government. Two alternative forms, one older and one very modern, have stressed the idea of the organic community rather than the more mechanistic doctrine of individualism. The first of these forms, an extension of medieval doctrine, incorporates Catholic beliefs in the context of a decentralized state. This includes various specific approaches to democratic government, such as Christian socialism and Christian democracy. The second form is democratic socialism, which emphasizes the democratic state as a means of fulfilling conditions of equality and freedom in conjunction with the development of the moral and material basis of the community.

Both of these forms see an inadequacy in democracy, resulting from a contradiction between private ownership of the means of production and the maintenance of civic obligation. How can government be secular and decentralized yet retain authority? If the achievement of democratic government is that it is secular in practice and therefore free of formalized commitments to a higher set of priorities than those desired by a majority, the problem is how to retain that self-control implicit in Calvin's formula. One answer is to study the new roles in government, particularly those which provide a "calling", such as the roles of civil servants, of members of professions, and of scientists, whose sense of responsibility and commitment to the exchange of free ideas is perhaps one of the most important characteristics of democratic government in highly industrial societies. (*See* Friedrich 1937; Jouvenel 1963; Sartori 1962.)

Types of democratic governments. Democratic governments require further differentiation. First, they can be divided into unitary and federal forms. Unitary governments are based on the position that all powers not otherwise reserved belong to a central government. Federal governments take the position that residual powers lie with the component geographical units which make up the federation.

Second, they can be classified as presidential and parliamentary forms. In a true presidential system, a president elected by the population is responsible to them, rather than to the legislature. The legislature, in turn, is responsible to the population which elects it, and not to the president. This provides checks and balances, with the public acting as arbiters during periodic elections, held at fixed intervals. The parliamentary system shows parliament supreme, with a prime minister responsible to it and holding office at its pleasure. Through votes of confidence and changes in parliamentary party membership, a government can fall, in which case a new general election to parliament is necessary; the majority or plurality of seats won by a political party provides a mandate to form a government. Under such a system the president (or monarch) is largely a figurehead. Where the parliamentary government is a constitutional monarchy, the transition from earlier forms of monarchy has generally been smooth, rather than abrupt, and has been achieved by virtue of internal structural changes. Notable cases are Holland, Denmark, Sweden, Norway, and Great Britain.

Much of the present concern of democratic government lies with the problems associated with the growing complexity of modern life and the increasingly broad responsibilities which individuals expect a secular government to take upon itself. Whereas the problem in the first half of the twentieth century was the improvement of electoral and representation methods and of local government and administration, the present emphasis is on the work load of parliaments and congresses. Both federal and unitary systems today accept the principle of one man, one vote, and "popular sovereignty" tends to mean a form of parliamentary representation embodying territorial and demographic bases. How to maintain debate on important issues and get through a heavy legislative work load is therefore a critical matter. In Great Britain, for example, the widening of the franchise was accompanied by the decline of the role of the private-member bill as the work load of the committees increased. Parliament divides according to the lines laid down by the party whips, and a free vote, each member voting according to his conscience, becomes rare (see Wheare 1955; McKenzie 1955). Discipline in parliament has given rise to the term "cabinet dictatorship".

How well parliamentary or cabinet forms of decentralized representative government work depends a great deal on how political parties carry on the work of government. Different structural rules obviously affect this. Since all decentralized and democratic forms of government have some means to control the executive, this may lead, in multiparty systems, to cabinet instability, as it did in France and does in Italy. The stability of such parliamentary governments, therefore, depends on the stability of coalitions. Where two parliamentary parties are characteristic, instability is rare, partly because of rigorous party discipline. (*See* Laski 1951.)

How to improve decentralized and democratic government has posed serious problems of political theory. It is not surprising, therefore, that highly individualistic conceptions of democracy have been replaced by notions of group representation, block voting, and the responsiveness of government to various groups, such as professional bodies, business lobbies, trade unions, co-operative movements, civic and veterans' organizations, churches, and educational and cultural groups. (*See* S. E. Finer 1958.) Indeed, so important have group theories become that interest groups have been called in Britain an "anonymous empire".

All of these questions relate directly to the relations between community and government. More precisely, they are devoted to an examination of intervening variables between community and government, such as political parties and interest groups, and even of subgroups within government itself. (See Figure 3.)

GOVERNMENT IN NEW NATIONS

Governments formed in new nations—those achieving independence after 1945—present some of the most interesting and challenging material confronting constitutional experts. political theorists, and politicians alike. New governments tend to include characteristics of all the forms we have discussed (Apter 1965). For ex-

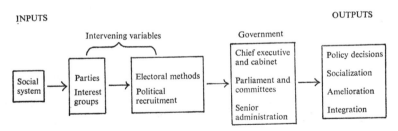

Figure 3.   Intervening variables relating to democratic government

ample, in Africa and parts of Asia there are attachments to primitive governments, which remain in competition with central government for the loyalties of the population. Regional clusters associated with a religious or linguistic affiliation may represent powerful primordial loyalties, denying legitimacy to a central government or countering it with a preference for local primordial attachments. Thus, unity and legitimacy within the context of a nation are urgent problems facing political leaders. Inasmuch as certain aspects of primitive government represent a rightful heritage, it may be that traditional qualities of legitimacy should be applied to modern governmental forms, as has been attempted under such ideological forms as "African socialism" or "communocracy".

Furthermore, new nations commonly emphasize the positive role of government as the great "engine" of social change, actively intervening in all aspects of life, from family relationships to educational opportunities, from road building to the development of local airways. Government in this respect is seen as an independent variable, much as it is, for example, in the Soviet Union.

At the same time, most constitutional patterns follow the line of Western parliamentary government. With sufficient control over parliament, through the instrumentality of party discipline, it is possible to retain popular government, based on parliamentary practice and a cabinet system, with few formal checks on executive authority.

In a very real sense, then, the governments of new nations tend to become amalgams of the other types we have discussed—theocratic, communist, fascist, and democratic. Their roots in primitive government become identified in normative terms, with a mythical past providing a national identity. The communist emphasis on puritanism, public ownership, and discipline is represented in the recruitment of a developmental elite and in its method of exercising power. The representation of corporate functional groups has much in common with fascist governments. And, the populist democratic emphasis and the pattern of parliamentary government represent Western democratic ideals and some of its procedures.

All this is confusing because the various systems of government described appear to be so antithetical that it would seem impossible to blend them into a viable and effective system. This is to a certain extent true; hence, virtually all new governments are in the process of changing into some more stable type. It is not surprising that quite often what holds such a government together is allegiance to a particular political leader, associated with revolution or the development of a mass movement. Indeed, the outstanding common feature of these new governments is their dependence on a personalized leader supported by a dominant political party. This tends to be the case whether or not the system is *formally* a single-party state, as long as there is a dominant party which is capable of controlling large regional areas. In the special case of new governments, therefore, the crucial factors are the relationship between the leader of the government and the leader of the party, and the role of the party. Ordinarily the first two are the same person, and the party operates government.

In terms of the various models employed here, new governments incline in theory to the position that government is an independent variable. In practice, however, government is likely to be an expression of an elite which manipulates a mass party that is itself a reflection of a wide diversity of interests. In other words, government and social system tend to become incorporated into the broad concept of a single party. Party becomes the independent variable, with government the intervening one, and social system the dependent one. (Even where there is more than one party, the situation is not very different. There may be several dominant regional—tribal or linguistic—parties, rather than one party; however, none are deeply committed to a single ideology, and in this they differ sharply from communist or fascist parties.)

The situation illustrated in Figure 4 is found in its clearest form under conditions of radical transformation from dependent to independent status or directly after a revolution. Since the framework within which the parliamentary and cabinet systems operate is not entirely eliminated, it intervenes between government and changes in the social system. In other words, the role of government, derived through the formal decision-making process, is the making of technical decisions, while the main lines of policy are generally laid down by governmental leaders, who are also senior party leaders. Classic examples are Nyerere's Tanzania, Ghana under Nkrumah, Nasser's Egypt, and Algeria under Ben Bella.

INPUTS   OUTPUTS

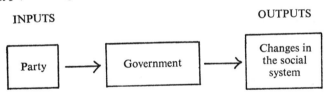

Figure 4.   Government in the pluralistic single-party state

How can new governments be evaluated? Normative criteria involve those associated with democratic systems and would include the adequacy of the protection of individual rights, and the degree of pluralism tolerated in government and parliament. On this score governments in new nations show a mixed record. Some, such as Ghana under Nkrumah, have a declaration of fundamental principles to which the president has sworn adherence, but these declarations cannot be enforced in the courts. Nigeria has a bill of rights. Burma emphasizes the social ownership of the means of production. Ghana and India have preventive-detention ordinances. It is safe to say that the protection of civil rights and liberties varies less with governmental form than with the general spirit in which government functions.

Since the legitimacy of new governments tends to be rather weak and is often associated with highly personalistic leaders (a very vulnerable structural condition), another normative criterion is how successfully a government develops primordial loyalties. The quality of such attachments provides a basis for evaluation of new governments and describes the depth of its emerging political culture.

Primordial attachments tend to become linked to problems of economic growth. Planning, technical skills, manpower surveys, and the like, are important areas of governmental decision making. In addition, they are moral or normative concepts associated with the objectives which commonly take the form of socialism, since socialism explicitly validates a development ideal and is represented, through party and government, in evolutionary ideal terms. Socialism also justifies political demands for personal sacrifice and loyalty. How well socialism (or its variants) can embody new economic rationality and enforce commitment to savings, work, education, and development becomes a third evaluative criterion.

Behavioural consequences of normative beliefs thus emerge. A combination of political norms, nationalist primordial sentiments, and philosophical ideological expressions of socialism combine to form the motivational system of the society. Structurally these elements are organized less frequently in parliamentary or representative institutions than in functional or corporate bodies within and around a political party. Party wings and various related interest groups are the devices that link individuals to the government.

Despite all the integrative efforts, the most striking feature of new governments is the behavioral weakness in their population *vis-a-vis* government. Changing allegiances and ritualization of authority, not to speak of the stresses and strains of rapid economic change and industrialization, all require much study of motivation, of the sources of personal identity, and of learning. Indeed, what is now called the identity problem, involving examination of the conditions under which individuals are able to establish a set of personality boundaries compatible with changing normative and structural conditions, is a growing concern. Only a few studies of the relationship between government and identity have been attempted, though many problems of governing derive from the search for identity (Pye 1962; Erikson 1958; Edelman 1964).

CONTEMPORARY RESEARCH AND THEORY

The author has tried to demonstrate a few of the emphases associated with the study of government and has employed both normative and structural variables to differentiate types of systems. Historically, the most elaborately studied aspect of government has been its normative side, which is still important in trying to determine how governments will evolve because it helps us to relate political means and ends. The structural dimension, almost as well studied in the literature as the normative, has been heavily weighted in favour of the study of the constitution as the foundation of government. Different constitutional systems have been distinguished through enumeration of their characteristics. More recently, work on the structural dimension, developed along the lines of institutionalist analysis and heavily influenced by the work of Max Weber, Karl Mannheim, and others, has related government to art, religion, philosophy, education, and other social institutions. The main concern of these scholars has been to study democracy as a universal system originating in Western civilization and to contrast it with less evolved forms of government, such as monarchy or oligarchy.

This work led to the development of functional analysis in the study of government, with its emphasis on the derivation of more-universalized comparative categories. Such studies have by and large employed one of two forms of systems theory. The first tends to follow the organismic analogy. Government is seen in its intimate relationships to society. A good set of functional categories for government will do the following: allow comparison of widely diverse forms and actions in terms of their implications for government as a whole; segregate critical activities from less critical ones; allow one to observe explicit levels of explanatory theory (Almond & Coleman 1960; Apter 1965).

The second emphasis in contemporary systems theory follows a mechanistic tradition. Some of the recent work, based on theories of coalitions, is originally derived from economic theories and attempts to use principles of rational calculation and maximization in order to predict political group behaviour. Several of the efforts to deal with coalitions begin with the group basis of politics and draw their original inspiration from the writings of A. F. Bentley. The most powerful form of systems analysis following this tradition is to be found in cybernetics models and game theory. These represent more generalized structural models than the ones used for functional analysis. The rules derived for one unit apply to all group behaviour. In the game-theory approach these deal primarily with the consequences for action of communications and information. Systems analysis of this type involves analysis of attempts, according to explicit rules, to maximize gains and minimize losses. Formulation of such highly rationalistic models can help us to understand political competition and government actions in priority and other settings. (*See* Downs 1957; Snyder 1961.)

Emphasis on groups has also given rise to an important literature with behavioural, as well as structural, implications. Behavioural and structural aspects of government depend on the analysis of government as a group, with reference to its size, its patterns of communications, and the ways in which motivation and memory are structured within it. Work in this area draws on the theories of psychologists (e.g. Kurt Lewin, R. Lippitt, and Theodore Newcomb), concerning leadership, interaction processes, cohesiveness, control over deviance, internalization of norms, etc., and tends to treat decision-making as the main object of analysis. (*See* Cartwright & Zander 1953.) Today such an emphasis can be integrated with informational analysis, group theory, and game theory in certain cybernetics models applied to government. This form of systems theory uses the concept of an information grid, in which a political system represents the flow of messages or of "cues" and government the critical "transformer", i.e. a coding and decision-making instrument. It is concerned with adaptability, and emphasizes the capacity of different systems to learn and adjust, with government performing an essentially creative role. One modern political theory which attempts to bring together these functional and other emphases very systematically is Karl Deutsch's application (1963) of the general cybernetics model, which is an attempt to solve problems of learning, creativity, and adaptation in politics.

INPUTS   OUTPUTS

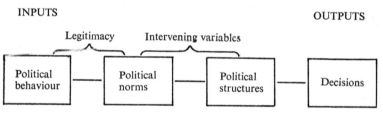

Figure 5. A generalized model of government

To account for these new developments, a more general way of analysing governments is required. The formulation illustrated in Figure 5 helps to move the analysis of government to a highly generalized level, incorporating the various approaches, new and old, in a single model. In this model political behaviour is the independent variable. Political norms and structures can therefore be treated as intervening variables. Their effectiveness is subject to change because political structure is bound and limited by the legitimacy pattern established by the relationships between political behaviour and political norms. Political structure can be seen in terms of its consequences for decision making, which in turn is designed to maintain a sustained pattern of political behaviour consonant with the maintenance of norms.

It is possible, of course, to enlarge the complexity of this model. More important, it is necessary to rotate these variables for different purposes and to hold each of them independent in turn, in order to estimate their effects. Many of the variations in approach to the study of government derive from holding different of these variables independent without realizing the specific methodological implications of doing so. The selection of variables to be held independent is entirely arbitrary. To estimate the effectiveness of different forms of government, however, it might be useful to treat political structure as the independent variable and see how various types—democratic, totalitarian, centralized, decentralized, monistic, pluralistic, monopolistic, competitive—affect both political norms and political behaviour. How does each of these alternative types allow political learning to take place? How does government preserve continuity? How does it affect the course of change? In addition to rotating the variables, it is possible to add new intervening variables. These may be normative ones, such as ideologies, or structural ones, such as political parties, administrative organizations, and the like.

Any general theory of government will require a model which is sufficiently explicit to account for the limits of variation, sufficiently flexible to handle diverse methodological emphasis, and empirical enough to be fully operationalized. We are still far from able to construct such a model, but the foregoing discussion shows that at least the foundations of the model and the theory have been laid. Still needed are improved techniques of gathering data, as well as analytical paradigms by means of which such data can be related to the appropriate theory. These concerns connect the analysis and study of government to the philosophy of science by emphasizing logical and epistemological problems, and also cause us to speculate about the application of highly advanced mathematical and statistical techniques and computer programming to the careful mapping and testing of propositions about government. The concept of government thus remains a critical point of departure for both the evaluation of the normative issues of political life and the structural and behavioural analysis of politics.

BIBLIOGRAPHY

Adams, Brooks. 1898 *The Law of Civilization and Decay* (New York: Macmillan).
Adams, Henry. (1904) 1963 *Mont-Saint-Michel and Chartres* (New York: Collier).
Almond, Gabriel A., and Coleman, James S., eds. 1960 *The Politics of the Developing Areas* (Princeton University Press).
Almond, Gabriel A., and Verba, Sidney. 1963 *The Civic Culture: Political Attitudes and Democracy in Five Nations* (Princeton University Press).

Apter, D. E. 1964 *The Politics of Modernization* (University of Chicago Press).

Barker, Ernest (1942) 1958 *Reflections on Government* (New York: Oxford University Press).

Barnard, Frederick M. 1965 *Herder's Social and Political Thought* (Oxford: Clarendon).

Bryce, James. 1921 *Modern Democracies*, 2 vols. (New York: Macmillan).

Brzezinski, Zbigniew K. 1962 *Ideology and Power in Soviet Politics* (New York: Praeger).

Cartwright, Dorwin, and Zander, Alvin, eds. (1953) 1960 *Group Dynamics: Research and Theory* (2nd ed., Evanston, Ill.: Row, Peterson). A good review of the psychological materials on group behaviour.

Davies, Reginald Trevor. 1937 *The Golden Century of Spain* (London: Macmillan).

Deutsch, Karl W. 1962 *The Nerves of Government: Models of Political Communication and Control* (New York: Free Press).

Dicey, Albert V. (1885) 1961 *Introduction to the Study of the Law of the Constitution* (10th ed. with an introduction by E. C. S. Wade. London: Macmillan; New York: St. Martins). First published as *Lectures Introductory to the Study of the Law of the Constitution.*

Downs, Anthony. 1957 *An Economic Theory of Democracy* (New York: Harper).

Easton, David. 1957 "Political Structures and Processes", *World Politics,* 9, pp. 383–400.

—— 1965 *A Systems Analysis of Political Life* (New York: Wiley).

—— ed. 1966 *Varieties of Political Theory* (Englewood Cliffs, N.J.: Prentice Hall). See especially "An Individualistic Theory of Political Process', by James M. Buchanan.

Edelman, Jacob M. 1964 *The Symbolic Uses of Politics* (Urbana: University of Illinois Press.)

Erikson, Erik H. (1958) 1962 *Young Man Luther: A Study in Psychoanalysis and History,* Austin Riggs Monograph No. 4 (New York: Norton).

Fairman, H. W. 1958 "The Kingship Rituals of Egypt", pp. 74–104 in Samuel H. Hooke, ed., *Myth, Ritual and Kingship: Essays on the Theory and Practice of Kingship in the Ancient Near East and in Israel* (Oxford: Clarendon).

Fallers, Lloyd A. (1956) 1965 *Bantu Bureacracy: A Century of Political Evolution* (University of Chicago Press).

Finer, Herman. (1932) 1949 *The Theory and Practice of Modern Government* (rev. ed., New York: Holt).

Finer, Samuel E. (1958) 1962 *Anonymous Empire: A Study of the Lobby in Great Britain* (London: Pall Mall).

Friedrich, Carl J. (1937) 1950 *Constitutional Government and Democracy: Theory and Practice in Europe and America* (rev. ed., Boston: Ginn). First published as *Constitutional Government and Politics: Nature and Development.*

Friedrich, Carl J., and Brzezinski, Zbigniew K. (1956) 1965 *Totalitarian Dictatorship and Autocracy* (2nd ed., rev., Cambridge, Mass: Harvard University Press).

Gash, Norman. 1953 *Politics in the Age of Peel: A Study in the Technique of Parliamentary Representation, 1830–1850* (London and New York: Longmans).

Gierke, Otto von. (1881) 1958 *Political Theories of the Middle Ages* (Cambridge University Press). First published as "Die publicistischen Lehren des Mittelalters", a section of Volume 3 of Gierke's *Das deutsche Genossenschaftsrecht.* Translated, with a famous introduction, by Frederic William Maitland.

Hignett, Charles. (1952) 1962 *A History of the Athenian Constitution to the End of the Fifth Century B.C.* (Oxford: Clarendon).

Jouvenel, Bertrand de. 1963 *The Pure Theory of Politics* (New Haven: Yale University Press).

Laqueur, Walter, and Labedz, Leopold, eds. 1962 *Polycentrism: The New Factor in International Communism* (New York: Praeger).

Laski, Harold J. (1925) 1957 *A Grammar of Politics* (4th ed., London: Allen & Unwin).

—— (1935) 1956 *The State in Theory and Practice* (London: Allen & Unwin).

—— (1951) 1962 *Reflections on the Constitution: The House of Commons, the Cabinet [and] the Civil Service* (Manchester University Press). Published posthumously.

Lasswell, Harold D. (1930) 1960 *Psychopathology and Politics* (new ed., with afterthoughts by the author, New York: Viking).

Lewis, Ewart, ed. 1954 *Medieval Political Ideas*, 2 vols. (New York: Knopf).

McKenzie, Robert T. (1955) 1963 *British Political Parties: The Distribution of Power within the Conservative and Labour Parties* (2nd ed., London: Heinemann; New York: St. Martins). A paperback edition was published in 1964 by Praeger.

McNeil, John T. 1954 *The History and Character of Calvinism* (New York: Oxford University Press).

Ostrogorskii, Moisei I. (1902) 1964 *Democracy and the Organization of Political Parties*, 2 vols., edited and abridged by Seymour M. Lipset (Chicago: Quadrangle). An abridged edition of a 1902 English translation from the French.

Payne, Stanley G. 1961 *Falange: A History of Spanish Fascism*, Stanford Studies in History, Economics and Political Science, No. 22 (Stanford University Press).

Pipes, Richard. (1954) 1964 *The Formation of the Soviet Union* (rev. ed., Cambridge, Mass.: Harvard University Press).

Pye, Lucian W. 1962 *Politics, Personality, and Nation Building: Burma's Search for Identity* (New Haven: Yale University Press).

Riker, William H. 1962 *The Theory of Political Coalitions* (New Haven: Yale University Press).

Sartori, Giovanni. 1962 *Democratic Theory* (Detroit, Mich.: Wayne State University Press). A paperback edition was published in 1965 by Praeger.

Snyder, Richard C. 1961 *Game Theory and the Analysis of Political Behavior* (New York: Free Press).

Talmon, Jacob L. (1952) 1965 *The Origins of Totalitarian Democracy* (2nd ed., New York: Praeger).

Ulam, Adam B. 1960 *The Unfinished Revolution: An Essay on the Sources of Influence of Marxism and Communism* (New York: Random House).

Wallas, Graham. (1908) 1962 *Human Nature in Politics* (4th ed., Gloucester, Mass.: Smith).

Weber, Max. (1904–05) 1930 *The Protestant Ethic and the Spirit of Capitalism*. Translated by Talcott Parsons, with a foreward by R. H. Tawney (London: Allen & Unwin; New York: Scribner). First published in German. The 1930 edition has been reprinted frequently. A paperback edition was published in 1958 by Scribner.

Wheare, Kenneth C. 1955 *Government by Committee: An Essay on the British Constitution* (Oxford: Clarendon).

6

Why Political Systems Change*

I intend to follow an abstract line in answering the question why
political systems change. That is, I am not concerned with the in-
finity of descriptive reasons why change occurs in any concrete
case. It may be argued that now is not the time to bother with
such a trivial approach, particularly when the language of crisis is
what must be used, and also understood, and not the language of
abstraction.

I think the answer to this is that for too long the evaluation of
politics, and of government in particular, has become a "pseudo-
activity" in which descriptive categories like "parliamentary control
over the executive", or "reform of the committee system" are com-
forting shibboleths which, although meant to contain some inner
profundity have lost much of their original meaning. The truth is
that the balance between normative givens and structural conditions
is becoming so altered that the common-sense foundations of the
discipline seem almost irrelevant.

Of course this is not a new situation, but as old as politics itself.
Only the form is bizarre. But if the discipline is to be improved it can
neither remain stuck at the level of shibboleths which pass for concepts nor succumb to the attack of anti-intellectuals who would, out
of perversity or innocence, destroy government itself. The problem
to tackle then is the political predicament both in industrial and
modernizing societies. These we cannot attempt to understand by
sliding well-worn political science categories around in the great
shell game which passes, particularly in Britain, for political science.
The point of view taken here is that in order to deal with practical
questions of basic reform, we first need to revise the categories used
for understanding politics. If the particular theory offered here will
not do the job, perhaps it can serve as an illustration of the sort of
thing which is needed.

* Reprinted by permission from *Government and Opposition*, Volume 3, Number 4, Autumn 1968.

GOVERNMENT AS A CONCEPT

Concrete variations in arrangements and mechanisms of government appearing in standardized format can be called regimes. Regimes constitute a specific linkage of government to elites. Regimes are normally differentiated on the basis of executive, judicial, legislative, and administrative functions in which the role of each is contingent upon the role of the other. The particular arrangement can then be examined in terms of its internal workings, as with parliaments, cabinets, committees in regard to legislative and executive functions, and courts, administrative tribunals, and other forms of adjudication with respect to judicial functions. This draws our attention to the many ways in which all these are organized and their members recruited, their relation to constituencies, etc. A large literature already exists on just these subjects which is invaluable as a source of data, commentary, and analysis of the properties of specialized instruments of government.[1]

One difficulty with this general line of approach, however, is that it demands too much of the concrete mechanisms. Form may follow function, but in ways that are general not specific. It is very difficult to specify the conditions under which a concrete mechanism will have the consequence in a different original setting. Parliamentary government in England in a democratic regime may turn into cabinet dictatorship in Ghana with an autocratic regime. One party government may be democratic as it evolves in Czechoslovakia or Tanzania and autocratic in China or the U.S.S.R.

This invites two caveats. First the danger of reification which results from elevating concrete units to the level of analytical ones. Second, and contingent on the first is the difficulty of detecting affinities between regimes and stages of development. At the concrete level then we want a narrow definition of government which allows intact the analytical relationship of linkages between society, elite, and government without telescoping these into mechanisms characteristic of regimes. This was avoided in an earlier and more philosophical period. Let us take a quick look back before proceeding.

For a political scientist, or anyone concerned with politics as a variable, government is the heart of the matter. Whether we speak of government by men, or government by laws, we deal with a certain kind of 'entelechy", the capacity of applying intelligence to specific problems arising within society or abroad, to be handled, if possible, with despatch. It is, in an ancient manner of speaking, part heart and part head. Perhaps it is because of this that Plato emphasized a state governed by the wise or superior men in his *Republic*, or Aristotle even when he supported the supremacy of law, made special pro-

H

vision for exceptional men whose superior qualities were such that they could be regarded as above law. The relations of government to society are embodied in this problem.

That is why much of the original stuff of politics was devoted to the relationship of man to law, action to rule. The argument over law and its limitations embodied all the larger issues. Law represented a series of regularized procedures, which applied more or less universally to the body of citizens, forming the basis for reciprocal rights and duties between governed and rulers. This meant that when actionable boundaries were set and remedial procedures established, the result would be a "meaningful predictability" providing on the one hand continuity in the society yet allowing for changes in the composition of government on the other. Indeed it is this relationship between the slow moving alteration of society and the faster moving and more immediate responses of government which, specified in a set of legal relationships and powers, constituted what is meant by the state. It is as if the generalized relationships which obtain in society with all its myriad strands and links to resources, human and material, were tied together at one point, knotted and gripped firmly, in the sense that law presumes power, and power presumes force or compulsion. Whether the strings were tied to puppets, or themselves were delicate threads, easily snapped if the pull became too great, was another matter. Over such issues centred the original debates over political forms. When was the time for a strong lead? When would such a lead result in violence and revolution?[2]

Traditional theorists had many answers to such problems. It is precisely because their reasoning was so persuasive that principles of majority rule, of government by consent, and all the rest of the liberal pantheon has come to embody a hortatory character and a descriptive holiness. But their defence as virtue is one matter. Their employment as models are another. It is in the latter case that new theories are necessary. Mindful of such matters we will deal with government as a highly generalized concrete unit. It represents, however, the least general of three concrete units with which we deal, society, elites and government. To analyse government we will not employ the distinction which separates the "rule of law" from "the rule of men", nor the usual typologies of government which may follow from such distinctions. Nor will we distinguish here between the exercise of power as compulsion and the application of power as a responsibility of office, although we are of course aware of the importance of such matters. Our preference is to deal with them in the context of certain political systems types which we plan to develop on the assumption that only then does it become possible to compare (within such types and between them) the consequences of specific mechanisms of rule and isolate their variable significance. For the moment then, our emphasis is on the relationship of government to elites and society.

Seen in this light, government is the recipient of inputs received from the other two more general concrete units, which it converts into a set of outputs which are decisions of various kinds. For example, the problems of industrial and modernizing life can be summarized as the "meritocracy" problem in the first instance, and the *embourgeoisement* problem in the second. Confronting these in the context of our political systems suggests a variable capacity of government to deal with them. In all political systems, however, whether there is or is not a government of laws, the capacity to deal with the problems of the meritocracy and embourgeoisement are a function of the effectiveness of authoritative decision-making. It is to assess that effectiveness under different types of political systems that we pursue the present formulation.[3]

THE GENERAL MODEL

The concepts employed to analyse these matters are taken from a series of books and articles which I have already published.[4] The point of departure is the problem of choice. Choice we divide into three components, normative, structural, and behavioural. The first two contain and limit choices. The third deals with which alternatives are selected. How choices widen is what we mean by development. Industrial societies are those which create choice alternatives. Modernizing societies are a result of the spread of roles developed in an industrial society without much of an industrial infrastructure. In the two types of situations modernizing and industrial the political problems are substantially different. In the first, the goals are to widen choice through greater development. Norms and structures are related to each other in terms of this object. In industrial societies the problems are different. It is the meaning of choice which becomes important—its morality. The normative structural situation becomes increasingly complex, and imbalances arise. How a political system responds to these conditions will vary specifically from place to place, but particular types seem more suitable for various stages of the process and less suitable for others. This implies a theory of political systems, i.e. a deductive typology which can form hypotheses, and a general model which combines all types.

The theory offered here begins with the following summarizing proposition which is generally accepted in our discipline: choice is to allocation as equity is to order.

$$\frac{\text{Choice}}{\text{Allocation}} = \frac{\text{Equity}}{\text{Order}}$$

This simple formulation leads us to the statement that *equity of allocation equals orderly choice*. The concept of political norms derives from the concept of equity. The concept of political structure derives from the concept of order. If we take one more step and characterize norms as *consummatory*, i.e. embodying ultimate ends, and *instrumental*, i.e. embodying empirical ends, and structure as hierarchical and pyramidal, we have the basis for a deductive model of political systems types, analytical not concrete, which forms hypotheses in relation to development. This model is as follows:

Political Structure

		Hierarchical	Pyramidal
Political Norms	Cons.	Mobilization System	Theocratic System
	Instr.	Bureaucratic System	Reconciliation System

Figure 1.　Political system types

From this formulation several observations can be made.

1. Each concrete society will show several of these political system tendencies simultaneously, hence we can only speak of predominant types.

2. Each predominant type produces a "political ceiling" for governments after which a pressure to alter the predominant political type arises.

3. That political instability in this special sense constitutes creativity and innovation.

4. That affinities exist between stages of development and predominant types of political system (but not on an evolutionary, unilineal, or permanent basis). Specifically, bureaucratic systems are likely to be most suitable for early to middle modernization periods, mobilization systems most suitable for carrying late stage modernizing societies into industrialization, and reconciliation systems most likely in highly industrialized societies. There are many reasons why we put forward these propositions but here we shall focus the discussion on government.

THE FUNCTIONS OF GOVERNMENT

Our main process variables will be industrialization and modernization. These can be translated into normative and structural inputs. Such inputs when undertaken specifically by elites, represent linkages to government. They use group claims to representation. The degree of access by elites can be measured in terms of certain functions of the elite and structures of government. More specifically, we suggest that there are two structures which are a result of the operation of elite functions, (1) the structure of *information*, which is a description of the conversion of messages into knowledge by elites, and (2) the structure of *coercion* which we suggest results in the conversion of actions taken by governments into outputs which then affect the society as a whole. Hence the intimate relationship between government and elites.

But as government is confined to a lower level of generalization than the elites, so the relationship described allows us to make another more specific formulation, namely, that the structures of information and coercion formed by the elite *are functional requisites of government*. No government can function without information. No government can function without coercion. Both are necessary ingredients if governments are to act as an "entelechy", i.e. to engage in meaningful activities. Both information and coercion are functional requisites because governments by their actions seek to rid themselves of as much uncertainty as possible. That is they try to eliminate random factors as much as possible in order to make decisions affecting the society with predictable results. What the business of the day shall be is determined by the information obtained from elites. What decisions can be carried out, depends largely on the coercive opportunities available to them and of which they have an originating monopoly.

Although the purpose of this formulation is not merely a matter of logical elegance, there must be a logical roundness to it. If, on the one hand government is the recipient of inputs, by its ability to create its own outputs it affects the inputs in a next stage or sequence of relationships. This capacity is exactly what gives government its importance. Indeed, we can go further and say that such a role defines the character of the relationship between concrete units, inputs and outputs, but also its actions should vary with the predominant political system type which prevails. By analysing how information and coercion work it is also possible to identify two structural requisites of government, *authoritative decision making* and *accountability and consent*. Hence in our formulation it can be seen that the unit government not only completes the system of relations between concrete units, it also closes the analytical system. This brings the analysis to an extremely important point, namely the determination of independent variables.

From the standpoint of analysis, we treat the concrete units society, elites and government in descending order of generality implying that each larger unit sets the concrete boundaries of action for each smaller unit, and on a cumulative basis. That is, whereas government is bounded by elites and societal variables more generally, elites are bounded by societal variables, and societal variables themselves are bounded by the processes of modernization and industrialization, with the latter the dynamic element. In this concrete formulation, government is a dependent variable "responding" to inputs generated outside of its immediate boundaries, although as a sub-system, the varieties of arrangements within enable it to deal, in each case, somewhat differently with these inputs. The same would also be true of incumbents to office. As these change, within a given sub-system type of government, some alteration in response to inputs will occur.

From another standpoint, however, industrialization, modernization, characteristics of stratification, patterns of elites all of which accumulate and identify inputs, are the result of government actions which are themselves dependent and intervening variables. Thus, in terms of the concrete units employed, whereas government is independent, elites would be intervening variables and society a dependent one despite the level of its generality.

Now from a purely analytical point of view, which unit is regarded as independent is quite arbitrary. It is quite possible to link the concrete units as first described, i.e. society—elites—government, and then turn these around, with quite useful results. Or for that matter, it is possible to consider elites as independent with the others dependent or intervening as the case may be. Such arrangements are entirely arbitrary and at the discretion of the observer.

In our treatment of political systems, the relationships of power to values suggests a classificatory division which can serve to separate two main arrangments of the concrete units involved. Theocratic and reconciliation systems, since they rely less on coercion and more on information would involve government as a dependent variable, elite as intervening, and society as independent, with any change in this relationship depending on an increase in coercion which would shift the position of government from dependent to independent. Mobilization and bureaucratic systems would, in contrast, require government to be the independent variable, with elite intervening and society dependent. Indeed, the ambiguity of the bureaucratic system on the one hand and the theocratic system on the other derives from the position of government. In bureaucratic systems, what must be clear in theory is not always clear in practice, i.e. the role of government as the independent variable. And in theocratic systems the same condition would apply, only it would not be clear whether in fact society was the independent variable and government dependent.[5]

What criteria do we have to demarcate between these two conditions? The two structural requisites of government can serve as indicators. These, the structure of accountability and consent, and the structure of authoritative decision-making, depend in the first instance on elite representation and in the second on elite access, both of which have already been described. In turn, the two functional requisites of government, information and coercion, would be affected as follows:

1. Where accountability is low and access limited, the political system will show a high degree of hierarchy and a reliance on coercion. In this situation the predicament for government is caused by the need for accurate information.

2. High accountability implies low hierarchy, widespread representation (by one means or another) and elite access to decision-making. This results in high information. The problem then is the inability to make necessary but unpopular decisions, or to carry them out, both of which would require greater coercion. This simple formulation is not a very surprising one or very novel. Nevertheless, it is at the centre of the structural theory of politics.

We have already suggested that despite its central role in political studies, and the lengthy descriptive literature that exists at present, there remains associated with the term government an elusive quality because we are never quite certain who actually governs or why. Indeed, in the sense that government can refer to participation by the entire body of citizens, at least in a democratic society, the various devices by means of which they delegate their authority to representatives constitutes a good deal of what political science is about. Thus government in the sense of the group of individuals responsible for making and carrying out the decisions necessary to sustain the society is an ambiguous unit and its boundaries are by no means clear. What is "the government" in the United States? Is the Congress part of the government or does the term refer primarily to the executive branch? Do we include the judiciary or not? And in Britain, does "the government" consist entirely of members of the cabinet with the rank of minister, or does it include the Queen in Council or Parliament? The answer is that the unit "government" will shift depending upon how the question is asked. Similarly in the case of "totalitarian" governments. No government is truly one-man rule. There is always some sharing of power and some consultation. Despite the arbitrary quality of his decisions, Hitler did consult with his generals in wartime, so did Stalin. This vagueness about the unit despite its central role in the study of politics is one of the more important anomalies of the subject. Accordingly we will need to establish some guide lines for dealing with government as a concrete unit. We prefer a "minimal" unit, in contrast to elites which are a "maximal" unit. A minimal unit of government refers to the smallest number of individuals responsible for wielding executive authority on a consistent basis, i.e. the smallest group with a defined responsibility for maintaining the balance between equity and order. The peculiar and central characteristic of this group is that it constitutes a sub-system role. It is a concrete sub-system with a defined responsibility for the maintenance or adaptation of the system as a whole. Such maintenance or adaptation has its concrete aspect in the sense of boundaries in space and time, a membership with legally defined rights and responsibilities. In other words the unit society and its equity—order relationships, become the concern of government, which remains the minimal unit possessing executive authority.

Where government is a dependent variable, it is the minimal which we say responds to the chain of inputs described (those arising through processes of industrialization and modernization, reflecting on society through the formation of various types of stratification groups, translated into specific forms of participation by means of elites, who convert demands into inputs for government response). With government the independent variable, it, that is the minimal unit, is a source of inputs affecting the industrialization and modernization processes, which in turn determines the pattern of stratification and group representation, and defines the character of elite participation. By dealing with a sufficiently small group, governments can be treated in these various capacities as dependent and independent variables and by examining both these alternative conditions it is possible to evaluate the extent to which a political system follows in the direction of mobilization and bureaucratic systems on the one hand, or reconciliation and theocratic systems on the other.

Government then not only stands as the strategic concrete unit in the present analysis (for reasons just suggested). It is also the concrete unit which defines the character of the analytical units described. The way in which elites and government interact in terms of access, information, and coercion, defines the type of political system which predominates in any concrete case.

WHY POLITICAL SYSTEMS CHANGE

When does a government reach its "ceiling" beyond which it cannot take effective action? The answer is when functional and dialectical changes in society are so excessive that either the structure of accountability and consent or the structure of authoritative decision-making fails. By "fails" we mean that the structures no longer result in government being able to obtain adequate information, or being able successfully to apply effective coercion, i.e. failures in the structure requisites result in failures in the functional requisites. When information and coercion no longer function for government, then they also fail as structures of the elite. In turn, when the structures of the elite no longer operate, neither do the functions of the elite, i.e. goal specification, central control, and institutional coherence. The result is the randomization of relationship between groups, a condition which is the opposite of order, producing at the same time competition between various sets of values, which confounds a stabilized system of equity. This brings us back to our original point of departure in the form of a general structural proposition. If a political system is to work, equity must be structurally integrated with order. When a political ceiling is reached and the system breaks down, then order is not integrated with equity. The problem is to find this point.

The point at which the equity–order balance is upset is described as that in which uncertainty, coercion and information become fixed in their relationship to each other. How this relationship becomes fixed will vary depending upon whether government is the independent or dependent variable in the relationship between our three concrete units, society, elites and government. The greater the amount of functional participation by elites in the government the greater the degree of information available to government. The smaller the degree of functional participation by elites in the government, the more coercive is the role of the elites. Information means that type of knowledge which reduces uncertainty. Uncertainty in turn means the capacity or ability to predict a reasoned sequence of events. As modernization increases, so does complexity, so does uncertainty, and so does the need for information *and* the need for coercion. Since the relationship between these variables is inverse, attempt to solve the paradox by an increase in coercion transforms those governments which are dependent variables into independent ones, and attempts to increase information by those governments which are independent variables transforms them into dependent ones. Or, to put it another way, when reconciliation and theocratic systems attempt to maintain the structures of accountability and consent and authoritative decision-making by increasing coercion, they become changed into mobilization or bureaucratic systems, and when mobilization and bureaucratic systems attempt to maintain their structural requisites by increasing information, they change into reconciliation or theocratic systems. The response to uncertainty, whether in terms of coercion or information, is thus the key to political system change.[6]

To summarize, (1) the greater the degree of modernization, the wider the range of choice. (2) The wider the range of choice in a system, the greater the degree of normative and structural imbalance. (3) The greater the degree of normative and structural imbalance the greater the likelihood of alteration in the equity–order relationship, and legitimate authority, resulting in greater uncertainty. How each political system responds to such uncertainty, reaches its ceiling and alters, is the problem.

Let us take two political systems types, the mobilization and reconciliation systems and see how they handle these matters. Confronted with uncertainty, both seek to maximize the information at their disposal in order to increase the efficiency of their decision-making, and strengthen the attachment of populist, interest, and professional groups and their elites. Remembering that at any point in time the total amount of information available in a system derives from these, with steady increases in the instrumental and technical spheres as modernization increases we can suggest the following propositions:

1. The lower the degree of hierarchy, the greater the difficulty confronted by government in acting on information unless there is a high degree of consensus. 2. The greater the degree of hierarchy the easier it is for government to act upon the information at its disposal. 3. Technical information is easier to obtain than other forms. 4. In mobilization and bureaucratic systems, governments tend to maximize technical information and employ coercion to reduce uncertainty in the spheres where information is lacking. 5. In reconciliation systems the attempt is made to maximize populist, interest, and professional forms of information and to find an acceptable common denominator to validate increasing coercion for carrying out authoritative decisions. 6. Theocratic systems represent idealizations in which a unanimity of beliefs create a high information voluntaristic system in which coercion is unnecessary.

Hence two of the four systems need higher degrees of nontechnical information, but need more on the populist and interest side; one has plenty of information of all types but needs to increase coercive opportunities in order to resolve its competitive conflicts, and the last tends to be a non-functional ideological goal as for example in socialist mobilization systems.

In other words, in both the situations in which government is the independent variable and the dependent one, governments either do increase or want to increase their effectiveness through the application of coercion. In the case of the mobilization system, coercion takes the form of governmental control of the elites, and is applied in terms of information already available. It is coercive, particularly in the sphere of consummatory values. Normatively, it restricts political values to a highly symbolic set of consummatory "templates" creating a special language or code. A high degree of symbolic coercion is prepared for violators of this code. They may be "cast out" of the community or put to death for violations of symbol. Political "witches" are publicly burned, especially those representing counter-legitimacy consummatory values. Instrumental values, more easily contained by police controls or a political party (the so-called single party system being one device employed), tend to be concentrated in two forms of interest: economic and political; but these interests stand for the community as a whole, rather than particular sub-groups.

In reconciliation systems political leaders also desire to use centralized coercion. However, the key characteristic of pyramidal authority is limited power; and such limitation on coercion is imposed by the diversity and strength of accountability groups. Nevertheless, the tendency to coercion exists for many reasons. In the absence of coercion, there is likely to be considerable private corruption. Dislike of the government as well as other forms of resentment are common. Many interests compete; but this may weaken rather than strengthen the system as the danger that interest conflict may be converted into value conflict arises and prepares the groundwork for either a mobilization system or some other alternative, including take-over by groups with a high coercive potential and instrumental values best represented in the military. Cases in point have been Burma, Pakistan, the Sudan, and most recently Nigeria.

In each case—mobilization or reconciliation system—the key to system-change is a functional change in the political system itself.

THE INFORMATION–COERCION RELATIONSHIP

Increasing coercion will result in losses in information. Such losses are not necessarily direct and immediate; nor are they all of the same type. Losses in information from increased coercion are likely to occur in the following order: highest, in the sphere of counter-legitimacy consummatory values; and lowest, in the area of technical information resulting from industrialization itself. However, instrumental conflict is likely to be disguised and increasingly converted from interest conflict to value conflict. In other words, a two-step process takes place, including the loss of information about counter values and the increasing political significance of what would otherwise remain in the category of interest claims. This is the particular problem of the mobilization system.

The problem is the reverse in the reconciliation system. Thus, information about instrumental conflict is likely to be very high—so high, indeed, that it cannot be screened and evaluated. In addition, the content of the information is likely to be so confusing that a government is at a loss about how best to act upon it. With its sphere of action limited by diverse accountability groups, government is likely to find compromise necessary—itself a cause for that stagnation. This creates groups in favour of populist consummatory values which repudiate government or act as a regenerative movement against the government. If coercion can be applied against representatives of this moral force, it only reinforces their claims and gives them wider legitimacy. We can diagram these tendencies as follows:

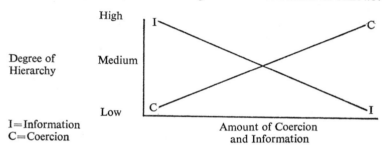

Figure 2. The information–coercion relationship

Now, we can restate these assumptions in several hypothetical propositions:

(1) All governments engaging in modernization show a tendency to increase coercion to maximize the efficiency of decision-making. (2) The point at which this tendency terminates is where coercion causes such losses in information that effective decision-making is reduced. (3) Changes in the relationship between coercion and information produce changes in the type of government involved, not only in terms of mobilization and reconciliation systems, but also into two intermediate types involving hierarchical authority and instrumental values or pyramidal authority and consummatory values (the latter change occurring much less frequently than the former).

We can diagram these points as follows:
The tendency "A"→"E" illustrates the need for greater information on the part of a mobilization system; while the tendency "B"→ "E" indicates the need for greater coercion on the part of the reconciliation system.

Quite aside from their theoretical interest, there are several reasons why these tendencies are significant. As a practical point–particularly

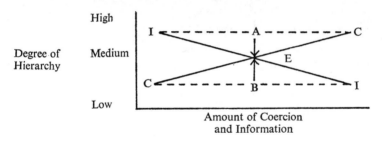

Figure 3.   The information–coercion relationship

for countries in the early stages of modernization—erstwhile mobilization systems, such as, Ghana, Guinea, or Mali, which showed a high degree of hierarchy through the mechanism of the single party state as a vanguard instrument, did not apply much coercion in the first stage of their regimes. Moreover, having replaced colonially sponsored reconciliation systems (at least in the last stage of colonialism) they were exceptionally high information systems. However, as the pressure to pursue rapid modernization created problems of organization and discipline, the coercion outputs rapidly increased and the process of declining information manifested itself in several ways. In the Ghanaian case the conversion from "A" to "C", as in Figure 3 above, occurred through a military *coup d'etat*; while in Mali and Guinea it resulted in bureaucratic formalism and the drying up of sources of activity and enthusiasm.

In the case of a reconciliation system, the problem is too much information. The failure of the federal government of Nigeria to act on information received was a result of the excessive degree of regional and local accountability, which made necessary action impossible. The recent succession of military take-overs have resulted in the formation of a more hierarchical system with corresponding increases in coercion. Information previously available through the reconciliation system is still available for the new regimes; while the newly present coercive opportunities have been manifest in domestic military action against the Eastern Region.

I cite these cases because their theoretical formulations were worked out well before the actual changes in government occurred in both Nigeria and Ghana, and they are perfectly explicable by the model. Both new regimes have medium hierarchy and medium coercion and conform to the type I have called bureaucratic, which includes as sub-types military oligarchies as well as neo-mercantilist and modernizing autocracies. These can be described as ABCD below:

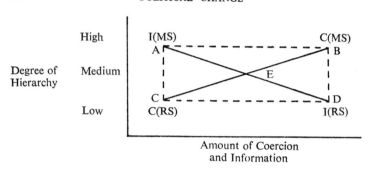

Figure 4.   The information–coercion relationship

The reasoning underlying both the concrete cases and the theory can be described in a number of propositions emerging from this formulation: (1) Increasing the degree of hierarchy narrows the circle of decision-makers and enlarges the excluded range of representational elites. (2) The greater the degree of hierarchy, the more concentrated the power of the decision-maker. (3) To maintain this power, decision-makers may employ coercion or pay-off. (4) To the degree to which potential representational elites are eliminated, competition for power between remaining decision-makers becomes greater, as does the need for manipulative skills on the part of the central leadership. (5) The greater the loss of representational elites, and the greater the competition between remaining decision-makers, the greater the loss of reliable information. (6) The greater the loss of information, the greater the need for a regulative coercive force, such as an army or police unit. (7) The greater the reliance on coercion, the more significant the role of the army and police, and the greater the need to control them.

To summarize:

(1) Increasing hierarchy—lower accountability
(2) Lower accountability—greater coercion
(3) Greater coercion—lower information
(4) Lower information—greater coercion
(5) Greater coercion—increasing hierarchy.

CONCLUSION

Let us conclude by restating the general hypothesis: as modernization grows in a system, the greater the complexity of differentiation in stratification-group competition, the more quickly a political systems type will reach its "ceiling" of effective response, and the greater will be the need for coercion. Thus, in early and middle stage modernization, we can expect a succession of political system-types, with the bureaucratic type providing the greatest degree of stability. If the goal of industrialization is central and overriding, during late modernization a mobilization system will emerge to "take" the society over the "hump" from late modernization into early industrialization. Subsequently the need for information will grow and coercion will become increasingly dysfunctional to the system.[7]

If these assumptions are correct then the long run tendency towards a reconciliation system is fundamental to conditions of high industrialization. Political system change however will not end there in some final sense. Various differentiations need to be made within the reconciliation category to cope with the problems of representation and participation to enable us to take a fresh view. But that would be the subject of yet another paper.

REFERENCES

1 See the valuable discussion of typologies of government by Bernard Crick, "The Elementary Types of Government" in *Government and Opposition*, Vol. 3, No. 1.

2 Weber's distinction between *Macht* and *Herrschaft*, between the capacity to impose will and powers that are legally given is particularly relevant here. See also the extremely useful discussion in Alexander Passerin d'Entreves, *The Notion of the State* (Oxford, 1967), pp. 1–81.

3 See the discussion of these matters in D. E. Apter, "Notes for a Theory of Nondemocratic Representation" in J. R. Pennock and J. W. Chapman (eds.), *Representation, Nomos X* (New York, 1968).

4 These include *The Politics of Modernization* (Chicago, 1965); *Some Conceptual Approaches to the Study of Modernization* (Englewood Cliffs, N.J., 1968); and *Choice and the Politics of Allocation* (New Haven, 1971).

5 We are not talking here about the legal primacy of government and the right of a sovereign government to rule. All governments assume a certain priority. Rather, the limits of authority vary to the extent that the primacy of society is expressed through checks on executive powers of government, or whether these are feeble or non-existent.

6 We have stressed the predilection of mobilization systems for coercion and reconciliation systems for information. But there is a limit beyond which increasing coercion creates uncertainty, just as there is a limit beyond which increasing information can create certainty.

7 It is precisely this type of situation which we see emerging in certain socialist industrial countries like Czechoslovakia, Poland, and the U.S.S.R. The result may be a far cry from democracy as we have come to understand that term. But certainly the move in that direction is under way.

7

Development and the Political Process: a Plan for a Constitution*

David E. Apter and Martin R. Doornbos

I

The word "constitution" has many meanings. Friedrich has suggested some of them. In their political sense, he calls them a set of rules insuring fair play. Other characteristics can be emphasized: philosophical, legal, and historical. And, as if the technical status of the term were not sufficiently questionable, mechanical questions arise which also make the intent of such fundamental laws and the scope of their application ambiguous. These include the form of the constitution, centralized or decentralized, its method of determination, its method of expression, written or unwritten, and its ultimate objects, i.e. whether it is built upon the established principles of a community, or a framework on which such principles can be established. As objects, methods, and forms change, so our evaluation of constitutions requires a shifting of ground, a different perspective. Because of all these factors it should not be a surprise to anyone that the term "constitution", while not lacking in repute, carries with it rather less respect than it did a generation or two ago. We expect less from fundamental laws than we did in the past. But we continue to use them none the less.[1]

We do so despite the fact that it is in the very nature of constitutions to be found wanting in one respect or another. And how abundant is the evidence for that! For in the matters they are drawn to contain they must provide just the right mixture of rigidity and accommodation. Rigidity is necessary to establish common norms and sanctions, accommodation to allow for disparate goals and interests. But rigidity and accommodation can only be achieved at the price of one another. Challenge and change of constitutions is a continuous review of the costs and benefits of those two variables.

* Reprinted by permission from *African Review*, Volume I, No. 1, 1971, Dar es Salaam.

When the cost is too high the constitution becomes a dead letter. One needs only to glance through the back issues of Peaslee's *Constitutions of Nations* to see the debris of so many monuments men erected in the hope of improving the basis of their relationships. The record of constitution-making plainly demonstrates that the search for the indestructible political order is vain, the ideal state an illusion. Constitutions everywhere have left goals unanswered and groups aggrieved, even if they were designed with the best of intentions.

But if all constitutions are imperfect, some are better than others. Some have been successful in giving shape to society where others have failed. Some reflect a capacity to strike out into new directions and incorporate emerging vital concerns where others do not. The quality of constitutions appears to hinge on two standards, of which the exact balance struck between rigidity and accommodation and the congruence this exhibits with societal requirements is only one. More fundamentally, the pertinence of constitutions depends on the functional relevance of the relationships they seek to establish. The ultimate test of a constitution must lie in its conduciveness towards the achievement of the most generalized goals of society combined with the creation of meaningful instruments for the formulation of goals. In other words, the relevance of constitutions cannot merely be judged by the neatness of the checks and balances they provide, but should be considered especially in terms of the kinds of objectives and aspirations they are designed to further.

These points need emphasizing because if the record of constitutionalism is a sorry one in the recent past, in developing areas it is disastrous. Probably never before were so many constitutions drafted in such a short time as in former colonial societies, and probably never before have so many been abrogated so soon. This chain of events cannot fail to leave a sense of disillusionment. For expectations had (perhaps not unlike those in Polybius' time) been rather exalted. Most of the independence constitutions had had an air of solidity about them which seemed to hold their own with that of their more aged and time-honoured counterparts. Quite a few featured preambles surpassing almost anything of that order in sophistication and expression. Indeed, on the face of it, it had all looked rather promising. But very soon the first round of constitutions lost its lustre and fell into oblivion.

Lack of concern is hardly the answer. Even if the constitutions were ignored or followed one another in sequences, the time and thought spent on their preparation was considerable. This continues to be so today in Pakistan, Ghana, Uganda, and elsewhere, and the pattern is similar in most cases. An extensive series of consultations precedes the launching of a new constitution. Constitutional com-

I

missions, elaborate reports on relationships, interim conventions—all end in a usual grand finale, a local version of Lancaster House or Paris. Jurists and men of experience ponder over concepts of justice and search for a sensible way of bringing a diversity of groups, ethnic, interest, and professional, into a common framework. The result is at best an aesthetically appealing structure of institutions and procedures, safeguarded relationships, delegated powers, and the rule of law. Needed is only the touch of a magic wand to bring the whole edifice to life. But the magic stroke fails to materialize. No matter how carefully designed, constitutions cannot, by themselves, create the necessary integration between norms and structures, values and functions. Time and time again the checks proved out of balance, and the balances not properly checked. Virtually all the new frameworks turn out to be shortlived and are soon followed by a new round.

As we have suggested, the dimensions of this failure go back a considerable way into constitutional history. In this connection, for example, it is worth recalling that shortly after World War I, President Wilson helped to stimulate a sizeable crop mainly in Eastern Europe, none of which proved particularly successful. There was a kind of innocence about constitution-making in those days, the idea being that if justice could be defined in some meaningful manner and participation organized so that a diversity of groups and individuals were represented, prosperity and growth would follow as the day follows the night. Christianity plus commerce was to be realized as law plus industry, with the framework defining the opportunities.[2] This is what we can call the "viability approach" to constitutional engineering.

There remains, of course, a certain wisdom and necessity in the search for viable constitutional structures. But the preoccupation with viability has obscured another emphasis—a more developmental one. It draws attention to the design of frameworks primarily concerned with law and order (on the assumption that viability can be legislated into being by tackling the problem at its own level). Today we can no longer accept the view that if one achieves some effective way of dealing with public demands by means of representative institutions, progressive development will follow logically. A framework of law and order is not a sufficient prerequisite for further development. We will therefore entertain an opposite view, and reverse the sequence. We want to consider a framework in which the concern with development is the *central* theme and is the prerequisite of viability.

Such a changed focus needs a hearing if only because new constitutions continue to be based on the worn-out assumption that conditions of viability lead to development. As a result, in country after country, the pattern is to replace one constitution by another whose main characteristic is merely the opposite of the previous one. Where the earlier constitution said "yes", the next one says "no". Decentralized forms substitute for centralized ones, federal set-ups are replaced by unitary arrangements, the delegation of authority by concentration of powers. What is new about such constitutions is their arrangement of the standard stock of elements. Each is devised in reaction to the previous one on the mistaken assumption that the previous round failed because the emphases had been wrongly placed. The larger premise is rarely questioned.

The tenacity of this premise is due to at least two main factors. One is the immediacy of the viability issue itself. In Africa, for example, where ethnic and other cultural divisions are endemic the very existence of state structures is precarious. Obvious examples are Congo and Nigeria, but there are many others. The ethnic situation in Kenya is already serious. In Uganda a basic Bantu–Nilotic conflict is slowly taking shape. The power of nationalism to bridge such cleavages and create unity has been grossly overrated and hardly papers over such cracks and fissures in society. It is only natural that a preoccupation with finding ways of containing such primordial disputes and conflicts should have priority over developmental concerns.

Another factor which continues to have an important bearing upon the pattern of constitutional development is the historical character of the previous colonial system. In former British areas and also in the French, law and order were key norms of colonial governments manifested in the devolution of authority by staged constitutional steps (in most instances, a precondition of independence). A considerable carry-over from colonial times, particularly in the early years after independence, significantly affected the type of institutional order particularly in the new African states not only at the top but also at the lower levels of the political structure. The colonial system, backed up by the force of the metropolitan power, was instrumental in linking central government, voting constituencies and local authorities in a single network. It is not surprising then that when the colonial authorities depart, the linchpin of the system gives way. Recognition of this weakness after independence has led to a desire in many cases to reject or reverse some of the institutional structures and tendencies carried over from the colonial period. Such reversals have taken the form of radical centralization for national unity, the bureaucratization of decision-making, or various mixtures of these.[3] But if these different avenues seem to contradict the liberal ideal of constitutional government it should also be remembered that the relevant frame of reference includes in its not too distant past an earlier period of colonial rule which was basically authoritarian. It was only in the terminal phase that powers were devolved or being devolved in considerable degree. This has led to some interesting historical parallels. At a normative level what was once seen as grassroot participation in nationalist movements and a refutation of authoritarianism, can also be combined structurally with political centralization (as the replacement of "divide and rule") in a new populist autocracy. Whatever the constitutional reversals effected after independence, regimes like these could be looked upon as the very achievement of nationalist aspirations, perhaps as the consummation of independence itself— a matter of no small importance for the direction of constitutional development in Africa. Of course, such a sense of achievement wears off very rapidly, while the problems of viability remain. Despite many appearances to the contrary, therefore, the frameworks handed over at independence have prompted quite distinct patterns of constitutional development with constitutional revision reflecting not only a confrontation of norms but also an underlying opposition of political interests disguised in the form of national coalitions. Conflict over these issues has stimulated immobility rather than change because it has been hidden, disguised, and secret.

II

Some of the problems posed here can be illustrated by the recent constitutional experiences of Ghana and Uganda. As for Ghana, Nkrumah's dictum "Seek ye first the political kingdom and all other things will be added unto you" acquires a new and tragic meaning in the light of the above. For this vision was based on the notion that a viability framework based on nationalism plus commerce as its central principles would create the conditions for development and prosperity. And, significantly, when Ghana's first constitutional arrangements turned out to be unsatisfactory, it was not thought that the viability-for-development postulate might need reappraisal, but rather that viability should be established by more revolutionary means. Revolution plus development was the new normative combination embodied in 1961 in a constitution which placed high emphasis on centralization and unitary government as an alternative way of promoting stability. This constitution put extensive powers into the hands of the chief executive on the grounds that he needed to be immune to the capriciousness of the parliamentary machine, particularly in moments of crisis, and therefore, in effect, above the law.

If in 1961 Ghana was among the first to opt for a strongly centralized framework, she is now attempting to reverse the situation. Attempts are being made to design a constitution which will contain every conceivable safeguard against the return of autocracy. In the proposals for a new Ghanaian constitution which have been circulated for discussion, every single person or group who might possibly have some access to power is to be checked by some other group. There are provisions for councils at all levels and elaborate elective arrangements and mechanisms for control—all of which reflect a basic desire to make public participation the central element in the decision-making process. But the suggested popular checks on power at all levels are so many that chances are there will hardly be an executive authority to speak of and that viability will be stifled (though not necessarily from lack of air).[4]

About the time that Ghana adopted her centralized and unitary constitutional framework (1961), Uganda got her independence constitution, which was federal and decentralized (1962). By 1967 Uganda had proclaimed her second,[5] unitary and centralized, constitution (1967). This was rendered inoperative by a military coup in 1971. Ghana restored parliamentary government in 1969 with a highly decentralized, constitutional structure which in its turn was overthrown in 1972. On the surface, these dates are merely a historical coincidence. However, they illustrate a significant point: that the various constitutional turns or pirouettes have a similar origin: the problem of viability. Here the problems of Ghana and Uganda have been similar, at least in one respect, ethnic and regional dominance by one group over another. Ghana's most pressing viability problem for long has been the appropriate means of incorporating the Ashanti confederacy, and in 1961 the attempt was made to achieve this through the total negation of Ashanti as a distinct unit and the establishment of a strongly centralized unitary state. Uganda's overriding requirement was to devise a way to bring the Buganda kingdom into the national fold, and, in 1962, the solution adopted was a federal structure with high decentralization which provided a number of important concessions to Buganda, including a special relationship to the political centre, and in 1963 it was the Kabaka of Buganda who became the first President. Thus, for some years between 1962 and 1967, Ghana and Uganda tried diametrically opposed remedies to ease their common predicaments.

After each arrived at a deadlock they opted for the opposite structural solution. The ballet continues. When Ghana moved from centralization to decentralization, Uganda did exactly the opposite. The constitution which Uganda adopted in 1967 not only considerably expanded the jurisdiction of her President, but it also attempted to eliminate Buganda and the smaller kingdom states from the map.

The constitutional experiences of the two countries can be found elsewhere, Nigeria, Tanzania, etc. The pattern is to change from centralized to decentralized structure and back again and with the appropriate radicalization or instrumentalization of norms, as the case might be. If any basic advancement is to take place, however, it will be necessary to break out from this circle, for if their accomplishments to date are any indication, there is no *a priori* reason to believe that these solutions are likely to solve the problem of creating viable government. Ghana's set of elaborate checks and balances needed to be handled with extraordinary skill and good sense to make it work with any degree of effectiveness. Uganda's centralized structure was not used with the necessary constraint to prevent its breakdown.[6]

It is, of course, interesting to speculate about the timing of constitutional steps. There is a whole school of second-guessing spawned in the wake of these events—the "if only" school. "If only the colonial authorities had stayed on a bit longer . . ." "If only the leadership had been different . . ." etc. We too can speculate along these lines. If only what appears to be a new phase in the development of the industrialized world had come only ten years earlier (or independence ten years later) it is conceivable that constitution-making in Africa might have taken a somewhat different turn. Since 1960 in the West, there has emerged an insistent demand for a more positive concept of the political system. But the "if only" approach is futile. We use it to underscore our point that a constitution must be more than a framework for law and order. During the last decade in particular, ethnic and religious violence, racial conflict, and student demands for participation all have constituted different ways of making the same point. What they share is a symbolic rejection of political order as the supreme value and a practical demand for specific reform. In industrialized societies this is leading to the integration of economic and social planning bodies into the very heart of political structures. In the Netherlands, for example, the Social and Economic Council, which consists of representatives of labour and management and government-appointed experts, plays a most interesting role. Constitutionally, the Dutch cabinet is required to hear this body on all social and economic policy matters. So important is its expected influence on decision-making that its establishment was seen as a potential curtailment of the role of the First Chamber of Parliament (Senate). Another illustration is provided by the Yugoslav Chambers for Economics, for Education and Culture, for Social Welfare and Health, and for Organizational-Political Affairs. Jointly, these chambers discharge the kind of social and economic planning functions which elsewhere may be performed by a single body. In the Dutch as well as in the Yugoslav case, these institutions have been made integral parts of the legislative structures. In a good many other countries, France, Italy, and elsewhere, technocrats and planners have in recent years made a dramatic entry into public organization and have gained a considerable amount of influence in a variety of ways, formal or informal. Their functions are associated primarily with the conditions of the welfare state.

These are portents of things to come in industrial societies. But, it is often argued, the services offered by a welfare state are at the present time a luxury which developing countries can ill afford. Perhaps not, but no one would argue that institutions which are concerned with the planning and creation of welfare can be dispensed with in developing countries—all the more reason then that political leaders feel that a more direct assault on the problems of development is more urgently needed in modernizing societies than industrial ones. In that sense, recurrent welfare expenditures are a function of the larger developmental picture.

If the primacy of developmental goals has become more recognizable in recent years, it cannot be said that the need for development has found expression in the new constitutions (except in some of the preambles). Yet if developmental objectives had been given some suitable institutional framework in the past there would have been a better chance for development-oriented policies to succeed. Structural mechanisms do after all have a certain capacity to give direction to behavioural processes; so do appropriate legal codes. In the absence of development frameworks, however, short-run viability pay-offs have resulted in long-run crises, while long-run development aims have been dealt with on a short-run basis, mainly by means of *ad hoc* decisions of politicians who rely on scattered planning agencies and other executive bodies for a veneer of rationality. Given the urgency to solve both the development and the viability problem, it is important to reappraise the relationship between them. Together they comprise the most sensitive issues that face governments in developing societies. The solution of the one is intimately linked up with the fortunes of the other. For if it is true that genuine development is not conceivable without some minimal viability, no lasting viability will come about without basic development. It is thus essential to define the proper context for each requirement and to restructure the relationship between them. In other words, instead of a viability constitution, it is necessary to turn our attention to the overall design a development constitution might take.

III

It is clearly difficult to suggest a general development constitution which could, without much further specification, be applied in any particular case. On the other hand, to describe a constitution for any single country would mean that it will fit no other country. One can do little more, therefore, than indicate some rough contours which a development framework might have, and leave the description of detailed arrangements for more specific cases. How, then, do we specify the basic ingredients which a meaningful development constitution must contain?

It will be useful to approach this matter from the standpoint of choice. What choices are available to societies in the process of modernization? The answer to the question implies boundaries for a development framework. For example, most African countries find themselves in the early or primary stages of the modernization process. In this situation their choices are clearly very limited. Lack of resources, particularly as regards the available manpower structure, poses an obstacle to any immediate and dramatic change. Such constraints make themselves felt in almost any type of situation, and their effects are present irrespective of the particular political framework applied to societies at this stage of development. This is one reason why development plans so often remain of limited consequence, despite all the expertise and good intentions by which they are inspired.[7] Meanwhile, rising popular demands heighten the pressure upon government to come forward with dramatic solutions. Unable to cope with these demands, the fragility of government is soon apparent. The political leadership thus finds itself confronted with an unrewarding set of dilemmas. It faces enormous hindrances to the achievement of viability as well as of development, but it must none the less create the conditions for both. Moreover, the leadership cannot realistically regard them as alternatives because in the long run viability and development are inseparable.

These complexities only seem to be multiplied if translated into practical political actions. If, in order to promote viability, government allows a certain amount of freedom of action and expression of interest but finds itself the victim of cross-pressures, ethnic, civil service vs. party, factions, etc., it will lose control and viability will break down. To further development, government may need highly centralized executive powers, but may find itself none the less dependent on popular co-operation and the unhampered flow of information relevant to planning. If this flow is lacking, there again, viability will break down. These most highly contradictory tendencies derive on the one hand from the need for a free flow of information so that politicians know what to do and, on the other, the necessity of coercive capacity in order to ensure adequate action. The difficulty is that these requirements together form an inverse relationship. High coercion results in a loss of information.[8] Low coercion may only be obtained at the cost of increasing corruption, the dissipation of energies and resources, and political stalemate. Such a structural paradox does not provide a way out. Instead, it brings us up sharply against the boundaries of possible action and underscores the need to find some optimal relationship between coercion and information. It is on such a relationship that a development constitution will be derived.[9]

On the basis of a more general model from which these postulates are derived,[10] it may be argued that for societies in the early and middle stages of modernization (such as most of the countries of sub-Saharan Africa) the optimal relationship is provided by systems which combine a considerable amount of information with a relatively moderate degree of coercion. Many African systems are characterized by a pronounced hierarchy in the decision-making structure and highly instrumental norms. On these accounts they can be categorized as bureaucratic systems. It is postulated that to promote a moderate coercion-moderate information ratio in bureaucratic systems of this type may enhance a capacity for more or less open-minded goal searching which can be conducive towards individual and collective improvement. However, a margin of flexibility along the coercion-information axis constitutes about the only scope for manoeuvre open to government.

Of course, the viability-development paradox is such that no easy solution offers itself. But rather than disregarding it, let us see what happens if we build the paradox right into the institutional framework itself rather than attempting to resolve it. Structuring a confrontation between the *contrasting* needs and demands of viability and development promises to be quite meaningful in so far as it creates a kind of dialectic based on competitive needs.

We can now attempt to specify more clearly how this might work out in terms of constitutional methods. The dialogue between viability demands and development requisites would need to be given institutional expression both at the normative and at the structural level, which are characteristic of any constitution. All constitutions contain normative statements, largely of an aspirational quality, about the potentiality of the nation as an innovative force and about the desires of the citizens to develop their capacities to the full. And all constitutions contain structural prescriptives with respect to the powers of government and the obligations and rights of its citizenry. At each of these levels there is an inherent contradiction between the interests of the system and those of its members. The distinction between viability and development requirements run largely parallel to this contradiction, since the viability problem is basically that of according sufficient scope of action for individuals and groups, whereas the development problem is essentially concerned with raising the prosperity of the whole.

A development constitution, then, which recognizes the contrast between these principles and which might even draw its strength from it needs first to state them normatively with a preamble that refers to two types of values. One is that of the needs of the individual in society, his rights to representation and individual expression, and the necessity to protect him against the overweening power of the state. The other speaks of the responsibility of the state to further the welfare of all and stresses its need to act as an educational force, to create new conditions of life, and to grant to individuals satisfaction by means of their identification with national goals. Basically, to incorporate these two concerns amounts to weaving Locke and Rousseau into a single covenant with, perhaps, Marx and Weber. From a narrowly philosophical point of view this would seem to make little sense. But we have in mind the considerable advantages that occur when a preamble embodies in itself the contradiction in a manner giving coherence to the basis of conflict and debate over norms and values in the society.

Each of these types of values is intrinsically relevant. It is in the dialogue between the two that the formulation of ultimate goals can be made. A preamble which juxtaposes those principles as principles may thereby provide the very basis for their reconciliation as practices. It does not dispose of the problems of choice and neither does it offer a substitute for conflict. But precisely because conflict over these normative issues is always concrete and particular, their recognition in the constitution opens up possibilities to frame the debate in a positive sense. As members of the society are able to turn to the constitution for normative support, the contradictions and conflict will make up the moral basis of the constitution itself. The significance of this is that no constitution can be meaningful without reference to these moral issues, because it is on these that basic legitimacy depends.

So much for normative considerations. Turning to the structural side, we find that the problems posed here present a mirror image of the normative paradox we have just encountered. The ethical dialectic between the notions of national potentiality and popular preference is reflected in a structural problem of executive power versus public demand. One dimension of this consists of the need to make provision for some capacity for coercion on the part of government. The point is not to provide sanction for random violence or capriciousness by those in power, but essentially to find a basis for the executive to function and, where necessary, to function in such a way that not all its energies are dissipated in wasteful controversy. One major consideration underlying this criterion is the need for government to embark upon long-term development policies and not to find its projects thwarted in the bargaining of the day. If development is to be achieved at all, it will generally be as a result of sustained efforts rather than as the outcome of competition for immediate gains. This, then, implies a necessary capacity for government to act strongly and at times to act in ways so as to protect itself. But this requirement is countered by the problem which was noted earlier, namely, that the excessive use of coercion will lead people to transmit information which is pleasing to their superiors, and suppress the kind of information that will cause embarrassment and consternation. An absolute prerequisite to sound development planning is the unhampered flow of planning information. Moreover, if the need for popular engagement is not taken into account in development programs, the chances are great that results will prove meagre. A recurrent difficulty is that plans which are devised in a technocratic manner and handed down from the top tend to work out badly in practice, even if they look well thought out on paper. In many instances, this is not so much because people are opposed; quite often they are indifferent and simply ignore proposals because they are not involved.

Thus, the problem is to devise means by which an executive will have sufficient freedom and autonomy to act and engage in compulsion where necessary, while at the same time there will be no less of the information needed in the execution of development policies. Moreover, ways need to be discovered which would allow a government to consider long-range alternatives and to make plans which are not always and entirely subject to immediate political demands that may bring the whole process to a halt. Finally, the question is how to arrange an institutional structure which does provide for the requirements mentioned here, but which none the less does not allow a government to engage in undue coercive activity. On the contrary, it should make provision for popular participation in development policies so as to enhance the relevance of plans of the society.

To translate these various contradictory criteria in terms of a constitutional framework we will try our hand at arranging organs of government in such a way that a maximum compatibility between the ingredients will result. For this we now have some guidelines. We turn first to information. If we distinguish between two main types of information, popular and technical, there are at once two channels of communication which need to be built into the structure of the constitution itself. Of these two, popular information can be conveniently accommodated in a way which has been familiar in traditional structures of parliamentary government. This requires a representative body which is popularly elected and through which the general public can voice their interests and raise questions about government policy as this affects patterns of daily life. In principle, the concerns put forward here can cover the whole range of government involvement, but in practice the demands will commonly tend to be of a short-term nature and be concerned with immediate issues of constituent groups. The principal function of such a representative organ is to keep popular representation informed about government policies and to make government aware of public responses to its plans and performance. The structure needed for this function is of the type generally found in viability frameworks, known as Legislative Assembly, Lower House, House of Representatives, or by other terms. In terms of the present model, its utility lies particularly in the contribution it can make towards creating a realistic relationship between planning and public demands, namely by allowing popular information to be freely expressed.

For channels of technical information, no such familiar context is present in modernizing societies. One common characteristic, however, is the involvement of a wide variety of technical experts in the design of an equally wide range of development projects. Most of these specialists are employed by government departments or by one or another of many specialized planning bodies and research centres. A good number are civil servants, while others are primarily affiliated with universities, international agencies, or perhaps with less conspicuous organizations. But, whereas these experts have in common their engagement in the drafting of plans, very often the plans themselves have very little relationship to each other. Indeed, quite frequently these tend to reflect the special interests and preoccupations of particular departments and bureaux more than they are reflective of wider national objectives. And when, at regular intervals, an amalgam of such desiderata is compiled into a five-year plan, that often barely disguises the heterogeneous origin of the ingredients. At the same time, development plans all too often reveal another shortcoming, namely a serious lack of congruence with political reality. Five-year plans, or three- or four-year plans, as the case may be, seem to be destined for one of two fates: they either disintegrate under pressure of short-term and often particularistic demands or they become documents which are frequently and eloquently referred to on ceremonial occasions, but which even then cannot escape the spectre of unfulfilment that seems to haunt them. One major factor leading to this is the fact that there is usually no provision for the continuous review of development plans in consultation with politicians. To arrive at successful planning it is indispensable to establish this kind of link in such a way that development projections will retain significance both as plans and in terms of political relevance. The problem this poses is thus to make planning information relevant to politics and political realities relevant for planning.

Moreover, the proliferation of various technical bodies (not to speak of expatriate experts from other nations and international agencies) is more likely to give an appearance of modernization than its substance and produce both false expectations and public anger. The building of houses, facilities, and the stocking of shops with consumer products appropriate to a more industrial society superimposes a veneer of urban expatriate culture upon a population which is unable to share in its benefits. Modern office blocks may look like splendid monuments of modernity against the spare skyline of a game park, but the local population is likely to derive a rather limited satisfaction from looking at them from the outside. In a certain sense then the predominantly expatriate "development community" which creates an urban enclave which is self-consuming and self-sustaining adds little to real growth for the population. In Kenya, for example, the people (with a *per capita* income of £85 per annum) wait with their noses pressed against the modern glass buildings of Nairobi. They press harder and more insistently all the time. Forced to come to grips with this problem, short-run solutions turn out to be bizarre and costly. The government of Kenya (and Zambia) has begun to push Asians out of their businesses by refusing to renew commercial licences. Not only is it questionable whether Africans are in a position to take over distributive enterprises vacated by Asians, but the developmental consequences may make the situation worse. The reasons for political pressure are clear enough. Too many noses against the glass and not only the window but the whole edifice caves in. But the likely solutions are to provide the immediate satisfaction of negative distribution, the removal of an "alien" enterprise, instead of more positive developmental benefits.

Let us take a somewhat different problem, i.e. the administration. With it, too, political pressures arise and there is a loss of technical information. After independence a civil service experiences great expansion. Promotion for good men is rapid. Those with sufficient education and some experience rise rapidly to the top of the hierarchy at relatively early ages. They reach maximum earning power and opportunity early in their careers. This stimulates and challenges the energies of young and aggressive bureaucrats. But such liberating effects are short-lived. The success of rapid promotion wears off and the senior civil servants become cynical, lose their initiative, are resented by juniors, and come to be regarded as out-of-date by university students and others oriented toward the civil service as a career.

Under such circumstances professional knowledge which represents a form of critical investment in the future tends to be misused, misplaced, and misdirected. If it were to be co-ordinated better and rendered into a politically useful form by the politicians they in turn would need to be concerned with more long-term interests rather than the day to day response of a society to policies. Moreover, the technocrat and civil servant would need to be more concerned not only with long-term planning and overall objectives but political considerations as well. But politicians distrust the future, and as they do so the civil servants become politicized, not in terms of their work but their careers. As a result, the politicians become more and more distrustful of expertise, both expatriate and local. They see in it not only a threat to their own power but as a commodity for sale to the highest political bidder. Their efforts to safeguard their positions include building a following or a faction based on grievances (although in so doing they may become a threat to a superior political leader who is afraid of factions which whittle away his own power). The result is to bureaucratize the party. This is one reason why so many politicians come to favour the single party format. It seems to safeguard authority and provide the weapon for reform and development.

The civil servant, in turn, for somewhat different reasons, does the same thing. He turns for protection to the norms and standards of the bureaucracy. The old colonial administrative system, based on class, education and organization of the files, becomes reconstituted in new forms. More stable promotion, secondment, review procedures, hierarchy, all these become front line defences against the politicians rather than means to facilitate administrative work. Viability breaks down in the competition between bureaucracies, party and official, in which a few individuals, capable of exercising capricious power, become the sole innovating elements, while a few senior officials dream of a civil service state.

The single party as an instrument of development is also caught on the horns of the information-coercion dilemma. It builds in its own opposition as it tries to coerce the population, and in so doing finds itself in a precarious position. Nor does bureaucratization of a party lead to the professionalization of leadership and the ending of factionalism. Rather the latter is hidden behind sycophancy, and conflicts, particularly at a local level, proliferate. If a party bureaucracy is to be integrated with a civil service bureaucracy, particularly for purposes of regional and local administration, what usually occurs is bitter animosity between representatives of each. For example, the local education officer resents the party ideological officer and his attempts to change the school curriculum. The party official is irritated by the magistrate when the latter stands up for a minimum standard of justice, etc.

Yet such attempts at integration appear to make sense if only because the politician who is not in contact with the technician or civil servant will fail to see the rationale by means of which the latter work. Equally, the technician or the civil servant who sees the politician as a local satrap, preening himself in hypocritical statements of firm purpose and no resolve, or worse, as a cynical manipulator of the fortunes of the society for his own private objects, himself becomes a schemer in order to outwit him. Technicians and civil servants thus engage in a continuous warfare in developing countries to the detriment of all. Where the ideological context is revolutionary, the way out is to form a "red guard" or "green guard", or committees of vigilance representing a new generation mobilizable by the political leaders against civil servants, technocrats and other sections of the population bitten by the "embourgeoisement bug". But this produces low performance and mutual contempt.

Add to these difficulties the problems created by the muddled intermediate sector of manpower where inefficiency and poor training grind down the best laid plans, and it is no wonder that information fails. In this sense constitutional solutions have failed to come to grips with reality. Perhaps the only solution is to change the system as frequently as possible; that is, when a political ceiling has been reached to hope for a fall in the regime so that a circulation of the elites will take place. Political instability may indeed be a source of political creativity. As constitutions fail, new options are opened up for new political leaders where previous options had been foreclosed.

Such a theory of political instabillity has a great deal to be said for it. But it is a rather costly and socially disruptive method of approach. It is precisely because political instability is the actual consequence of the political predicament found in most developing countries that some more efficient solution is a challenging prospect. How to blend these conflicting tendencies into a more general process where the technocrats and civil servants can be made more political (without being politicized) and the politicians made more sensitive to the professional considerations of development (without being bureaucratized) is the main object of the development constitution. How to combine long-term and short-term interests in a manner which would help keep the civil servant alive to his expertise, fresh

in his participation (rather than bored and corrupt), and to subordinate the whims and elevate the skills of an expatriate class of
technicians is another.

All of the problems mentioned are well known. Solutions to them
have tended to follow lines which range from the remedial to acts of
desperation. The remedial approach is favoured by Americans whose
institutional solutions particularly favour the establishment of public
administration programs which, using largely obsolete administrative
theories, manage to do very little at great cost. They do, of course,
create a professional jargon capable of mystifying (or even better,
intimidating) adversaries of a civil service. And they help convince
the trainees of their own professionality, which is good for morale.
On the whole, this approach is more successful in building training
centres than effective cadres. It remains a favourite solution among
A.I.D. officials (and also teachers of public administration).

The more desperate solution is to decry the possibility of partial
reform without total revolution. Root and branch change is the
answer of many who regard the existing state of affairs as immoral
or, at least, corrupt, and therefore not worth saving. Amelioration
is thus regarded as the worst course since it can only end in failure.
This approach, favoured by a variety of present day neo-Marxians,
has among its deficiencies the rather awkward problem that few root
and branch revolutions seem to take hold root and branch. They
circulate the elites, change the ideological symbols and recreate the
old system in a new image. Few developing countries in Africa have
the inner resources, human or material, for such drastic overhaul of
the community, although some Latin American countries such as
Argentina or Venezuela, may have reached the point where revolutionary solutions are the only ones open to them.

A current solution seems to be a bureaucratic one. It is the result
of a military takeover where the hierarchical authority of the army
is superimposed upon the civil service to blend the two into an
authoritative chain of command. The difficulty is that few military
regimes seem to be successful in handling political questions and
tend to remove themselves from the direct burdens of government
when this becomes apparent.

Hence the three standardized solutions (administrative training
programs, revolution, and military takeover) all have obvious weaknesses. Although each begins with brave words, some kind of
groundbreaking ceremony, and the desire for a fresh start, the result
is that various forms of tyranny and corruption follow in the wake
of each attempt.

Is it possible to devise solutions which will prevent these gloomy
outcomes? It is illusory to suppose that a constitution can specify

the correct way to deal with the problem. But let us entertain the idea of a constitution as the embodiment of a larger theory and without going into the theory itself, sketch out some lines of approach which perhaps can open up a somewhat different reference point for discussions of the larger issues just described.

IV

When devising structural arrangements for a development constitution it is essential to recognize two kinds of information, populist and technical, which need to be meaningfully combined. In addition, we can start with the assumption that there is a need to generate long-term goals and objectives. These should not, or at least not in the first place, be of the specific type as is characteristic of many current development plans. Rather they should be in the nature of general priorities which lead in the direction one hopes to go in order to develop the society. One of the few pertinent steps in this respect is the Tanzanian recognition in the Arusha Declaration that theirs will be an agricultural society for a long time to come and that, given the constraints that are present, industrialization is at this moment not feasible. To generate such generalized specifications basically requires the location of meaningful focal points to which several development efforts can be related. For an effective engagement in the search and determination of broad objectives it is essential to have institutional arrangements that will promote the development of such perspectives. Once broad priorities have been established, it is not only necessary to adjust these over time, but also to make sure that the plans devised are consistent with the general targets already set. This implies a stringent need to safeguard plans from degenerating in any of the directions mentioned above and to ensure that a maximum relevance is kept between planning and politics. All this requires adequate institutional structures which will provide a continuous relationship between planning review and the establishment of main priorities.

One critical contradiction between these requirements should now be restated. In order to make planning realistic and effective, there is a need for popular involvement, to be expressed through political representation. On the other hand, if plans are not to be compromised and allowed to degenerate, they must be protected against the vagaries of political pressure, or, in fact, against political involvement. In terms of information, this poses the necessity of free exchange of popular and professional (or technical) data. In terms of decision-making, however, it implies a need for balanced powers

K

between the structures for technical information and popular information.

The solution to this puzzle seems to be implicit in the problem itself. In societies where the primacy of development is generally pledged to be paramount, the only realistic approach is to give proper expression to the two main lines of information and interest which are needed to make development planning possible at all. For each of these lines an adequate organ of government should be devised. What suggests itself, therefore, in addition to a representative house which functions as an organ of popular representation, is another body which one might, for the sake of convenience, call a development upper house. Through such a development house, technical information could be channelled into the political arena with policy a result of the dialogue between technocrats and politicians. A development house could be linked to a series of three or four research commissions which would function as central data-gathering services for such fields as fiscal and census statistics, education and manpower data, and other basic infra-structure information. Such research commissions need not be attached to a university, nor to a single ministry. Sustaining direct relations with government as well as members of the development house, it should retain continuous access to them for planning information and review. Let us discuss the development upper house a bit further.

Clearly, the warrant of legitimacy for such an upper house could not reside in popular appeals or even more narrowly defined interests. Its rationale is in functional information at its disposal with such functionality determined by development needs. We envisage such a house with a relatively small membership consisting of highly skilled individuals, drawn from appropriate ministries, technical bodies and the like. Since the knowledge available to this group is itself primarily technical, the quality of information, and the degree to which new data is available for planning, imposes obligations on the members if they are to sustain their professional qualifications. The important criterion for determining who would be eligible to sit in the house (if its legitimacy were not to disappear in the heat of conflict and controversy) would be technical proficiency.

We would also see the development house linked to four main functional commissions both for recruitment and technical knowledge with each commission representing some important development dimension. The following are suggested but they by no means exhaust the list of relevant possibilities: (a) manpower and education, (b) demographic and fiscal, (c) resources and communications, (d) military and police. Each commission would have a double link—

one to a relevant ministry or ministries, and the other to a specialized research branch. The latter, in turn, would have an association to a university both for training and recruitment purposes.

The objects of these commissions should be to concentrate on long-term evaluation and continuous review for the purposes of policy-making. The manpower and education commission might be concerned with projections of anticipated skills and occupations according to the general priorities of development which become policy. Attempts to undertake such projections are still rare, but they are becoming more common. The Carnegie-sponsored Ashby Commission Report and the Harbison Manpower Report were pioneers in this respect some years ago in Nigeria. Even in poorer African countries such attempts are being made.[11]

The demographic and fiscal commission would be engaged more directly in economic planification and assessment. The relationship between population, population distribution, urbanization, etc., and various forms of investment would be one obvious emphasis. In addition, the evaluation of alternative priorities for development would be another. Such a commission would undertake periodic economic surveys, prepare census materials, etc.

In every developing country various research stations such as cacao research, geological surveys, animal husbandry experimental stations and the like have built up considerable knowledge and expertise. The integration of such research in a resources and communications commission would not only involve the assessment of material resources but also the efficiency of their exploitation, the costs of extraction, and the shaping of transportation and communications accordingly. Obviously such a commission would have links to several ministries such as agriculture, commerce, transport and communications, etc.

Finally, the military and the police in developing countries are rarely called upon to participate in planning. However, they are prone to intervene when a political situation begins to deteriorate. In addition, since the strategic interests of many developing countries are matters which are subject to change with ideology, contingency planning by the military is likely to be more defensive strategy. For example, more security provisions might be necessary in view of a political emphasis on pan-Africanism—a cause which has more priority in certain African countries than others. A greater sense of the political relations between developing countries can thus be brought into the context of long-term military planning.

Also the military, since it has a considerable proportion of available resources at its disposal, may be used as an instrument for internal development. This may include literacy classes, road building, or any number of developmental activities. The re-evaluation of the potential role of the military in a variety of developmental programs may have the effect of involving them in the work of the country and relieving them of the boredom and inactivity characteristic of peacetime armies. In a developing area if the military has nothing to do, it is more likely to turn its attention to the inadequacies of the politicians and intervene.[12] Such professionalization, providing a basis for drafting long-term plans in the upper house, would find its outlet in the form of political solutions. This is why the association of the commissions with universities becomes important. Wanted is a direct link to the sources of new information created or disseminated in professional departments; for it is in the intellectual or technical institutions that the appropriate norms of professionalism and the safeguarding of standards are built in. Moreover, such institutions also bring association with relevant professional bodies overseas where major innovations are more likely to be made. Hence universities, military academies, international conferences, research institutes, all form a basis for exchanges abroad, both on unilateral and multilateral lines, and including U.N. and other international bodies, all of which can be directed towards the commissions and their research centres. In all this the universities cannot help but play a very important role, increasing their relevance to the needs of the country and preventing them from being isolated centres of privilege and antagonism.

Such a relationship would have an additional advantage for both students and staff of the research commissions, to train and be trained. This would not only augment curriculum by practical work, it would also serve as a bridge for recruiting well-trained students into the relevant specialities. Hence the upper house would provide a venue for professionals to make policy in terms of their expertise. In turn, these would be recruited from commissions made up of the best professionals available. Greater control would be possible over the myriads of expatriate or foreign aid specialists who descend in droves on developing countries to work, quite often, at cross purposes with the host personnel. Integrating their efforts is itself an important political need since it is becoming increasingly necessary to maximize the utility of experts and minimize their (often disguised) disutilities. All this, in the context of a continuous emphasis on research for planification in which the technocrat or civil servant is obliged to maintain his professional skill (or he will not be able to compete successfully with others) is involved in the institutional framework of a development upper house.

The details of how precisely such a development house should be composed will necessarily vary from case to case. Generally, however, one could conceive of this organ as having a membership which is partly representative, partly appointed. Members might also be affiliated with planning bodies, research organizations, universities, ministries, as well as perhaps, co-operative structures and other functional organizations. Whatever the exact arrangement in each case, it is clear that to have these specialists serve in a development house is realistic in more than one sense. The people who are presently engaged in planning and research in modernizing societies by and large constitute a potentially very capable elite. Despite their immediate job descriptions, the members of this elite now find themselves relatively isolated from the general developmental process. Their skills and insights could instantly be drawn upon, however, to fill the critical leadership vacuum that generally exists in the institutional set-up for long-term development.

V

We have said very little about the organization and composition of a lower house. Here we have little new to offer. There are many ways in which a lower house organizes its business. Mainly the choices are limited to types of electoral systems and the organization of constituencies. Whether there is a single-party system based on a single list, or a multi-party system based on proportional representation is of less importance in this kind of constitution than in the more straightforward type advocating constitutional democracy on the Western model. The reason is that even if there is a single party, there are multiple types of power being represented; hence the monopoly exerted in the contemporary one-party state is likely to be averted. If professional power constitutes an important part of the policy-making process, it competes with populist power based on numbers of the population organized in a political party. Of course it can be argued that the politicians will always win out over the technocrats in any showdown. That may be true, but in so far as the political condition of most developing countries is in large measure a function of developmental progress, the importance of professional power will grow over the years.

But the point is that it need not grow at the expense of the power of the politicians. We are not, after all, dealing with a zero-sum situation. More likely, if the upper and lower houses are in continuous relationship over policy making, professional power can be used to enhance populist power, and populist power can be made to support professional power. Embodied in this view is an assumption that the relationship between politicians and technocrats will create a mutually reinforcing system of legitimacy based on the utilities each side gains from the other's knowledge—the one technical, and the other populist, i.e. the popularity and absorptive capacities of the population.

Whether the lower house is on a one-party or two-party basis becomes a less significant question because, to a certain extent, built into the proposed political mechanism of professional and populist power is a relationship which in the past has been the preserve of competitive popular politics in a two or multi-party pattern. We refer to the provision of checks on executive power. One of the reasons why the single-party system emerges out of representative government in developing areas is that political leaders have too little flexibility—so bound are they by the condition of under-development. Under the circumstances, it is not the restriction on power *per se* which is beneficial, but the control of its capricious exercise. If a development constitution is able to provide more specific power to accomplish specific objects, better cadres, more resources, and in general better means to deal with their difficulties, then the desire to exercise autocratic rule will be minimized. If it is true that under conditions of underdevelopment a political ceiling is rapidly reached so that leaders exhaust the obvious means available to them, it is not surprising that they try to transform a multi-party system into something else in order to give them greater flexibility and to allow them to make mistakes without paying some immediate political price in the loss of support.

If such an approach to political rule is its choice of weapons, it is clear why politicians have opted so often for a single-party system, or, where this gives way to *coups d'etat*, the bureaucratic-military regime. The latter after all has some of the coherence of the colonial pattern to be reimposed by army officers whose concepts of good government are modelled after a governor and his regional and district officials, meting out administration and justice with some pretence of personal austerity (or the presumed austerity of the barracks).

The present approach then is presented not only as an alternative to the military regime but also the one-party system as it is commonly found, and the multi-party parliamentary system which so frequently fails. The idea is to increase the political importance of professional knowledge through application to policy, while drawing the attention of politicians to these larger issues and educating them in the process. At the same time the professionals need to know the human limits, sensitivities, reactions and other "political" responses of a population to policies.

VI

If this is the emphasis, we can now turn more precisely to the development constitution as described by means of the following diagram.

It is not only from the creation of a development house as such that important innovations might be expected. The diagram indicates a resolutions committee between the two houses. This is so that the discussions between the development house and the representative house can be appropriately structural. If we expect the mandate of the development house to be long-range planning, members of the representative house would need to consider proposals in terms of the immediate implications they contain for the people in the constituencies. Moreover, the development house will on the whole be concerned with technical soundness (though not exclusively so) and the representative house with political relevance. At present, there is a rather uncomfortable fusion of these functions in the existing representative bodies and in most African countries; for example, legislators are expected to assess plans both in terms of long-term objectives and technical criteria and in terms of their political implications for their constituencies. To separate these two aspects of plan evaluation will greatly enhance the clarity and effectiveness of the legislative process and will enable all organs involved to relate their tasks more meaningfully to broad national priorities. Bringing these divergent emphases into a single draft proposal for planification as well as the drafting of subsidiary legislation would require a resolution committee to function as its name implies. Here conflict would need to be resolved or the proposals returned to each house for further debate and comment.

It would be the task of the resolution committee then to establish one or more policy plans out of the drafts proposed by the respective houses, working back and forth between them until either some agreement is reached, or until a number of agreed alternatives are established. These then can be forwarded to government. The creativity of political leadership at the governmental level would consist in making the appropriate selections among various alternatives, the identification of main priorities among several, and the selection of appropriate strategies to ensure that the policies are realized. Government then would be able to operate in a high information environment in which the maximization of information is organized in a manageable form and not a welter of conflicting "inputs" impossible to screen or evaluate.

Hence, behind the concept of the development constitution is the notion that the political ceiling can be lifted if high information is

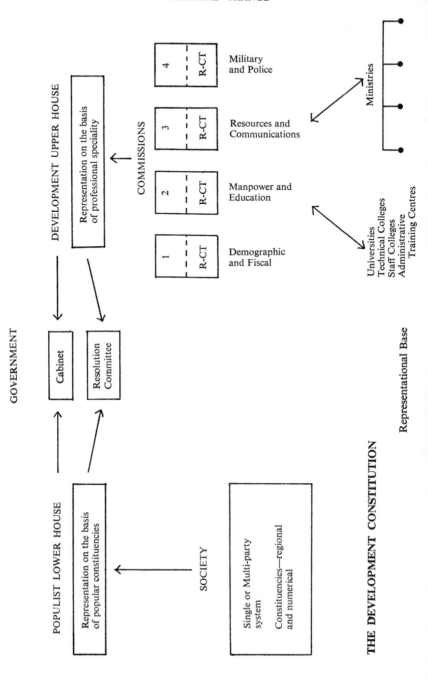

THE DEVELOPMENT CONSTITUTION

available. But mere information, unscreened and uncodified, may produce little more than political confusion and result in capricious acts by politicians or serious mistakes in policy, both of which tend to drive a new government in the direction of autocratic rule. Needed is a mechanism to better identify certain kinds of information as priority knowledge, professional as well as populist, and render it into policy alternatives so that governments are better able to act.

Although the actual scope of jursidiction granted to each of the two houses would be largely determined by the specific type of political system and local conditions, it would generally be useful to allow both houses some initiating as well as delaying powers in respect to specified areas of government policy. One of the main functions of the resolution committee would be to act as a go-between for the two houses and if necessary throw its weight on the side of one or the other, depending upon the government's own appraisal of the merits of the plans and the need of the public. One important effect this would have would be to shift the burden of policy formulation to the key representative groups in the society and to make government itself less vulnerable, although not less involved. The form of the legislative flow could then be as follows for matters concerning development, plans would be prepared in the research commissions and proposed through the development house. In matters for which the development house would not have reserved initiating powers, the representative house could be given a similar autonomy to make proposals. In either case, proposals which would have passed through the initiating body would be forwarded to the other house where they then become issues for scrutiny and debate. If the second house did not accept proposals, government would be able to refer them back to the initiating body. In this way, each house could alert its counterpart to possible shortcomings in the plans as seen from its perspective and each could protect the essence of its proposals against excessive demands of the other.

It is of considerable importance that the dialogue between the two houses be conducted publicly. In that way possibilities for pressing particularistic interests, both on the technical and on the popular side, would be severely reduced. Rather, the engagement in public dialogue might induce each side to anticipate the concerns of the other to the extent that initial proposals would already bear an awareness of the realities on the other side. A development house concerned to see its objectives adopted is bound to take likely popular responses into account, while members of the representative house would generally feel obliged to relate their views to wider and long-range goals in order to avoid the onus of parochialism.

In this fashion, then, one could expect a useful dialogue to begin on the issues of how society should be restructured. The dialogue would be between short-term and long-term objectives, in which the principle of expertise would form the legitimacy of one side and the principle of public propriety and the notion of equity the legitimacy of the other. A government which promotes this process will immediately derive some significant benefits from it in its efforts to create viability and development. For while the representative house will be supplying popular information and the development house technical information, the government can put itself in the strategic position of manipulating the exchange to the advantage of society at large. It can use public reaction as a weapon against the experts and it can use expert advice as a weapon against the politicians. In this way it would be able to work on the basis of high information while employing a minimum of coercion. That, generally speaking, is as desirable a situation as any political system can hope to attain.

Our object in this discussion has been to put the issue of development into a constitutional framework. We emphasize in this manner the need to create more opportunities whereby governments can deal with problems that confront them. In modernizing societies these crowd in at every turn until, overwhelmed, political leaders take actions designed to protect themselves against the people rather than work with them and for them. To harness technocratic resources is a way of making responsible and efficient knowledge which relates to development. Today governments are not able to adequately control those whose special knowledge gives them exceptional access to the resources and means of power, without substantially reducing their usefulness.

However, and this point should be made very clear, a development constitution such as the one suggested here, should not be seen as a long term affair or a permanent political framework. It is suggested as an interim measure, a temporary device designed to coincide with what should be a transitional period in which a society is making particularly strenuous and special efforts to increase its choices, its developmental infrastructure, and its public opportunities. After that the development constitution should give way, especially when a different ordering of social preferences becomes possible—one which places lower priorities on development than distribution, and is less concerned with growth than with equity. Indeed, the latter might be called an "equity constitution" to emphasize the stress on new and alternative ways of representation, and the need to deal with the problems of the modern meritocracy, which places its emphasis on the functional rather than the humane qualities of life.[13] In these matters the new industrial society poses far more serious threats than the modernizing ones and the traditional frameworks of representative governments are not equipped to handle them. To deal with the deficiencies of the constitutions of industrial states requires a fresh look. But this would engage us in another discussion.

Professor Apter wishes to acknowledge the support of the West African Comparative Analysis Project, which, under a grant from the Carnegie Corporation, enabled him to visit Ghana and discuss constitutional problems with various members of the Constitutional Commission in the spring of 1967.

1   For a good statement of various meanings of the term "constitution", see Carl J. Friedrich, *Constitutional Government and Democracy* (Waltham, Massachusetts: Blaisdell Publishing Company, 1968), Chapter VII.

2   For a review of these see Agnes Headlam-Morley, *The New Democratic Constitutions of Europe* (London: O.U.P., 1929), *passim.*

3   See, for example, the analysis by W. B. Harvey, *Law and Social Change in Ghana* (Princeton: Princeton University Press, 1966). For a different view see Geoffrey Bing, *Reap the Whirlwind* (London: Macgibbon and Kee, 1968).

4   See Yaw Tumasi, "Ghana's Draft Constitutional Proposals" in *Transition*, 37, pp. 43–52.

5   This was actually the third as in 1966 an interim constitution was adopted. But this document was introduced to make some immediate arrangements for the emergency situation in Buganda and basic constitutional changes followed only in 1967.

6   A dangerous situation in Buganda obtained when the area was divided into districts, each under a politically appointed district commissioner. The present military regime in Uganda which overthrew the government of President Milton Obote, has indicated that a restoration of the Kabakaship and some measures of local autonomy is envisaged. We can therefore expect a new round of decentralized constitutionalism.

7   Very few countries have based their development plans on the realities of the situation. Most set excessive standards of industrialization. The Arusha Declaration which recognizes that Tanzania will continue to be an agricultural country for the foreseable future is one exception to this.

8   See the discussion of these matters in D. E. Apter's "Political Systems and Developmental Change" in *Some Conceptual Approaches to the Study of Modernization* (Englewood Cliffs, N.J., Prentice Hall, 1968).

9   See Chapter 4, "Why Political Systems Change", pp. 00–00. See also "Notes on a Theory of non-Democratic Representation" in D. E. Apter, *Some Conceptual Approaches to the Study of Modernization, op. cit.*

10 See D. E. Apter, *Choice and the Politics of Allocation* (New Haven: Yale University Press, 1971).

11 See, for example, *Rapport sur les Problèmes Posés par la Scolarisation dans la Republique de la Haute-Volta* (Paris: Société d'Etudes pour le Developpement Economique et Social, and Institut Pédagogique National, Service de la Recherche Pedagogique, n.d.).

12 See John J. Johnson, *The Role of the Military in Underdeveloped Countries* (Princeton: Princeton University Press, 1962); William F. Gutteridge, *Military Institutions and Power in the New States* (London: Pall Mall Press,

1964); and Morris Janowitz. *The Military in the Political Development of New Nations* (Chicago: University of Chicago Press, 1964).

13 Contrasts between a "development constitution" and an "equity constitution" are suggested in D. E. Apter, *Choice and the Politics of Allocation* (New Haven: Yale University Press, 1971).

8

Political Theories and Political Practices: a Critique of Overseas Aid as Social Engineering*

I INTRODUCTION

The discussions so far have dealt with various aspects of government, political theory and development. We suggested in the previous essay that there were some applied or instrumental consequences to such ideas which could provide guidelines for new nations in their search to maximize development on the one hand and political stability on the other. The key variable was the use of information and how a political system could maximize its various forms without becoming bewildered or penalized by so doing. Here we want to extend that notion of information, in the form of a critique and some suggestions, to the practice of overseas aid. Such aid represents the most direct way in which theories and ideologies held by one country are applied to another. In all major industrial countries, experts in the social and applied sciences have served as consultants to government. In this respect, the administration of aid is a kind of test for the status of theory as it is understood by political leaders and administrators.

Despite its singular importance, however, the matter of aid, that is, assistance for development in modernizing societies, remains very controversial, especially in the United States. One would have expected that by now, the practice of aid would have become broadly institutionalized in a developmental service which could enlarge its experience, increase its expertise, and embody both in a cumulative lore, text and procedure. Instead, programs of assistance are at a crossroads, and the reasons are entirely political. Our conceptions of aid and its consequences have been naïve to the point of innocence. Our hopes were too simple for the complexity which follows from

* This paper was written under contract with the U.S. Agency for International Development. The opinions expressed are the author's, not necessarily those of the Agency.

even the most successful programs. If there is a visible correlation between aid and politics it must appear to politicians and to the general public that the more aid is increased, the more things fall apart. The result is that after over a decade of hard effort, instead of trying to improve the practice, many prefer to question the principle.

The reasons for such innocence are not too hard to find. Aid, in its original conception, was a kind of promissory note for the future. Wanted was a suitable investment, an appropriate set of institutions, and the natural inclination of people overseas to want to improve themselves. The technique did not seem difficult. Given an initial impetus the rest would take care of itself. This after all had been the effect of Marshall Plan aid to Western Europe. There was no reason why, with suitable modifications, the process could not be repeated in the less developed countries. Indeed, even the term itself, "less-developed", implied, in a delicate way, the urge towards development, particularly of the economic kind.

Behind this idea was the success of American technology. It had proved its worth during the war. What remained was to promote freedom through development in other parts of the world. Such freedom was twofold: political, the right to national independence and economic, an escape from poverty. U.S. policy favoured both decolonization and economic development, the latter to prevent communism and the former to promote liberty. With technical assistance to prime the pump the resulting infrastructure support to developing countries was envisaged with or without the collaboration of former colonial powers. What was not anticipated was that aid in such varying fields as education, manpower training, assistance for commercial and industrial development and the like, might be seen in a more total and abrasive perspective in years to come and indeed as a form of imperialism.

If the practice of U.S. aid was spawned in politics, made concrete in growth, with nation building for democracy its rationale, these ingredients varied in emphasis over the years. Packenham suggests that an economic emphasis was predominant during the years 1947–48. Security was the uppermost concern during 1951–60 and again between 1964–68. Building democracy more or less in our own image was the object most significantly in Latin America, especially during the period 1962–63 and again after 1966. Title IX of the Foreign Assistance Act is perhaps the most explicit statement of the political rationale.[1]

Whatever the emphasis, however, what is clear is that developmental assistance in terms of large goals like building stable democracies, have not been very satisfactory. In Latin America for example, the region where this object was most explicit (and which received the largest share of economic aid under the Foreign Assistance Acts), only one country, Venezuela, is in an improved condition as compared with 1961. Four countries operate under military regimes which in 1961 were at least nominally democratic, including some of the most important in the region, Brazil, Peru, Bolivia, and Argentina. The Dominican Republic, Colombia, Panama and Uruguay are in much greater turmoil and with more authoritarian regimes, than before. Chile has taken a major step towards a socialist solution which American policy makers regard at best somewhat lugubriously. Even Mexico has taken a turn for the worse recently in political and social terms. Similarly in Africa. Today one-third of the African governments are military regimes. It would appear that the politicians are correct. Aid is a disaster. However, whether a disaster or not we are stuck with it. There is no going back. As the Committee for Economic Development put it,

> More rapid growth and rising incomes will not necessarily win friends and allies or ensure peace and stability in the less developed countries. On the contrary, real progress involves a break with the past and may induce highly destabilizing political and social change. But profound changes are already under way in the less developed world regardless of what the United States does or does not do. The long-term political rationale for aid, therefore, rests on the calculated risk that accelerating the modernization process, and reducing the sacrifice required to achieve it, will enhance the odds in favour of an earlier evolution of responsible and independent states in the low-income regions of the world. By the same token, the risk of involvement by the great powers in crises and power vacuums abroad will thereby be reduced.[2]

II HAPPY MYTHS AND THE UNDERWORLD: DEVELOPMENT AS IDEOLOGY

The point is that building democracy by developmental means is not a cumulative or sequential process. Political instability, increased tension, the prospect of new social and political strategies abroad are all to be expected. We live in an infinitely more complex world than either politicians or their publics have been led to believe. Nor is this an exclusively American problem. A certain "demonology" has played a large part in the thinking of all those engaged in developmental politics. Myths of the "withdrawal and retrieval" variety have been common among former colonial powers seeking to retain their political influence after their territories have obtained independence. Others of a more "universalistic" variety have been preferred by highly developed countries like the United States or the

U.S.S.R. both of which assume that the pattern of their domestic development is capable of application abroad and should be promoted as such.

The British were closest to ours in the original emphasis on "nation-building". They favoured commercial development overseas by means of private enterprise, while politically the "mother of parliaments" reproduced in its ruder offspring those ideals of freedom and association which constituted the triumph of English civilization. In these terms "decolonization" became an achievement rather than a failure of empire especially when this took the form of a preference for constitutionalism, a disinterested civil service, and common bonds of association.

The French have been more practical, relying on a culturally attractive style (Paris is after all the capital of the world), French language, egalitarianism, and the broad qualities of French culture as supplements of direct economic aid to whatever regimes remain more or less friendly to France. Indeed, the French have given a larger donation from their social product than any other nation in the world, the bulk going to former members of the French community, particularly the one country which caused the greatest French post-war agony, Algeria.[3]

The American approach is not so different from these others except that its stage is world wide, its arena universal. Such universality competes with the equally universal claims of socialism, centred in Moscow and Peking with Havana and possibly Santiago as peripheries. It is anti-planning. Americans believe as a practical matter that aid should be of the self-starter variety; stimulating workmanlike responses should generate the eventual growth of a middle class as a natural haven for upwardly mobile workers while withering away an obsolete aristocracy. The U.S. myth is the establishment of a workmanlike (rather than the worker's) state, in turn a function of expanding manufactures, an improved agriculture, increased education, technical skill, and effective public administration. These, encased in a community dedicated to mild welfare (a welfare floor rather than a ceiling) private enterprise and representative government constitute the American liberal ideal. The place to begin is with loans for investment. With growth of the self-sustained kind, all other benefits will accrue (although the route may be circuitous).

Such a view is not merely for export. It is the basis of the American belief in itself. Its vision is a world of nations combining freedom and trade as the basis of mutualism. This was made explicit in President Truman's Point Four doctrine, the main purpose of which was to establish a program for "making the benefits of our scientific and industrial progress available for the improvement and growth of underdeveloped areas".

The *deus ex machina* of technical assistance may have failed in the large but it has succeeded in the small. New scientific knowledge has been made available. Educational, infrastructure, and capital projects have broken through many of the inhibitors of growth. Americans have to their credit a large number of shrewdly designed programs. American expertise has perhaps not produced the 2% or more increase in the standard of living in the rest of the world (an increase which, President Truman hoped, would keep factories and businesses in the United States working overtime because of the demand). Nevertheless, it has accomplished a very great deal. The key word has been *self*; self-sustained growth, self-government, self-help. The American ideal has always smacked of the self-start. One problem that has arisen in this regard is that a temporariness pervades the American practice of aid giving. This has prevented a career development service.[4] A lack of quinquennial or other long-term grants by Congress makes long-term planning impossible. As a result hasty careerism pervades "temporary" agencies. Senior officials continuously jockey for power and position. Programs have a patchwork quality. Standards are lacking for measuring success or failure. Faith in experts declines and with it conviction about the efficacy of technical assistance. Planning is seen to magnify blunders.

Above all, what continues to dominate much American thinking is fear that socialism will spread to more and more parts of the globe, the ultimate threat to a middle class democratic solution for a world of poor nations. The exact opposite prevails in socialist countries. Terrified of U.S. imperialism, in the U.S.S.R. the universal expression of virtue is the working class. Developmental priorities are assigned to the development of those infrastructures likely to produce a proletariat. The image of the brawny worker, secure in his job, bending over the blast furnace, is the Soviet equivalent of the responsible burgher, American style. (For China the moral image is embodied in the snub-nosed peasant equally at home with scythe or gun.) Indeed, one can almost speak of aid in such terms as a form of symbolic class conflict, to build a middle class, or a proletarian class, or a peasantry becomes a stratagem of international aid.

We need to recognize that the world of aid must be more modest in its objects. It must be relatively limited in its programs. Its only long run rationale is basically moral. Programmatic aid for development is a cost for which the benefits are partly psychic and partly concrete. The mixture will depend above all upon the realism of policy-makers and politicians. In a world populated by good neigh-

L

bours and bad villains, any policy which turns the latter into the former is obviously a good one. The trouble with the myths we hold and the demons they define is that they lead us to errors about who is good and who is villainous. All too often the "goods" turn into the "bads" (after a long period of developmental support).

III IF YOU SEE THE FUTURE
CAN YOU DOUBT THAT IT WILL WORK?

American development ideologies are perfectly understandable in the context of its history. U.S. political institutions from the start enjoyed sufficient popular political participation to allow for the more or less free play of economic interests and successfully reconciled the conflicts which resulted. Underlying this view of politics is a belief in an essentially economic interpretation of history.[5] Society is composed of various classes and interests: merchants, industrialists, agrarians, urbans, workers, immigrants, etc. As the polity becomes more popular, it needs to reflect the needs of these and other groupings. More adequate representation equals political development. Unlike the Marxians such a view defines no unique value-generating class (such as a proletariat). Moreover, a government which serves a diversity of classes and interests is not the executive committee for the bourgeoisie. Between the polity and this diversity of interest are elaborate institutional mechanisms embodying the conceptions individuals have of what is right and proper.

Indeed, from this standpoint development is first and foremost constitutional engineering. The polis comes first, as occurred in the political evolution of England and the United States. Growing popular participation and the extension of effective legal rights and safeguards are preconditions for successful entrepreneurship and an expanded commerce. "Economism" plus constitutionalism is thus the formula for success, and political democracy the key.

"Economism" plus constitutionalism has been tried twice. It has not worked any better after World War II after than World War I. Like Weimar and the Eastern European "democracies", the post-World War II constitutions, with few exceptions have proved to be ephemeral. This has affected the political study of development. As democratic political institutions dissolve in the developing areas the entire corpus of knowledge in the field becomes problematical.[6] The emphasis on political development declines in favour of the analysis of the social and economic prerequisite of the polis.

Indeed, most development experts in the Agency for International Development today believe that the failure of democracy is due to the slowness of economic growth. Hence to support growth regimes which may be autocratic, such as Brazil, becomes legitimate because it leads to an improved prospect for democracy in the future.

Political science as a discipline, although not rejecting such views, tends more and more to explode the more simplistic expressions of them. Questioning economic self interest in terms of the larger matter of norms and values has been one impact of what might be called the "Parsonian revolution", sociologizing the study of politics means studying the contrasts between ways of life in poor countries and rich ones by focusing attention on the value prerequisites for institutional change. The "Lasswellian revolution" with its strong concern with psychological variables generated interest in more experimental studies of political and social motivation including the "disposition to be democratic". These influences, sociological and psychological, when applied to developing areas raise the question of the relation of culture to behaviour in studies which go far beyond both economic self interest and the analysis of constitutionalism. Indeed, the discipline of political science has become virtually separated from its traditional focus. New methods and theories have helped to shatter the coherence of the earlier tradition. The present situation bewilders many practitioners of aid and others interested in using modern political science for policy purposes.

This brings us to the question of what political science can do generally in the study of aid policy. The general political science literature dealing with development has burgeoned.[7] Political development is seen as a total social and economic process. Lucian Pye suggests that modernization brings about certain universal values embodying similarities in outlook and behaviour among all peoples. "Tradition-bound villages or tribal-based societies are compelled to react to the pressures and demands of the modern, industrialized, and urban-centered world."[8]

Some see political development in stages which are not determined by economic growth.[9] Others see it as a form of disequilibration leading at times to revolution,[10] or concentrate on "underdevelopment" as a consequence of economic growth.[11] Still others are more concerned with the dynamism of the industrialization process itself as a kind of "permutation matrix" or an engine of continuous transformation.[12] Whatever the view, the need to conceptualize the process of political development is bound up with two questions: what are the social and economic preconditions of political development and what is the political precondition of social and economic development?

Some scholars outside political science have been able to stimulate new thinking about the first question such as David McClelland's notion of achievement motivation.[13] It seems to explain why development occurs both historically and as between various groupings depending on the degree of n achievement distributed within the group. This turns out to be a slippery idea which if it were translated into political planning would produce many difficulties.[14] For example DeVos discovered that in Japan, scores for individual achievement were low but group achievement was high.[15] I cite this because it illustrates a problem related to the question of prerequisites for political development, namely what might be called the "fallacy of misplaced abstraction". Any specific theory, related to the basic principles of individualism and its connection to entrepreneurship, innovation, and adaptive skill, raises more questions than it answers. From a policy standpoint, even if it were possible to train a people in "achievement motivation" we could not assume that their innovative skills would be enhanced.

This kind of difficulty affects most of the psychological, cultural, and social structural factors which political scientists have borrowed. Nor does history serve as a guide. For example, it was widely believed during the days of colonial empires that to Christianize a population meant also to educate people instrumentally. Religious conviction transferred to educational competence should stimulate the desire for social mobility (rising up the scale of "civilisation") and lead to greater innovative participation. However, such "connections" appear to be more "systemic" than they really are. What is the independent variable, religion or education? If you substitute Islam for Christianity would the same sequence occur? The answer is, sometimes yes and sometimes no. Geertz found that in Indonesia Islam was innovative, modern, secular while in Morocco it was the opposite. In short, how religion works is too complex. "The religious perspective, like the scientific, the aesthetic, the historical, and so on, is after all adopted by men only sporadically, intermittently. Most of the time men, even priests and anchorites, live in the everyday world and see experience in practical, down-to-earth terms— they must if they are to survive."[16] Perhaps this is the reason why the search for an equivalent to Weber's Protestant ethic, whether in broad cultural values or their internalized achievement, turns out to be elusive.

Similarly with education. Education, by changing the horizon of specific opportunities for individuals ought to be predictable in its consequences. Here again the experience is confusing. What type of education will produce an improved agriculture? Is the production of lawyers or a literati dysfunctional? If we know that education generates class distinctions, social cleavages, and a sense of relative deprivation as a function of opportunity will the solution lie in "people's education", European style universities, teacher training, the "land-grant approach", the creation of scientific specialists or the production of rough and ready improvisors?[17] Such questions are crucial for political development, affecting as they do the role of the bureaucrat or civil servant, the character of national elites, the civic culture itself. But if omnibus socio-economic variables are too complex to tell us very much, either by themselves or in relationship to each other, is it possible to speak intelligently about prerequisites of political development?

Nor do political variables help. If, as we have suggested, a liberal political framework designed to balance individual and group preferences with social policies and aimed at maximizing the greatest good for the greatest number, is advocated by many (including the more sociologically sophisticated economists like Albert Hirschmann or W. Arthur Lewis) is it not also the case that such a polity produces economic stagnation, political stalemate, marginal pay-off and overwhelming inequality and corruption, i.e. precisely the conditions which destroy developmental projects or lead to their gross abuse? Under such circumstances what good does it do to favour the establishment of parliamentary government or checks and balances, or judicial review, or proportional representation, or single member plurality voting constituencies, or bills of rights, or political parties. These turn ephemeral when confronted with hard interests, ethnic and primordial; class, linguistic, religious, and the various combinations of these which occur most in periods of increasing development. For example, to put Ghana on a firmer economic footing the parliamentary government cut back military allocations by 16%, favoured rural development, attacked the trade unions, devalued the *cedi* by 44% and promptly was overthrown. If it is very difficult to speak of the social and economic requisites of economic and social development, how much more difficult is the political.

It is not surprising therefore that social scientists trying to escape such dilemmas look for means to hook up variables into sequences and sequences in systems. No single factor in isolation can possess definitive significance. No empirical combination of factors is likely to be repeatable. Rarely does a sequence of steps successful in one social environment repeat itself in another. Because of this social scientists have increasingly moved in an analytical direction, toward abstraction the exact opposite to the position taken by most government officials and politicians.

Practitioners of assistance remain rightly suspicious. The manipulation of given combinations of variables which cannot solve the predicaments of any specific situation remains an empty exercise. Moreover, even where there are policy successes it is difficult to turn a programmatic success into a formula. The best administrators like the best politicians are people-oriented. They seek out the individuals who can be relied upon, not doubtful theories. They rely on individuals whom they expect to have good judgement and competence. Leadership is the alternative to theory. Leadership training followed by experience is the preferred method of recruitment.

Moreover, as any practitioner knows whether one works in a village resettlement scheme in Pakistan or a *barriada* outside Lima or in a community development project in Kenya, human situations are similar all the world over. Such typicality will allow an experienced man on the spot to employ all his intuition as well as his technical skills in gaining co-operation, associating people with the developmental project, dealing with local officials or other bodies. The real skill involved is an individual matter. This kind of expertise cannot be written up in textbooks. Like the politician a sensitive development officer will rely on his combination of experiential cues, private intuitions, his capacity to relate to others, his judgement about associates and friends, and certainly not on the theories of social scientists. Indeed, the more he reads the literature the more suspicious he becomes of theoretical solutions. Every instinct tells him that they will not handle simple truths.[18]

Hence, starting from a similar concern, the search for an explanation about the how and why of development, social scientists and aid practitioners draw opposite conclusions. The one seeks a wider and more capable system and resists the notion of "applied" theory. Policy research is cast aside in favour of pure research especially in political science and sociology. At the same time the practitioner recoils from such theories as incomprehensible, unrealistic, or whimsical preferring to work with real people with real problems in the real world. Occasionally developmental theorist and development practitioner will meet in conferences. They have a common need for alliances which serve universities, help recruit and sponsor research. Despite their association, however, between scholars and practitioners are differences in language and outlook which is likely to worsen rather than improve.

The situation is, however, remedial. There are signs that both sides would like to bridge at least some of the conceptual gaps. Certain shibboleths of development have disappeared. Few nowadays wave the flag of "institution building" or "infrastructure development". We doubt that there is a linear relationship between poverty and communism (and that if you remove the first, you are not likely to have the second). We are less certain that a strong middle class is the prerequisite for democracy especially if imbedded in interest groups and voluntary associations, it creates a self-serving party system validated by representative institutions. We are even beginning to wonder about such sacred cows as the Millikan–Rostow emphasis on developmental loans and the "absorption thesis" of Hollis Chenery. The effect of specific aid experience has over-all been so vastly different from what any program design anticipated that practitioners need a fresh perspective. Attempts at comprehensive reviews such as the Country Assistance Programs and/or Long-range Assistance Surveys have provided one impetus on the practitioner side to comprehend the meaning of aid in a larger analytical context. The social scientists' urge to translate general models into projective or predicative "contradictions" which can be anticipated by forecasting has been stimulated by the opportunities opened up by the growth of quantifiable national index figures and computers. The question is whether the gap which at present is very broad, can be bridged.

A new emphasis on theory will not work unless it anticipates and resolves likely paradoxes or contradictions resulting from typical sequences of aid or patterns of development. The search for such a sequence or pattern requires first the application of analytical or abstract systems to concrete cases. It is on this point that theorists and practitioners must agree.[19]

IV   SYSTEMS FOR SALE

If our assumptions are correct theorists and practitioners need to rediscover each other for good practical reasons. As one practitioner put it recently at a conference, 'at the end of the development decade our ideas are bankrupt". Moreover, to reconsider what political development means is urgently needed not only for its own sake, but also to educate a reluctant public which is expected to pay for it. Only then is it possible to re-engage the interest of politicians who currently regard aid as a marginal interest. Indeed at the moment, aid is about as politically acceptable as taxes and far less inevitable.

On the other hand, faced with the loss of externally financed research support to universities, especially in the social sciences, scholars "rediscovered" an interest in policy research. Whatever the motives it becomes more and more clear that the next steps in the development of our analytical understanding will be through policy research and applied methods. Virtually every major center or institution of developmental or international studies is attempting to use the policy focus to salvage part of larger programs or to relate theory and practice in ways which will have programmatic consequence. Whether this trend will be salutary or not depends a good deal on the nature of the collaboration between practitioners and theorists. This in turn will depend on the policy questions being asked, and the hypotheses that these generate.

There are several ways to bridge the gap. One is to translate system into aggregate data, and to employ quantitative methodologies for projective purposes. Such data can be derived from many sources, surveys and interviews, national statistics, indicators. Quality will vary, depend on the calibre of data-gathering agencies as well as data-processing facilities. More and more sophisticated mathematical strategies are being employed to minimize the effects of incommensurabilities. There is great inventiveness in the development of bridging categories which encompass on a higher level of abstraction what seems to be simply different at a lower (the art of comparing apples and pears). Whatever the specific strategy of research, the broad rubric under which this approach can be discussed is that of micro-components.

Within the micro-component dimension are three overlapping activities. The first is simulation. The second is cross-cultural data analysis. The third is ecological analysis. Some of those most concerned with simulation include Ithiel Pool, Frederick Frey and others at M.I.T. Cross-cultural quantitative indicator analysis has been associated with Karl Deutsch, Bruce Russett, Richard Merritt and others during the period of their work at Yale, while the ecological approach has evolved out of the work of many including Stein Rokkan, Angus Campbell, Juan Linz, Robert Dahl.[20] All use national societies as their concrete "systems". All have an explicitly political focus. All employ quantitative aggregate data.

They rely on behavioural and psychological hypotheses and administrative or organizational theory rather than explanations based on social and political structures and functions. They share a mechanical model of feed-backs, dependent and independent variables, factorial techniques, and regression applications with simulation a substitute for experimentation. As much as possible statistical scientific techniques and procedures are employed. Although there are great differences between the three, all share in the following:

1. They use concrete units and subunits as common sense reality.
2. They employ conventional descriptive categories like "democracy" and "authoritarianism", and concrete units like parliaments and political parties, treating them as more or less constant in their qualities.
3. They restrict their generalizations to what can be directly observed or measured.
4. Their general approach is quantitative, empirical, experimental, and inductive.

In short, this approach maximizes comparative and quantitative methods. It is also empirical and within the realm of common sense. Some practitioners are drawn to it because it holds out possibilities for processing "common sense" and for allowing an observer to see the forest as well as the trees. Theoretical skills are technical, and require learning by mathematical study, survey method, computer programming and the like. It is, at every level, a method of theory which generates syndromes and patterns while remaining concrete. Such a way of looking at development has great appeal. It is similar to forecasting in economics. It uses indicator data. It has been employed by "futurologists" in a variety of research of the projective variety.

The second main dimension of development in theory has been a structuralist one. Using macro-components which do not easily lend themselves to the language of dependent and independent variables, it has tended to employ the political as a residual rather than a key variable in analysis since power is seen as a complex phenomenon embodied in all concrete units of a society (work groups, families, voluntary associations as well as political parties, bureaucracies, etc.). The critical unit of analysis is role. Role relationships are seen in terms of personality structure and values and beliefs. The object of the macrocomponent approach is to formulate systems which are sufficiently abstract to identify logically contradictory empirical conditions which in turn define hypotheses for research.

The origins of this tradition are to be found in several fields, the naïve functionalism of Radcliffe-Brown and Malinowski in anthropology, the analytical tradition of ideal type analysis (a normative emphasis) in the sociology of Weber, the method of structural differentiation and social complexity of Durkheim. Parsons undertook the job of blending these in a general system with three components (social system, social action, and culture) with each emphasizing different problems.

The anthropological was concerned with contradictions arising from the clash and penetration of cultures, particularly the European versus the "traditional" as well as how the "meaning" of such traditional institutions as kinship changed. This kind of theory came to have a direct significance for administrators interested in grafting anthropological ideas on to political-administrative doctrines. Amateur ethnographers as well as government anthropologists and sociologists were employed to provide more adequate information to policy makers and these in turn "plundered" the historical sociologists, particularly Weber and Durkheim, for general ideas about highly differentiated industrial and less differentiated primitive systems. Using general orientational dichotomies (like kinship versus contract) they sought to find in the contrast of tradition and modernity, tribe and state, sacred communities and secular ones, those contradictions which would help explain both the ability or readiness to change and the inhibitions placed by a community upon change. The behavioural emphasis embodied in such an approach is one of orientation load, or how much change a man is able to accept, the degree to which education increases personal efficacy or leads to trivial specialization and a withdrawal from participation. The political emphasis derives from the character of the contradictions at all levels, cultural, social, and personality and the abilities of governments to resolve these by remedial programs, training, building supportive institutional structures for new roles, and creating new ideological syntheses to make sense out of change. In short, for a structuralist politics is in the nature of a response to fundamental patterns of incongruence between ideologies, roles, and motivational patterns, the contradiction between old forms of these and new, and the resulting threats to power or authority which arise when these are insufficiently reconciled or changed.

Those associated with this form of analysis in development studies include Geertz and Fallers in anthropology, Eisenstadt, Moore, Levy, Bellah and Smelser in sociology, Easton, Almond, La Palombara, Weiner, and Binder in political science and many others. What the various groups within this approach share is the following:

1. a concern with the relationship of parts of a society as a whole;
2. a concern with normative and structural contradictions within whole societies;
3. a deductive and/or ideal typical method;
4. a qualitative rather than a quantitative set of variables;
5. hindsight rather than projective theorizing.

The structural emphasis when applied to development, then, is on contradictions created by change and innovation and the search for mediating institutions to create a new level of integration. Traditional societies are seen to have been highly integrated. Change breaks this down. Politics and governmental policy need to re-create it in more modern form. Modernity means urbanization, secularity, functional differentation of roles, universalism. While these highly generalized and global distinctions can be organized into specific hypotheses, what they lack is good operational definitions, clear measurement criteria, and a standardized methodological form. In short, the macrocomponent approach is weakest precisely where the micro-component is strongest. As a result, while the structuralists have been most influential in developmental analysis, it remains a frustrating approach. Indeed, for many practitioners it is something of a joke.

A variant of macrocomponent analysis is in the area of political socialization which steers uneasily between the Freudianism and social "psychologism" of some of the social scientists interested in behaviour *per se* and the perception and experimental schools of Hull and others concerned with individual behaviour. The relationship to structuralism is in terms of various forms of congruence theory. Congruence theory is based on the assumption that the better the fit between people's ideas and cognitions and the structural relationship of roles, the more adequate their developmental performance and the greater the likelihood of equilibrium in a system. The method that a society selects for improving that fit is political socialization. Hence, it becomes important to examine the means whereby roles are institutionalized in schools, religious bodies, ethnic groups, parties, etc. The examination of the efficacy by means of which such socialization is induced and the consequences for groups and individuals, thresholds of variance, etc., form some of the criteria for the examination of microcomponents in a method which relies heavily on empirical studies particularly of the survey research and questionnaire variety. Scholars concerned with developing this aspect of political studies in modernizing societies have included Sidney Verba in his pioneering work with Almond, *The Civic Culture*.[21] Others include Langton's work on Jamaica,[22] and Fred I. Greenstein and Sidney Tarrow, *Political Orientations of Children*.[23] The styles of such research have been strongly influenced by Robert Lane, David Easton, Charles Andrain and others interested in personality, behaviour and socialization. Their application to modernizing societies of political materials will depend a good deal on how much other structural data is available. Moreover, the emphasis in modernizing systems would shift from equilibrium to disequilibrium and the identification of boundaries of incongruity.

A third line of approach, "political economy", is both the oldest and the newest in political development and is uniquely concerned with development in its strictest form, namely the methods of accumulation and production. These it sees as the infrastructural base for beliefs, political forms and other "superstructures". It uses material development as the independent variable and embodies a theory of stages in which there are correspondences between developmental level and political and social forms. Like structuralists, those who follow a political economic approach also see transitions between these as contradictions, but they are concrete, arising from specific situations of conflict between competitive functional groupings, with functionality determined by their role in the productive process.[24]

The political is stressed in each subject field. Economists are preoccupied not with economics as such but rather with the political consequences of capitalist development, as in the work of Paul Baran. Indeed, philosophers like Sartre, anthropological linguists like Claude Lévi Strauss, psychiatrists like Fanon, all show a concern with the socially negative consequences of private and "imperialist" forms of development as compared with the positive opportunities embodied in socialist forms. Some monographic studies rely heavily on the application of neo-Marxist analytical and descriptive sociology as in James Petras' work on Chile, and Maurice Zeitlin's on Cuba.[25] Perhaps the best work on socialist development is Franz Schurmann's study of Communist China.[26]

Clearly the policy implications of this approach are at odds with the other two. Moreover, success for one group means failure for the other. In so far as American developmental assistance advances the cause of capitalism, stimulates entrepreneurship, induces effective socialization and produces an environment militarily, politically and financially benign to the United States it is by definition imperialist. The consequences of aid can only perpetuate American "hegemony". To acquire or create client states which protect local capitalists, to promote, as a form of capitalist accumulation, conditions of under-development among those who are forced to give up their means of livelihood and become squatters or marginals, or partially employed, to enlarge the circumstances of partially employed, to enlarge the circumstances of inequality and give rise to grossly manipulative political regimes—these are the consequences of "successful" aid.[27]

However one regards the neo-Marxist point of view in terms of policy or theory, it points up certain realities of the development process which the others treat as epiphenomenal. Theoretically, the greatest significance of neo-Marxist political economy is that it is a form of marginal analysis which can be applied to the political and social spheres. It establishes the link between functional superfluousness in economic terms, and social and political marginality. This is extremely important in the analysis of developing countries and differs from the more classical Marxian formula (which would regard the functionally superfluous more or less as "lumpens" and consider the proletariat, the creators of value and therefore the most functionally relevant as the dynamic element). In short, the critique of capitalism in developing areas as distinct from industrial ones is that the group possessing maximal functional significance, the working class, is small, while the functionally superfluous are large but restricted to marginal social and political shares by the state which prevents an appropriate social and political redistribution. In other words, in less developed countries the social and political marginals are also economic marginals, hence they fall outside the normal limits of societal obligation. A neo-Marxist theory of developmental assistance would imply at least that such assistance should be devoted directly to maximal improvement *at the margin*. Anything short of that is imperialism, externally induced and internally deployed.

It is an interesting theory and most relevant in highly modernized developed countries like Argentina where there are profound social cleavages, huge squatter populations victimized by ruthless exploitation, corruption and political helplessness. One reason it has not had sufficient attention is that it tends to invoke socialism as an incantational solution without recognizing "systemic" characteristic problems of socialism, such as a burgeoning bureaucracy, lack of innovative skills, political inequality, and, often enough, terror. What the political economists can point to is successful development in China, North Korea, and the astonishing performance of what is currently the most militant case, i.e. North Viet-Nam.

Each of the three main approaches can overlap. It is possible, for example, to employ some of the central hypotheses about marginality under developmental capitalism as derived by the neo-Marxists, translate them into structural theories, and test them by more quantitative or cross-national analysis. One effort to develop such a strategy is the remarkable work on *The Politics of Change in Venezuela*.[28] Combining multiple approaches, the authors are able to evaluate the global effects of change in a single case, a *tour de force* in what might be called "combination" analysis.

V   COMBINATION ANALYSIS VS. ECLECTICISM

Most ordinary work on development and social change occurs in a non-theoretical manner and on a more or less *ad hoc* basis. Quite often, especially in case materials, theory provides a check list of important items which, when pooled, serve to alert practitioners to ills the social body is heir to. The results are typically printed in conference reports written by developmental experts, each one of which describes some developmental problem or experience, utters a few warnings for the future and returns to work, secure in the knowledge that his remarks have been solemnly recorded by some A.I.D. or United Nations' scribe, to be published as the next collection of essays on developmental thinking. If these contributions are characterized by a certain gratuitousness and looseness or, even worse, utter unprofessionality, it is justified on the grounds that professionalism is a barrier to communications. Typical of such documents is a recent report of a meeting of experts on social and policy planning held in Sweden in 1969. Here are the new shibboleths to replace the old ones; "economic phenomena are also social phenomena," "development is a process," the "dualism of the sectors" (modern and traditional), "quantify with care", unemployment is "under-utilization of labour", "bottleneck research should be specific to a given country", "the need for dialogue between planners and politicians", the need to "engineer social change." Prerequisites of development (equally pious but equally lacking in substance) are "peaceful, radical social change" to permit "all human and material resources of a country", "full and dynamic participation in the process of development". Such hortatory platitudes abound in the literature. "Excessive regulation and procedures in matters involving economic or social organization and resource allocation often give rise to problems of corruption. Developing countries should rationalize their procedures for trade licensing and other forms of resource allocation, giving special attention to making them more effective instruments of social policy. . . ." One could go on.[29] It is precisely this kind of checklisting which practitioners have become expert in regurgitating and which, although fatuous, gives an intellectual gloss to their endeavours providing a certain moral satisfaction or smugness because it all sounds so wise and responsible.

A much more important kind of checklisting is the search for social indicators. This, although it tends to be eclectic, turns attention to critical variables and their identification and is thus a precondition of our first approach. With time and performance dimensions built in at the start, the question of system is expressed in the form of "vectors" and structures. Indicator analysis can be extremely helpful in organizing basic information.[30] The best practitioners of indicator and trend analysis are very much aware of the limitations of the approach.

> If . . . development is not a uniform linear progression but is characterized by changing patterns of relationship among factors, then a country's own past trends may not predict its future very well. Furthermore, the historical experiences of countries now called "developed" have limited relevance to the developing countries today. It cannot be concluded that the latter countries will or should repeat the historical development paths of the former—modern science and technology have made this quite unnecessary. The most revealing kind of cross-temporal analysis would cover modern periods and involve a large sample of countries, developing a well as developed. But, as noted above, the

statistical basis for quantitative studies of this kind hardly exists, except for a limited number of countries and a limited number of variables between 1950 and 1960 or 1965.[31]

Limited projections, short time series, and most of all, comparative reviews to see if replicable patterns are possible will become more likely as statistical services in less developed countries are improved in quality and expanded in scope. Indeed, as we shall discuss later on, there is perhaps no project more worth doing because of its manageability, and the varied nature of its consequence, than improving the scope and quality of research-statistical institutions.

The possibilities of more controlled analysis of developmental change will obviously depend first of all on the availability of data. But as well, "combination theories" will be essential, using all three forms of analysis which have been described. Clearly they cannot simply be "stuck together". The first involves strategies of time series and is above all a method for the analysis of microcomponents. The second generates a concern with macrocomponents, generalized variables like power, authority, norms, class, elites, information, etc. These, in order to be effective, will depend on the "sociological" content and form of their variables, as well as their capacity for translation into "surrogate" variables[32] or indicator variables. It is necessary for the macro theory to "engage" the micro in both methodological and empirical ways. Finally, since many of the specific propositions of the neo-Marxians deal with behaviour under capitalism, it is necessary to focus on particular issues raised by the theory itself, the hegemonic or imperialist consequences of aid, the causes of "under-development" along side of development, the marginal theory of social change, etc.

Combination theories, then, are specific analytical and empirical strategies self-consciously integrated in terms of particular problems. The criteria of combination are first of all the availability of data. That should go without saying. The other criteria are as follows. 1. Hypothesis formation: "The essence of any model is the hypotheses embedded in the relationships and structure. The social scientist can invest hypotheses relating to components of any desired level of aggregation, just as the physicist may promulgate hypotheses about the behaviour of gasses as well as about the behaviour of molecules or components of molecules." 2. Specification of causality: "We want models of social systems that will enable policy-makers to predict consequences of alternative actions. Furthermore, we want models that say more than that certain things have been associated in the past or even that, in the absence of control efforts, they will be associated in the future. We want models that will predict how the future will be different if particular actions are taken in preference to others." 3. Estimation and testing: "Social scientists do not yet possess a body of theory sufficiently developed and tested to permit the confident specification of variables to be included, of forms of equations to be used, and of appropriate lags for each variable prior to the estimation of parameters entering into equations. Existing theory offers some guidance, but it is the most fanciful kind of wishful thinking to believe that it offers much guidance in the above respects. It is obvious, therefore, that any effective testing and estimation requires very large numbers of observations."[33]

These criteria would hold for any system of analysis which tries to improve the science side of developmental policy-making. A parallel need to that of generating basic aggregate data, is in the translation of qualitative information into binary or ranked data so that the body of observational material in the fields of anthropology, politics, sociology, etc., can be employed in more than a monographic and unique context.

There is still very little emphasis on what I have called "combination analysis". Too many social scientists remain embroiled in parochial disputes over such large issues as the ethics of science in social matters, the degree to which computers sterilize knowledge rather than advance it, behaviouralism versus structuralism, etc. That these and other issues are of great importance, we do not deny. But far too often the actual debates take on a posturing aspect which prevents just those kinds of collaborative efforts necessary to build a better theoretical mousetrap. What is needed now is more organized research at centres inside or outside the academy devoted to various forms of combination analysis at a high level.

VI HYPOTHESES FOR HIRE

Obviously we cannot go into the question of which combination theories might work best for what purposes. Few such theories as yet exist, as Orcutt suggests. No such decision can be made about them until the hypotheses which they are supposed to test are specified. Taking several of the main political objectives of aid as our guide, what general hypotheses can we derive as guides to would-be combination theorists? The most general of these objects, namely the creation of a stable and prosperous world of nations with a capacity for self-sustained growth is too broad, but some of the other original assumptions can be reviewed in the form of hypotheses. The most obvious example is the notion that if there is poverty then there is likely to be communism. Far more sensible is the Lipset hypothesis that if there is increasing development, rising expectation, increasing educational opportunity and political participation, then there is also likely to be an increasing tendency towards radical movements. The real question for combination theory is among which groups and under what specific circumstances. A more interesting hypothesis is whether or not, with successful modernization, radicalization (that is, the rejection of roles values and practices previously institutionalized), will (a) increase, (b) be likely to be a middle-class phenomenon, carried by (c) bourgeois elites, particularly the (d) best educated and most rich. A subsidiary hypothesis is that such radicalization will suddenly increase at x degree of development among those with technical skills, in responsible positions in planning for agronomy, engineering, and increasingly the military, who feel frustrated by "the system" and see a need to transform key aspects of it, root and branch. Evidence for this is greatest in precisely the most advanced modernizing countries where development has produced great inequality, stagnation, and a pool of frustrated intellectuals and technicians, not all of whom dissipate their energies in romantic leftism but, as in the case of Peru and Chile, generate specific developmental programs of reform through nationalization.

Indeed, these hypotheses, simple enough to describe empirically, contain many of the key questions for the political study of development because they link to the development process, questions of political institutionalization and de-institutionalization and open up the opportunity for systemic analysis of how counter-norms and counter elites, form and the patterns or syndromes of radicalization *vis-à-vis* regime change and political system shifts. One of the few political scientists who have tried to deal with this problem directly is Samuel Huntington. "The revolutionary intellectual is virtually a universal phenomenon in modernizing societies", he points out.[34] But Huntington's form of analysis is institutional rather than analytical and descriptively impressionistic or illustrative rather than inductive and projective. It is precisely the next stage in combination theory that we are after.

What I have called the twin process of "radicalization" and "embourgeoisement" is merely illustrative. Questions about dependency, efficacy loss, and above all information creation and utilization are even more important. For each we need to know structural syndromes and to program and compute degrees to which structure at the macro level relates to the behaviour of micro-components. To what extent is radicalization a phenomenon that remains largely rhetorical (perhaps punctuated by violence and terror) and to what extent does it become elaborated and articulated in the expectations and actions of other sectors of a community? And,

M

to go back to the Lipset question, to what extent is radicalization a function of development?

I tend to regard much of the so-called radicalization process in modernizing societies as "radicalization for embourgeoisement". To put it another way, attempts to employ radical ideologies, planning, socialist methods, and the like, are essentially the present day versions of the catch-up phenomenon which in the past, particularly in Prussia and Japan, took a more "neo-mercantilist" form.[35] Today the emphasis on "mobilization" is more total, if only because the difficulties in catching up are so much greater. Indeed, to catch up will only be possible for a very few countries: China, Brazil, perhaps a few others. The political method becomes important as a system of development. Each generates its own set of difficulties. A mobilization pattern generates coercion; a more bureaucratic military one as in Brazil, not unlike the military neo-mercantilism of Germany and Japan, generates growth but becomes repressionist.

Our argument has shifted now from process (radicalization, or embourgeoisement) to political system type. If each contains built-in difficulties then we must rid ourselves of the accustomed thinking about political stability as a prerequisite of effective development. Political instability, i.e. changing not only governments but types of government, may be the only form of "entrepreneurship" open. Nor does this necessarily mean that society is unstable. For example, Argentina is a remarkably stable society on the social level, but has experienced a bewildering array of governmental changes since Peron. Here we need a concept like "political ceiling". To what extent is it possible for what kinds of governments to use what levels of resources to carry out what degree of development and what degree of alteration in the social system. This is precisely the kind of question which combination theory can address itself to. By dealing with the micro-components in the context of a generalized theory of political system change it can do more than illustrate but also project.

What sorts of theoretical constructs are available for such combination theory at a political level? The framework which I have found useful is one which combines the following ingredients: (a) functional components deriving from information creation relevant for development; (b) dialectical components relevant to the clash and transformation of norms; and (c) motivational components relating to learning, efficacy, and commitment. These I have called the normative, structural and behavioural components out of which a macro theory can be built. More specifically, the normative can be translated into ideologies about capitalism, socialism, liberalism, etc., at both societal and governmental levels. The structural component deals with emergent classes and elites, their functional significance, conflict and the discrepancies between the way they function and the ideologies people have accepted. Too big a discrepancy and the likely chances of a political system change increase. What chances or probabilities becomes a task for comparative analysis using microcomponents and indicator variables.[36]

Without elaborating the matter here, the question of political ceiling can also be related to two critical variables which have great policy significance. One is the degree of information (technical, interest, and populist) that governments have at their disposal. The other is the extent to which they can employ that information. Some political systems admit of very high degrees of populist information, namely public reaction and mood, but have very little technical information. Clearly it would be a policy objective of the United States to provide a better technical information-gathering base and improve the professional services a society can muster. Moreover, the more amenable to policy on the basis of information a modernizing polity is, the more likely is it to be democratic. Providing technical information and the infrastructure to obtain it would be a critical way to raise the "political ceiling" of a relatively democratic system.

But such policy would also require follow-through on the infrastructure side. Information may also show that a democratic government, with its obligations, cleavages, bargains, and commitments, is in an utterly fragile condition and the more information it has the more difficult it is to act. Then either the political system must change to a more coercive one, or massive support will be required. The recent coup in Ghana against Busia is a case in point. The full realization of what that implies, including amounts and forms of support, and the follow-up projects that might be necessary are rarely appreciated "systemically".

This leads to another query. Under some circumstances, what is necessary is not more information (unless we are prepared to do a total job of development), but internal coercion. We are more willing to accept this when it involves military or bureaucratic regimes which are anti-socialist or anti-communist. A more ruthless question (from a theoretical point of view) is whether or not forced draft methods of development by mobilization means, such as in Communist China, do not create conditions for "embourgeoisement" and generate conditions of trade, more effective political relations and the like, i.e. in a more stable manner, than other forms. (Nixon's visit to China may be one indication that it is, and would have appeared as unlikely a few years ago as a visit by Castro to San Clemente seems now.) The question of regime change in communist societies has itself become very central in political studies as the polycentric and pluralistic character of socialism manifests itself in Eastern Europe. Political system change as a basis for combination theory would at the very least require us to take a very different view of communist regimes.

All this suggests that process variables like radicalization and embourgeoisement, structural variables like political system can be examined empirically by microcomponent methods. Combination theories are always arbitrary. They do not exist in the abstract. They must be designed for a particular task. A policy emphasis is one way to bring them into fruition applied to major issues; with due regard for long-term and short-term tendencies, our conception of the real world of development can be enlarged. The result can help to educate politicians and the public about what to anticipate. To put it another way, since the accumulation of specific projects in any country will produce long-term contradictions out of short-term success, analysis of latent functionalities and dysfunctionalities, particularly those which result in political crisis, constitutes the most important questions for all of us. It is precisely this kind of understanding which is needed to off-set the mythologies and demonologies with which we have clouded the aid-giving process.

Putting the question in this form raises many issues, including fundamental ethical considerations. Developmental policy is inevitably social engineering, the more so as it becomes improved and predictive in its results. The political consequences include distribution of power based on unequal access and control over knowledge itself. Indeed, if the chief characteristic of industrial societies is the capacity to generate new information at an exceptionally rapid rate and transform it by means of a domestic infrastructure into a disposable output, then not only are modernizing societies increasingly dependent on information from abroad, but they are locked into an international stratification system in which they become "knowledge clients" of industrial scientific "patrons".

Such concerns turn our attention to an older tradition in political science but in a fresh form, namely to the concept of constitutionalism as political development. The question is, what forms of the polis will enable decision-makers in modernizing societies to expand the technical side of their own policy-making establishments, while improving the fit between political needs and demands? What is needed is a new concern with the forms of a "development constitution" to deal with such matters of information theory, e.g. the development within government of sensitive receptors of what might be called populist information (public reaction), interest information (the special demands of functional groupings) and finally professional information (particularly of technocratic and welfare character). How governments receive this information and employ it to widen their capacities for intelligent decision-making and find new and fresh alternatives seems to me to be the essential question for those interested in political development. To put it another way, how can the political ceiling be raised by means of expanded information and improved decision-making. That can be seen in its broadest sense as developmental constitutionalism.[37]

Combination theory is above all projective, and interpretative, a research tool to enable those in positions of policy planning to understand and forecast what a development program is likely to produce.[38] From a political science standpoint there are two broad strategies. The first is the politics of development, i.e. the political consequences of that accumulation of pressures, conflicts, discontinuities, competition, etc., arising out of development change. Whether such an accumulation is a primary, secondary or tertiary stage developmental problem, its consequences can be examined by studying counter-elites whose ideologies specifically challenge authority and charge it with being illegitimate, and the emergence of new kinds of interest groups, such as technocrats, who make demands upon the political system in a new way as a result of some policy program (agrarian reform, increased agricultural output, new technical bodies, etc.) This is certainly fundamental to the tradition of political studies and how coalitions form, make demands, and disintegrate. The fluid quality of politics in developing societies becomes less difficult to understand as our basic knowledge increases. Work load analysis of modernizing political systems in bureaucratism, nepotism, and corruption can all be studied by fairly conventional means. How these more familiar concerns relate to more behavioural questions is a task for combination theory, i.e. the effects of coalitions on the degree of willingness or unwillingness to innovate, a tendency to play a role in an "external" formal way, without performing effectively within it. Moreover, the assumption that modernization gives men a better control over their environment and lives may be true collectively but does not always hold for individuals, whose personal sense of efficacy may decline, causing them to retreat rather than participate effectively in change. One of the reasons for peasant or rural conservatism is precisely this sense of efficacy loss. Combination theory tries to blend such diverse concerns and levels and types of analysis into a single strategy.

The second major strategy is that of a politics for development, i.e. varying the political type and predicting the consequences. This requires abstracted systems which are themselves hypotheses. For example, what I have called reconciliation systems rely on increasing marginal pay-offs to new contenders for shares in the developmental process. Aid may be more effective in generating new contenders than in producing a developmental product. Indeed, as a particular program becomes shaky or lacks morale, or is confronted with internal conflict as is so often the case in community development, educational, or entrepreneurial and commercial projects, personalism leads to politics, both within the new institutions and as a work load of government. This does not necessarily resolve itself through marginal distributions of gain, but may reawaken old "primordial" loyalties of religion, tribe, ethnicity, language, etc., with all the fissionable consequences of that—civil war, separatist movements, etc. We have seen the effects of this precisely in those reconciliation systems where the prospects of democracy seemed fairly good, as in Nigeria or Ceylon.

On the other hand, mobilization systems tend to rely on a fixed set of developmental goals and to alter the social structure to fit such goals. In the first, government is essentially participatory and managerial. In the second, it is essentially hortatory and authoritarian. It generates coercion, and opportunism, but may be the most successful political system for converting late stage modernization into industrialization.

A third type is more bureaucratic. Its object is to retain the features of the social system more or less as they are, but to control the terms of bargaining and to restrict demands by the selective use of coercion. Most military regimes are of this type. They commonly result when the other two types fail.

Without going into an analysis of these types or others that might be suitable, it should be clear that when we are talking about the consequences of political systems *for* development, a variation in type must reveal the consequence for development rate and priorities. However, whether concerned with the politics *of* development or politics *for* development, what is required for combination analysis is a store of data which can be mobilized. The emphasis on the politics of development would include data about incongruities and political demands. The emphasis on politics for development would emphasize governmental strategies including the sequential analysis of planification.

VII DATA FOR BANKING

Combination analysis, then, is a specific strategy of macro and microcomponents. It can also provide the basis for an information storage and retrieval system in which analytical search categories can be built into a computer program. Again there are precursors for this. The Human Relations Area Files at Yale was the first attempt to organize such a data bank with qualitative data. It suffered from a primitive set of categories for use and the unevenness of the materials. Quantitative data around particular types of materials have been gathered in a number of places such as the consortium based at the University of Michigan. Survey data from all parts of the world have been accumulated in the International Data Collection Library of the Survey Research Center at Berkeley. Other important collections exist at Williams College, the Political Science Research Library at Yale, and at other places.

None of these can serve as models in a specific sense. They merely suggested that data banks built around specific subjects, using qualitative as well as quantitative variables, and employing retrieval languages, are possible. The relation between theory and practice must be made very explicit, however, if a retrieval system is to be useful for policy. In other words, a combination theory should provide the basis for a retrieval language in the politics of and for development. The first attempts to negotiate a bibliography on the basis of retrieval systems are extremely promising but they have necessarily taken the form of reviews of available materials rather than substantive accumulation of new data.[39] One basis for a development data bank, however, might begin with the materials already on hand in the reportage and statistical files of aid agencies. Such materials go back far enough to make possible time series analysis, regression analysis, etc. In short, the combined overseas development files contain the materials for a first-class data bank in which the statistical and qualitative materials translated into systemic variables in binary or nominal form, can be combined.[40]

VIII   MANY HAPPY RETURNS

The possibilities of effective information storage and retrieval combined with effective combination theory would be important enough for the development of social science policy. The question is how to translate such possibilities into a more institutional form. The organization and management of aid is critical if research is to provide policy returns. Clearly, to substitute a well-trained career service is one step in the right direction.

Another possibility is the organization of development teams similar in conception to the "integrated work unit". Unlike a differentiated service with its various types of experts, its line and staff men, its sub-specialists, all of whom constitute a division of labour which intensifies conflicts between individuals and expertise, the integrated work unit combines these various specialities in a more permanent arrangement or grouping, the developmental team. (The idea is similar to some of the new methods of work being experimented with in factories. Today the costs of assembly line practices are becoming excessive because of wastage, improper supervision, poor morale, and hostility on the part of workers. The result is sabotage, theft, and bad workmanship. Indeed, the assembly line is becoming prohibitively expensive as a method of production in the automobile industry, with some factories experimenting with permanent teams responsible for the entire product, i.e. engaged in all aspects of the production. These work together as integrated groups, sharing in the direct responsibility for the product.) The development team is a cadre composed of different kinds of experts, men with field and executive experience varying in composition according to purposes and scope of activity and jointly responsible for entire projects, from the original planning stage to the time when, as functioning entities, projects could be turned over to host country operatives. Teams would vary in speciality; some being composed primarily of, say, agricultural experts, while others might be more educational; but whatever their composition, the point is that the teams themselves ought to be more or less self-contained and responsible at each stage for planning and making needed alterations in conception and organization as experience and fortunes dictate.

Each team would be composed of area, subject or technical, and administrative experts. Not very large, they would employ language and other more specialized experts from a resource pool. They would begin work after completing higher level discussions over specific programs and when complete agreement had been reached at the appropriate policy levels of government. With the alternatives defined and priorities fixed between donor and host, a project would become the specific responsibility of the appropriate development team, the first task of which would be essentially an orientational one consisting of study and hearings on the area and its particular problems, and the significance, politically and economically, of the proposed project. As a second step, a survey party of the team might be sent to the host country for feasibility studies and to ascertain the responsible personnel overseas (preparing to train such personnel if necessary), and to specify what technical operations would be necessary. Thirdly, the survey party would need to report to the development team as a whole, enabling the team to draw up alternative schedules, projecting long-run and short-run consequences and assessing the multiple costs and consequences in each case. It is precisely at this stage that combination theory becomes crucial. What we envisage is the developmental team working out its own style and emphasis in combination theory and over time accumulating a body of theoretical experience on which to draw.

The development team approach makes a continuous group responsible for effective performance, and to take the blame for failure. It maximizes information and communication between specialities. We would expect, too, a much higher degree of solidarity between the members, which would grow with the record of accomplishment. In short, we want to maximize individual and group efficacy where today high specialization tends otherwise to isolate individuals, and make them feel vulnerable outside their speciality (and therefore less inclined to be flexible and innovative).

The developmental team idea is not new. It was used with considerable success at a district level in some colonial territories. In Uganda, district teams composed of various administrative officers, medical, community development, magistrates, animal husbandry, forestry, etc., worked in collaboration with district and local councils and district commissioners. This, of course, was at a relatively limited developmental level.

The Chinese in Mali and to some extent in Tanzania, and the Israelis in Africa more generally, have hit upon a somewhat similar format. With smaller resources and limited available technical staff their need is to maximize the impact and effectiveness of their programs as inexpensively as possible. The result is stable cadres moving from place to place somewhat in the fashion described. We suggest the development team as the nucleus of aid programming (the operating unit) in the context of a development institute, relying on data, working out combination theories in conjunction with its staff, negotiating the details of programming with host country nationals so that those who negotiate will also follow through the consequences, making provision for its host country successors and trying to train them in the shortest period of time, and finally, when its job is done, redeployed elsewhere. We do not suggest the development team idea as an all-purpose solution but rather as a mobile force capable of dealing with many projects more or less as they are presently conceived, and stimulating the organization of similar cadres among host countries.

This brings us to a final point. Much of our thinking about development is already outmoded. If our myths preserve our innocence, they also prevent us from considering the ways in which the relations and terms of aid are presently inadequate. Take, for example, the idea of a gap between rich and poor countries. Barbara Ward and other supporters of the "gap theory" are, of course, right when they say that the development gap between less developed countries is widening rather than narrowing. But it does not really mean much. Indeed, in such terms very few poor countries will ever catch up with rich ones. Moreover, why close the gap? Highly industrialized countries, faced with a series of lamentable and insurmountable crises; compacted urban densities, the intensification of internal disparities between racial and cultural groups, the survival of primordial attachments and hostilities, crime—all point to the inadequacies of contemporary industrial life. To an increasing extent developing countries will have all these problems without the benefits of full industrialization. The congested urban areas found in most Latin American cities are one example of what happens. Greater development will only compound the problem and closing the "gap" will only mean that the means of resolution will be ever more difficult. Instead of such "gap" notions, we need to see the world in development terms, i.e. as an ecological space organized around different kinds of developmental strategies and jurisdictions depending on the character of the problems. What is really obsolete is our thinking about rich and poor, capitalism or socialism, small countries and big ones. These categories are not likely to disappear in the near future, but their persistence prevents more rational plans for limiting population, decentralizing industry on a global basis, creating stable and limited industrial communities, expanding the range of educational strategies and diversities. If in the long run the problem of development is how to integrate the ignorant, the partially educated, and the highly educated, whether in our own societies or abroad, we need a different set of conceptions altogether. Indeed, if our present developmental objectives are not to produce a terrible international meritocracy, some of the concerns of the political-economy approach need to be given greater attention.

I am not suggesting that thinking outrageous thoughts should be the main purpose of combination theory and policy, but rather that the consequences of development are not ever likely to produce benign results. Our assumption of a good policy to produce a world of happy and prosperous nations is too simple. As André Latreille commented in a recent issue of Le Monde, " Seen in the most charitable light, the industrialized nations of today's world bear a striking resemblance to the wealthy middle class of the nineteenth century. Their shortsightedness—so thoroughly denounced today— accepted the wretchedness of the masses as the natural order of things, and bought its peace of mind with the odd handout to the poorest of the poor. What was needed, in fact, was an effort to seek and develop a basic structural reform, a program regarded as impractical in the last century."[41] What we are suggesting is more attention to the possibilities of basic structural reform.

1 See Robert A. Packenham, *Foreign Aid and Political Development* (Princeton: Princeton University Press, forthcoming).
2 See Committee for Economic Development, statement by the Research and Policy Committee, "Assisting Development in Low-income Countries", Sept. 1969.
3 For a discussion of French aid programs see Teresa Hayter, *French Aid*, London: The Overseas Development Institute, 1966.
4 Of course, such a service could easily become an empire composed of bureaucratic technocrats or a force to contend in a powerful way with other bodies concerned with overseas affairs, such as the foreign service and the military.
5 See Charles and Mary Beard, *Basic History of the United States* (New York: Doubleday Doran and Company, 1944).
6 See the description of the evolution of foreign studies in Cyril E. Black, "Foreign Area Studies: Emergent Challenges and Trends" in Fred W. Riggs (ed.), *International Studies: Present Status and Future Prospects* Philadelphia: mimeograph 12, American Academy of Political and Social Science, 1971.
7 The best recent review is Samuel Huntington, "The Change to Change: Modernization, Development and Politics" in *Comparative Politics*, Vol. 3, No. 3, April 1971.
Less recent is a review article I did with Charles Andrain, "Comparative Government: Developing New Nations" in Marian D. Irish, ed. *Political Science: Advance of the Discipline* (Englewood Cliffs, N.J. Prentice-Hall, Inc. 1968).
8 See Lucian W. Pye, *Aspects of Political Development* (Boston: Little Brown and Company, 1966). Political development consists of economic development as a prerequisite, modernization, the operation of the nation state, legal and administrative institutions, mobilization of participation, organizing democracy, and stability.
9 See A. F. K. Organski, *The Stages of Political Development* (New York: Alfred A. Knopf. 1965).
10 See Chalmers Johnson, *Revolutionary Change* (Boston: Little Brown and Co., 1966).
11 See Paul Baran, *The Political Economy of Growth* (New York: Monthly Review Press, 1957), Andre Gundar Frank, *Capitalism and Underdevelopment in Latin America* (New York: Monthly Review Press, 1967), and Irving Louis Horowitz, *Three Worlds of Development* (New York: Oxford University Press, 1966), pp. 47–72.
12 See Raymond Aron, *18 Lectures on Industrial Society* (London: Weidenfeld and Nicolson, 1961).
13 See D. C. McClelland, *The Achieving Society* (Princeton: Van Nostrand, 1961).
14 See Robert LeVine, *Dreams and Deeds* (Chicago: The University of Chicago Press, 1966). LeVine's analysis in Nigeria suggests that differences between Ibos, the most innovative and achievement oriented group in Nigeria, are not as great as might be expected when their achievement motivation is compared with Hausa or Yoruba groups.
15 See George DeVos, "Achievement and Innovation in Culture and Personality" in D. E. Apter and Charles Andrain (eds.) *Contemporary Analytical Theory* (Englewood Cliffs, New Jersey, Prentice-Hall, 1972).

16 See Clifford Geertz *Islam Observed* (New Haven: Yale University Press, 1968, p. 107). See also the analysis of values in relation to development in Robert N. Bellah, *Tokugawa Religion* (Glencoe: The Free Press, 1957).

17 See the discussions of such matters in John W. Hanson and Cole S. Brembeck, *Education and the Development of Nations*, (New York; Holt, Rinehart and Winston, 1966). See also the discussion of the political significance of education in terms of political orientations, congruence with other socializing agencies, and the specific effects of school environments in James Coleman's introduction to his volume, *Education and Political Development* (Princeton: Princeton University Press, 1965).

18 See the general critique by Michael Lipton, "Interdisciplinary Studies in Less Developed Countries" in *Journal of Development Studies*, School of African and Asian Studies, the University of Sussex, Reprint Series No. 35, n.d.

19 See James S. Coleman *et al.*, *Crises and Sequences in Political Development* (Princeton: Princeton University Press, 1971).

20 See especially M. Dogan and S. Rokkan, *Quantitative Ecological Analysis in the Social Sciences* (Cambridge: M.I.T. Press, 1969).

21 See Gabriel A. Almond and Sidney Verba, *The Civic Culture* (Princeton: Princeton University Press, 1963).

22 See Kenneth P. Langton, *Political Socialization* (New York: Oxford University Press, 1969).

23 See Fred I. Greenstein and Sidney Tarrow, *Political Orientations of Children: The Use of a Semi-Projective Technique in Three Nations* (Beverly Hills, Calif.: Sage Publications, 1970).

24 There is a huge developmental literature in this field (from Rosa Luxemburg to Paul Sweezy) employing three main variables, the division of labour, capital accumulation, and technical change. See Maurice Dobb, *Capitalism, Development and Planning* (London: Routledge and Kegan Paul, 1967).

25 See James Petras, *Politics and Social Forces in Chilean Development* (Berkeley: University of California Press, 1969).

26 See Franz Schurmann's *Ideology and Organization in Communist China* (Berkeley: University of California Press, 1966).

27 See James O'Connor, "The Fiscal Crisis of the State" in *Socialist Revolution*, March-April 1970, Vol. 1, No. 2, pp. 34–94, for an excellent summary statement of this point of view.

28 See Frenk Bonilla and Jose A. Silva Michelena, *The Politics of Change in Venezuela* (Cambridge: The M.I.T. Press, 3 Vols., 1967, 1970, 1971).

29 See "Social Policy and Planning in National Development" in *International Social Development Review*, No. 3 (United Nations, New York, 1971).

30 See the discussion in Raymond A. Bauer (ed.), *Social Indicators* (Cambridge: M.I.T. Press, 1966), pp. 19–48.

31 See D. V. McGranahan *et al.*, *Contents and Measurement of Socio-economic Development; an Empirical Enquiry* (Geneva: United Nations Research Institute for Social Development, Report No. 70, 10, mimeo, n.d.), p. 3.

32 Surrogate variables are different variables employed to identify similar phenomena. For example, evaluation of opposition to government may in a democratic society be based on electoral results while under totalitarianism by underground activities.

33 These three criteria are taken from Guy H. Orcutt, "Data Needs for Computer Simulation of Large-scale Social Systems" in James M. Beshers, *Computer Methods in the Analysis of Large-scale Social Systems* (Cambridge: The M.I.T. Press, 2nd ed., 1968), pp. 234–35. Orcutt would rely much more ex-

clusively on microcomponents where I would rely more on a blend of microcomponents and macro.

34 See Samuel P. Huntington, *Political Order in Changing Societies* (New Haven: Yale University Press, 1968), p. 290.

35 For a dicussion of these terms see D. E. Apter, *The Politics of Modernization* (Chicago: The University of Chicago Press, 1965), and the essay in this volume, "Radicalization and Embourgeoisement: Hypotheses for a Comparative Study of History".

36 For a full analysis of this see D. E. Apter, *Choice and the Politics of Allocation* (New Haven: Yale University Press, 1971). See also D. E. Apter and Charles Andrain (eds.), *Contemporary Analytical Theory* (Englewood Cliffs, N.J.: Prentice-Hall, 1972).

37 See a preliminary approach to deal with this problem by D. E. Apter and Martin Doornbos, "Development and the Political Process: A Plan for a Constitution" above.

38 See Bettina J. Huber and Wendell Bell, "Sociology and the Emergent Study of the Future" in *The American Sociologist*, Vol. 6, Nov. 1971, pp. 287–95.

39 See, for example, Frederick W. Frey, *et al.*, *Survey Research on Comparative Social Change: a Bibliography* (Cambridge: The M.I.T. Press, 1969).

40 See Kenneth Jaunda, *Information Retrieval Applications to Political to Political Science* (New York: The Bobbs-Merrill Co., 1968).

41 *Le Monde*, No. 143, Jan. 15, 1972 (Weekly English Edition).

9

Comparative Government: Developing New Nations*

David E. Apter and Charles Andrain

I INTRODUCTION

The study of new nations began to take its present form in a particularly fortunate intellectual climate, at a time when new patterns of social science thought in anthropology and sociology were beginning to have an effect on political studies. This impact, stemming largely from World War II, generated antagonisms within the field of political science; yet it also allowed considerable analytical experimentation, particularly in those cultural and regional areas where little previous work had been done.[1] Although political science orthodoxy reigned supreme in the comparative political analyses of Western Europe and American government, even here a previous generation had already attempted to employ institutional variables in analysis, as exemplified by institutionalists like Sir Ernest Barker, Harold Laski, Carl Friedrich, and Herman Finer.[2] Hence a tradition existed on which to build. However, it required a shift in research emphasis—to the comparative analysis of new nations—to allow sufficient scope for those who wanted to use different approaches and apply new concepts to the "fundamentals" of politics. Preoccupied with such matters, the "first round" studies did not compare but rather emphasized internal ingredients of novel systems. They sought to delineate the characteristics of authority in political systems, particularly in the context of change from a colonial-traditional to an autonomous-modern one, and to devise new field methods and research concepts needed for understanding the many levels of the process.[3] These monographic studies made possible comparative work in a "second round". The study of new nations stimulated comparisons not only between each other but also between new and

* Revised chapter reprinted from Marian D. Irish, ed., *Political Science: Advance of the Discipline*, (c) 1968, by permission of Prentice-Hall, Inc., Englewood Cliffs, New Jersey.

older ones. Analysts compared industrial societies (Western and Eastern Europe, Japan, the United States, Canada, Australia), the less industrialized, older modernizing nations in Latin America, and the newer nations in Asia and Africa. All these studies viewed societies in a new context—modernization and development.[4]

The problem focus and the concern with analytical methods evolved simultaneously. Indeed, the evolution of the comparative study of new nations took the following forms:

(1) Throughout Asia and Africa, comparative analysts focused on nationalism as a rising moral force against colonialism. A parallel was drawn between nineteenth-century working-class claims for rights of political participation and twentieth-century claims of colonial peoples for self-government. Nationalism was the ideology for dependent societies, just as some form of socialism tended to be the ideology for nineteenth-century trade-union demands with democratic institutions seen as the likely answer. In the broadest sense, this parallel was the silent major premise of most analytical work on new nations. Colonialism was thus studied in the context of democratic reform, constitutional devolution of powers, emerging interest groups, and increasingly well-organized nationalist organizations operating in a scene of struggle that created a moral centre.

(2) Overlapping with the first emphasis came the problem of consolidating new systems of authority. The changes in the power structures that accompanied national political independence encouraged leaders to articulate new moral justifications of the right to rule. Nationalism thus brought a new concern with forms of legitimacy, methods of rule under conditions of weakly institutionalized governmental forms, and effects of weak legitimacy on constitutionalism. How could authority sustain itself? What balance was possible between public participation and effective decision-making? Could change take place in a "natural" fashion, or did it have to be forced? What was the relevance of ideology, political beliefs, and personalistic leadership? How did the collapse of the colonial system of authority, the partial disintegration of traditional patterns, and the emergence of nationalist authority affect those individuals caught between conflicting notions of proper authority? Behind the concern with authority and legitimacy came a renewed emphasis on governmental forms and their relation to stability. Structural analysts formulated new typologies of political systems that were not linked too descriptively with Western democratic governments.[5]

(3) The emphasis on nationalism and authority focused attention on the relationship between the whole system, especially the nation-state, and its sub-systems. In what ways does the operation of the part, like an administrative bureau, an interest group, a political

party, or a village council, affect the whole society? How do characteristics of the larger unit, for example, multinational oil companies, influence the activities of Near Eastern states? What are the links between *political* organizations and *social* groups? Does government act as an independent agency creating changes in the social system? Or does government mainly respond to the demands of social groups? All these questions revolve around structural concerns; i.e. to see political things structurally is to perceive relationships. The structural analyst wants to see whole systems "from above"—in their entirety. The more sensitive the structural analysis, the easier it is for the observer to gain a sense of the whole and evaluate how the parts function.

(4) A fourth related tendency of those studying the new nations was an effort to close the gap between abstract conceptualizing and concrete data-gathering. The elaboration of abstract models of development reflects the need to reconceptualize the older typologies, in order to explain "systems tendencies". By examining a wide variety of cases throughout the world and by viewing contemporary events against a backdrop of historical sequences, social scientists have attempted to highlight the significant patterns of development, including both progressive and regressive trends. Here attention focuses on the theoretical links between changes in the content and interpretation of moral values, structural changes in the ranking of groups on stratification scales, and changes in motivations as they affect individual political behaviour. The abstractly formulated hypotheses about patterns of development try to move beyond the older, more concrete classifications of government. As the effort to re-conceptualize goes on, we also see an interest in quantitative techniques for collecting and analysing data. The use of both aggregate and survey data has increased, following the leads set by Karl Deutsch, Daniel Lerner, Alex Inkeles, and others. Here the new techniques and complex computers open up a dazzling range of possibilities. These two emphases (theoretical re-conceptualization and technical quantification) are at opposite ends of the same continuum. Theories suggest explanations for the flood of data uncovered by the growing technical sophistication. In turn, the new techniques provide mechanisms for testing theoretical hypotheses, for designating the key dimensions encompassed in the global concept of "development", and for weighting the relative importance of the key factors. Today, we see this attempt to combine theoretical simplicity with technical complexity as the most important tendency characterizing the comparative study of new nations.

As these four trends reveal, the study of new nations has covered a diversity of approaches and changes in emphasis since the end of

World War II. The many changes in subject matter, scope, and method have produced as well continuous controversy over what is a proper focus for current work and future analysis. Behind all these trends stand the larger problems of comparative politics. One problem is ethical. If the social sciences are, in the classical sense, moral sciences, then they should be concerned with the nature of the ideal political system, with the right relationship between the rulers and the ruled. Here a primary concern centres about the relationship between the values of the analyst and the values present in the new nations.[6] What structures and behavioural patterns will maximize particular sets of norms and moral beliefs?

A second problem concerns the policy needs of the American government. If since the end of World War II the areas of Asia, Africa, the Near East, and Latin America have been the object of much more scholarly investigation than before the war, this in part stems from the attention to certain policy problems which confronted the United States—the disintegration of the European colonial empires (first in Asia and the Near East, later in Africa) as well as the role of the United Nations, which emerged as a champion of independence from colonial rule. Bipolarity replaced the more complex, fluid balance of power system which had existed before the war. The cold war stimulated the United States and the Soviet Union to compete for support among these countries outside the two major blocs. As a reaction most of the new nations chose to articulate a foreign policy position of neutralism and non-alignment. The classification of national political systems into the "three worlds of development" obviously reflects the bipolar tendencies in the international political system.

A third problem deals with technology. From a policy standpoint, recent developments in technology are revealed in the military hardware granted to rapidly growing armies in Asia, Africa, and Latin America. From an analytical viewpoint, the construction of high-speed computers to store and process data portends a revolution in social science research. Because of computers, more and more data from the developing areas are becoming available to the social scientist.

Fourth, from our perspective the most important development in the study of the developing nations revolves around the evolution of more valid and useful analytical approaches. Because of computer technology the analyst now faces the possibility of becoming overwhelmed by his data. Theories are needed to give meaning and significance to the data, to isolate the critical elements—patterns and tendencies—so as to avoid the shortcomings of crude empiricism. By using explicit analytic approaches, the researcher finds it easier to

N

highlight the crucial relationships in his data, especially the relationships between political and social factors. To accomplish this objective, the political scientist has drawn on theories, methods, and data of the other social sciences, especially psychology, anthropology, sociology, history and economics. Today we see a search for broader analytical frameworks able to adopt the methodology of other disciplines. Whereas the old research tradition emphasized the study of documents, books, and recent history, we now use more precise techniques of analysis in field work. Interviews are more systematically conducted. Survey and aggregate data are increasingly used, analysed in the light of more explicit theoretical constructs. All these trends lead to the possibility of a "third round" emerging in the political studies of new nations. If we can now consider political science a "policy science", then extremely interesting problems are raised about the purposes and proprieties of political research itself.

With this background in mind, we can begin to examine the new tendencies in the comparative study of new nations in light of three analytic dimensions—the normative, the structural, and the behavioural. Each new system, each polity, can be seen as a system of choice. The normative, structural, and behavioural aspects of choice represent its components parts. More particularly, the *normative* dimension is concerned with analysing the values and norms influencing the choices which ought to be made. The *structural* dimension considers the patterns of social action, the relationships among individuals that affect the opportunities for making choices. Like values and norms, social structures outside the individual place limitations on his choices. The *behavioural* dimension deals with the choices individuals in fact do make, the perceptions of the alternatives available to them, and the motivations behind selecting particular options.

Viewed in light of the normative, structural, and behavioural dimensions, "development" obviously represents a highly global concept.[7] It has both empirical and evaluative connotations. When analysts contrast development as linear progress with "decay" or retrogression, they reveal an evaluative impulse. Studies linking development to social mobilization, such as the increase in literacy, education, urbanization, and mass media, deal with more empirical indicators. Development also conveys qualitative and quantitative meanings. For example, structural-functionalists conceive of development in terms of the growth in differentiation and complexity, whereas political economists focus on increases in productivity, output of goods and services, and occupational mobility. Moreover, development may be viewed as a process and a goal; the analyst must inquire "how does development take place and for what ends?"

Finally, development encompasses both individual and societal referents. It refers to attitudes and behaviour as well as to different subsystems within the society, like the polity, the economy, the family, and the pattern of cultural values, especially as revealed in religions, ideologies, and myths. Those studying the new nations have sought to explore the relationships among these several facets in order to explain how the "leads and lags" in different sectors produce overall developmental patterns.

In the following sections, the normative, structural, and behavioural dimensions will be analysed according to the following elements: (1) *analytic problem*: What is the topic under investigation? What relationships among the variables is the analyst studying? What questions does he want answered? (2) *framework of analysis*: (*a*) What are the key *units* for analysis? Units here refer to concrete membership groupings, including the individual, primary group, secondary group, organization, institution, society, and region. (*b*) What are the crucial *variables*, that is, analytical aspects or properties of the empirical behaviour of the unit? Variables are frequently classified into independent (assumed "cause"), intervening, and dependent (the effect or aspects of behaviour the observer is trying to explain. (*c*) What are the general *assumptions* or more specific hypotheses posed by the analyst? Hypotheses are statements of the assumed relationships among the variables. In this discussion, the main hypotheses will centre around the conditions of modernization.[8] (3) What *techniques* are used to collect data? (4) What *techniques* are used to process and analyse the data? Table I summarizes these three dimensions.

II THE NORMATIVE DIMENSION

The normative emphasis in comparative politics is by far the oldest tradition in the field. Its object was to find the "best" form of government by which the "best" community would be possible. For the Greeks, this view embodied the idea that the polis was a moral and educational community. In comparative politics this emphasis had an evolutionary component, in the sense that the development of constitutional democracy was seen as the advance towards modernization. In addition to exploring valid ends and means of government, normative theories considered the ethical aspects of recruitment to public office, primacy of group versus individual rights, and proper ways to secure representative government. Once a central emphasis in comparative politics, this tradition has, more and more, become the special concern of those interested in the history of political ideas and, more recently, the sociology of knowledge. Today those study-

TABLE I: ANALYTICAL DIMENSIONS

Element	Normative	Structural	Behavioural
Approaches	Political philosophy Analysis of values, norms, laws, ideologies Linguistic analysis	Institutional Structural-functional Neo-classical political economy Neo-Marxism	Stimulus-response, psychoanalysis, field theory, cognitive development models, cognitive consistency theories of attitude change
Analytic problems	Cultural prerequisites of modernisation Relationship between modern and traditional values Relationship between nationalism, constitutionalism, and modernity	Funcional and structural requisites necessary for maintenance and modernization of social system	Internalization of cultural values and norms Personal needs and motivations required for maximizing modernization Relevance of ideology to perceptions of changing world Role of dominant personalities in creating new patterns of authority
Units	Whole society: small-scale and nation-state	Macro-units: whole societies, nations, government institutions, organizations, groups, social strata, classes	Micro-units: individual and small group
Variables	Values, norms, myths, ideologies, political culture	System maintenance and development, structural differentiation and integration, stratification, allocation of goods and services, allocation of power and responsibility, representation, role conflict and consensus	Personal traits: attitudes, needs, emotions, motivations, perceptions Behavioural processes: learning, socialization, adaptation

ANALYTICAL DIMENSIONS—*Continued*

Element	Normative	Structural	Behavioural
Assumptions (examples)	Change occurs dialectically; conflicting values energize human activity. Man is a cultural being who seeks the meaning of events through ideology and religion. Shared values are the source of solidarity; they are prerequisites for democracy, modernization, and stable authority.	Political modernization depends on (1) the establishment of representative institutions, a binding constitution, and an effective civil service; (2) unified, flexible, complex, and political autonomous institutions, especially a strong political party; (3) a balance between structural differentiation and integration; (4) the political mobilization of the lower classes and equal distribution of resources.	Modern man has a clear and stable identity, empathy with others, a large number of diverse opinions about a wide range of issues, and an activist orientation toward social and political matters.
Techniques	Participant observation, intuitive examination of documents, content analysis, interviewing, review of ideological statements	External observation of concrete structures, multiple regression analysis, factor analysis	Sample surveys, oral interviews, written tests and questionnaires, experiments, intensive observation of small groups, content analysis

ing new nations are formulating a new normative language, which incorporates issues of building new states, coping with problems of uneven social change, ascribing meaning to complex events, and creating new forms of legitimacy. To a certain extent, this focus represents a new tendency; but historically speaking, it is a very old one, taking us back to times before philosophy became divorced from politics.

If we accept the proposition that political science is, unlike the physical sciences, a moral science, then the meaning and ethical evaluations people attribute to social behaviour cannot be ignored. The normative approach pays particular attention to the cultural values and norms found in a society. In the Parsonian sense, values are conceived to be generalized concepts of the desirable, the legitimate ends which direct action in certain channels. Considered to be more specific than values, norms constitute the rules (rights and obligations) which indicate how the values are to be realized. Norms range from the formal and explicit laws to informal and implicit customs.[9] Ideologies, which represent the most specific forms of moral beliefs, combine more general values and norms into programmatic guides for political action. In this sense, political leaders use ideologies to justify the exercise of power and to legitimate their public decisions.

Those analysts working within the normative tradition are not content merely to record the values and norms of particular societies. Rather, they are searching for a higher meaning and significance which transcends the crude empirical observations of events. To realize this objective requires a perceptive awareness of the relationship between one's own moral values (the values of the observer) and those of the society one is observing (the values of the political actors). A basic premise of the normative approach is that the observer can never really perceive the meaning of values to others until he identifies the significance of these values to himself. For example, it takes a good Lutheran to know a Catholic or a good Trotskyite to know a Stalinist. Whereas both can understand something about religion, a nonbeliever will never become a part of the dialogue.[10]

Analytic Problem. Those working within the normative approach identify as main analytic problems the following: What are the cultural prerequisites of modernization? What is the relationship between traditional and modern values? How can the modern values carried from the West be blended with the traditional values of the indigenous peoples? During the nineteenth century the Japanese expressed hopes of combining Eastern morality and Western technology. Many Latin Americans hoped to blend Indian and Hispanic values. In this century, the Africans and other Asians have voiced similar aspirations to blend the best features of Western colonialism with indigenous Afro-Asian culture. How effective will be this synthesis in forging modernization? No society has wholly modern or wholly traditional values; all societies contain mixtures of both types. What will be the consequences for modernization of reinterpreting tradition so as to make it congruent with modernity?[11]

A key problem related to the cultural prerequisites of modernization deals with the relationship between nationalism (a set of values) and constitutionalism (a set of norms). Both nationalism and constitutionalism are associated with modernity. The earlier normative tradition viewed the development of nationalism and constitutional government as the emergence from barbarism and the advance towards a modern form of civilization. Today, these evolutionary notions have been largely dropped. Political scientists no longer feel so sanguine about the prospects for reconciling democracy, constitutionalism, and modernization. As a number of analysts have pointed out, the nature of nationalism differs in Western Europe and the developing nations of Africa and Asia. Whereas people in Europe were bound together by similar values stemming from a common language and similar culture, in the new states today the major value uniting diverse peoples is opposition to colonial rule.[12] Faced by a lack of cultural unity, the new nations face problems in reconciling constitutional democracy and nationalism. Is national unity a prerequisite for constitutional democracy? Does national self-determination, with its emphasis on the collectivity, interfere with democratic self-determination, with its stress on individual rights?[13]

Units for analysis. Analysts using the normative approach usually take the whole society as their unit of analysis. Anthropologists, like Claude Lévi-Strauss and Max Gluckman, study small-scale societies, for it is in these societies that the observer can best perceive the personal relationships among individuals that illuminate the meaning they ascribe to social action. Political scientists are much more likely to study the nation-state, which since the last century has been judged the morally proper entity for human existence.

Variables. Normative thinkers have somewhat different ways of treating values and norms. Some examine the origin of values in the social relationships among individuals, especially in the kin system. They see values as the dependent variable.[14] Other analysts assume that values are the independent variable. For them, ideas have consequences; they choose to investigate the effect of values on the operation of social institutions. Seymour Lipset exemplifies this tendency.[15] Conceptualizing the relationship between values and social structure differently than Lipset, Barrington Moore argues that values should be viewed as an intervening variable intimately linked to historical social situations, not as a causal factor. Intervening between the "objective situation", that is, the economic and political stratification system, and human behaviour, values condition how specific individuals perceive changes in technology and the existing social situation.[16] Regardless of whether values are conceived to be independent, intervening, or dependent variables, the major focus of attention is on patterns of values and norms, as found in ideology, religious beliefs, nationalist sentiments, customs, constitutions, and systems of law.

Assumptions. Given the explicit value-laden orientation of the normative approach, most writers in this tradition articulate a set of general assumptions which guide their research, rather than state precise hypotheses to be tested. One key assumption is that a major source of change in a society stems from the conflict between opposing values and between groups articulating contradictory ideas. Thus, change and modernization occur dialectically. Every value gives rise to an opposite value. Some sort of synthesis emerges from the contradiction between opposites.[17]

A number of political scientists have pointed out the attempt of non-Western leaders in Latin America, Africa, and Asia to synthesize values dominant in the West with the values unique to their indigenous culture. Deriving the concept of the "colonial dialectic" from Hegel's notion of the conflict between master (colonizer) and slave (colonized), Clement Henry Moore has analysed the stages of nationalist development in three North African countries—Morocco, Tunisia, and Algeria. During the first stage the modernized youth assimilate rather completely the liberal colonial values of modern education, secularity, and legal reforms granting greater representation to the indigenous population. The second stage, characterized as a period of "traditionalist anti-colonialism", sees the pre-colonial elite reject colonial innovations to identify instead with a mythical golden age of the past. Finally, during the third "radical" stage, a mass nationalist party, such as the Neo-Destour in Tunisia, arises to synthesize the modern values of colonialism with the anti-colonial spirit of the traditionalists. Of the three North African territories, Tunisia best illustrates the constructive conflict and synthesis suggested by Hegel as the outcome of the dialectic. Under Habib Bourguiba, the radical Tunisian elite developed the value cohesion and organization needed to realize a positive national identity in opposition to French domination.[18] In his works dealing with the Near East, Leonard Binder has similarly sketched the nature of the nationalist synthesis. From his perspective, politics deals with the "legitimation of social power",[19] Reflecting this concern with how rulers legitimate their political rule, he has examined the attempts of Near Eastern intellectuals to fuse medieval Islamic law and ideas of rule with West European concepts, in order to produce a nationalist synthesis.[20]

According to a second general assumption made by normative analysts, man is a cultural being who seeks the meaning of events through ideology and religion.[21] Values not only interpret the world for the political actor, who subjectively defines the existing situation, but they also shape his behaviour. Thus, in the new nations both religion and ideology as statements of values and norms respond to man's loss of meaning and to his need for a moral guide to energize his actions. Confronted with a disintegration of the old authority systems, both traditional and colonial, developing man is in a state of conceptual confusion. Ideology provides a cognitive map to help him evaluate and perceive the meaning of complex, unfamiliar changes.[22]

A third assumption is that shared values constitute the most important source of solidarity in the new nations. Although integration can arise from several sources—the exercise of coercion, the exchange of economic goods, institutional co-ordination, and social group pressures—normative analysts focus on agreement on shared values as the prime basis of solidarity. In their view, divisive value conflicts, which reflect a weak sense of national identification, deflect energies from the push towards modernization and make difficult a compromising, bargaining, consensual culture assumed to be an essential component of a democratic society.[23]

Techniques for collecting data. Since the end of World War II, all the social sciences have undergone a technical revolution, in the sense that the techniques for collecting data have become less implicit and impressionistic and more precise and empirical. The normative approach is no exception. The older normative approach examined documents, like constitutions, laws, and parliamentary proceedings; relied on newspaper accounts; studied ideological statements; and carried out limited observation—often a rapid tour through the country, in the spirit, if not with the perception, of a Bryce or a de Tocqueville. The new techniques in this field still rely on written material and observation to discover the values and norms of a society, but these newer techniques are employed in a more systematic, self-conscious manner. Content analysis, rather than an intuitive perusal of documents, becomes common. Participant observation becomes more important than observation from a distance. In this respect, the work of Harold Lasswell and Cornell University anthropologists in a small Indian village in Peru is instructive. Following his long-held assumption that political science ought to be a policy science actively concerned with ethical issues, Lasswell and the group at Cornell sought to guide a peasant Indian community in Vicos, Peru from traditionality to modernization. The goal was to shape those values which further modernization. The Cornell staff, which held a lease in Vicos from 1952 to 1957, engaged in "participant intervention". Allan Holmberg, the head anthropologist in the project, acted first as a *patrón* (a tutelary leader) who articulated modern values and urged the Indians to share in these values through participation in democratically run institutions, like schools and representative councils. Against the traditional Indian values of elitism and self-deprivation, the Cornell project attempted to instill the more modern values of equality and self-respect.[24]

Techniques of processing the data. In the past, the data about values and norms were processed and analysed in a rather subjective manner. Often the search for meaning involved considerable metaphysical speculating. This orientation still characterizes the work of many normative thinkers, especially those like Lévi-Strauss, who are trying to discover some "higher meaning" behind concrete empirical events. Increasingly, however, the trend is toward more rigorous processing of data; computers will be used as both a descriptive and a logical instrument to codify social values. Already, the General Inquirer program promises a technical breakthrough in content analysis of a group's values and norms.[25]

Critique. The normative thinkers face a series of analytic problems not confronted by the structuralists or behaviouralists. These problems concern the rather "free floating" status of values and norms. Values are linked to the structural and behavioural levels, in the sense that values are institutionalized in social organizations and internalized within individuals. Yet, and this is the rub, we do not observe values directly but rather infer them indirectly through the overt behaviour of individuals and the activities of social structures. Thus the observer must impute values to societies. Given the great heterogeneity, vagueness, conflict, and contradictions of values, particularly in the new nations, this task becomes difficult. Different social structures may transmit different values or diverse interpretations of the same values. Some values like equality, freedom, and universalism are so highly general that they can be interpreted to legitimate any structure or behaviour. Moreover, for different individuals, the same values may lead to different behavioural consequences. Finally, when the analyst assumes that values influence behaviour, he may be using the same phenomenon to measure both dependent and independent variables.[26] For all these reasons, the causal links between values, social structures, and behaviour remain elusive.

III   THE STRUCTURAL DIMENSION

The structural dimension of comparative politics has been the most elaborately articulated, although in a descriptive rather than an analytical sense. Before the Second World War, much of the work dealt with specialized concrete structures of government, such as parliamentary organizations, bureaucracies, courts, and political parties. What "theories" emerged from this study of formal institutions were based on the notion that a particular structure, such as a multi-party system, has a particular function, i.e. the maintenance of democracy through competition for public office. In recent years the type of structural analysis has changed. The formal institutions associated with European and American democracies were found to be either nonexistent or else operating differently than intended in the nations emerging from colonial rule. Moreover, work in the developing nations required expanding the scope of analysis. Kinship, family structures, tribes, caste associations, lineages, and language groups suddenly became more relevant than before. These tendencies have led to a more abstract method of conceptualizing development from the standpoint of *analytic* structures, rather than from an exclusive focus on *concrete* structures. The latter are conceived to be separable parts of society, that is, membership units. Analytic structures, in contrast, refer to aspects or properties abstracted from the behaviour of the concrete structures.[27] Family and kin groups, government institutions, political parties, interest groups, schools, and churches are, of course, still examined. However now these concrete structures are studied in light of analytic structures, for example, sub-system autonomy and structural differentiation (Gabriel Almond), functional specificity (Fred Riggs), and authoritative decision-making and accountability (David Apter).[28]

Among the many structural approaches to the study of comparative politics, we can distinguish four related emphases. First, the *institutionalist* studied mainly legal and administrative institutions. Dominant during the inter-war period, this approach was stimulated by certain policy considerations. Throughout South-east and South Asia and sub-Saharan Africa, the British colonial officials in particular combined patterns of direct and indirect rule. As first articulated by Lord Lugard, the British were supposed to rule indirectly through the traditional structures to avoid producing unmanageable social dislocation. The British civil servants encouraged English anthropologists to make thorough studies of the Afro-Asian traditional institutions.[29] The early institutionalists examined how to most effectively blend African and European legal-administrative institutions, that is, indirect and direct patterns of rule. The legal emphasis centred around the writing of constitutions and the development of representative institutions, such as local authority systems and legislative councils. During the period of "terminal colonialism", to use James Coleman's phrase, nationalist leaders were to demonstrate their capacity for independence by successfully working within successive stages of devolution of constitutional authority and enlargement of local responsibility. But it was the administrative emphasis, rather than the legal, which was dominant. The methods of colonial administration, with the notion of the supremacy of the European civil service, became a central focus of attention.[30]

After the end of World War II and the emerging disintegration of European colonial empires, the *structural-functional* approach, as represented in the writings of Talcott Parsons, Marion Levy, S. N. Eisenstadt, Gabriel Almond, Fred Riggs, and David Apter, came to replace the more traditional institutional ways of perceiving development in the new nations. In the post-independence period, elaborate constitutional procedures seemed insufficient to check the arbitrary exercise of power. Legal, representative institutions exercised far less political power than in England, Holland, Belgium, or France. The civil service performed highly diffuse, rather than specialized, roles. The demands of social groups outside the formal institutions crucially affected governmental performance. Structural-functionalists thus expanded their scope of analysis beyond the narrower focus of the institutionalists. In essence, they perceived of society as a system of related parts, implying that the analyst had to know everything to know anything. As Gabriel Almond explained: "We mean to include not just the structures based on law, like parliaments, executives, bureaucracies, and courts, or just the associational or formally organized units, like parties, interest groups, and media of communication, but *all of the structures in their political aspects,* including undifferentiated structures like kinship and lineage, status and case groups, as well as anomic phenomena like riots, street demonstrations, and the like."[31]

For the structural-functionalists, the main analytic task is to highlight the relationships among these different structures of society and to show what functions these structures perform in sustaining the social system. Structures are assumed to have consequences that lead to either stability (adaptation, adjustment, system maintenance) or to instability. The analyst investigates those tensions upsetting the existing structural relationships and their consequences (functions). In this regard, the structural-functionalists pay particular attention to the stabilizing or destabilizing consequences of concrete groups on the analytic structures. Their attitude toward the causes of developmental change draws upon a form of requisite analysis. They conceive of change as arising from internal structural differentiation, from technological innovations devised by a society's members, from conflicts between ideal values and operating structural conditions, and from forces outside the system, as illustrated by the impact of a colonial presence on an indigenous society.[32] In their studies of the new nations, structural-functionalists articulated the following general concerns about the process of modernization: What are the prerequisites for securing a modernized society? What are the requisites for the maintenance of modernization or "sustained growth"? What are the social and cultural conditions that produce a breakdown in the system?

Dominant from the 1950s through the late 1960s, the structural-functional approach to political development has recently come under challenge from two different fronts: the *neo-institutionalist* and the *political economist*. Both groups attack the structural-functionalists for their overly abstract method of conceptualization, that is, for their elaboration of abstract models to the neglect of concrete data, their devaluation of concrete structures, and their lack of concern for the effects of governmental policies on social development.

Of these latter two structural frameworks, the neo-institutionalists place greater emphasis on the dominance of political organizations over social groups. Particularly as articulated by Samuel P. Huntington, a leading neo-institutionalist, the main assumption is that the state—the dominant political structure—plays the crucial role in the modernizing process. According to Huntington, modernization implies both a centralization of governmental power and an increase in the total amount of resources. The new states face an expansion of social group demands that outstrip the organizational capabilities for satisfying them. Only strong political institutions—a civil service and especially a political party—can control, channel, and moderate these demands to bring forth orderly change. Thus, in Huntington's model, strong political institutions provide order, whereas social groups, if uncontrolled, foment chaos, disorder, instability, and the lack of authority.[33]

As Huntington's assumptions indicate, the neo-institutionalists focus less on abstract functions and structures and more on concrete groups and institutions. Rather than stressing rather vague functional categories like interest articulation, interest aggregation, and political communication, they urge that political scientists give central priority to more concrete institutions, namely, administrative staffs, legislatures, courts, executives, military organizations, political parties, interest groups, even councils of elders. All these play a crucial role in making political decisions that may modernize the society. Since political institutions produce public policies (or "outputs") that shape the social group demands (the "inputs") into the political system, these governmental outputs represent a more powerful explanatory variable for development than does the social group "inputism" of the structural-functionalists.[34]

Another challenge to the structural-functionalists comes from the political economists, including those articulating neo-classical and neo-Marxist views. In contrast to the structural-functionalists, the political economists concentrate on the economic interests and policy positions of concrete groups, rather than on the stability of the whole social system, as the main variable. The analysis becomes less abstract, for political economists want to ascertain the costs and benefits of public policies accruing to particular groups and individuals. Which specific groups gain concrete benefits from governmental decisions? Which groups bear the greatest costs? How do the differential advantages affect the rate, level, and extent of development? In the economic exchanges between industrialized nations and less industrialized territories of Latin America, Asia, and Africa, which economic groups receive the greatest wealth and income? How do European-American investors penetrate governmental agencies in the Third World to protect their economic advantages? Although both groups of political economists pose these general questions, the neo-classical approach gives more weight to government as an independent agent affecting developmental output, whereas the neo-Marxists assume greater primacy for economic variables, like the demands by social groups for greater wealth. The neo-Marxists also stress the systemic relationships between the industrialized and less industrialized nations as these exchanges affect economic development, a concern downplayed by the neo-classicists, neo-institutionalists, and structural-functionalists.[35]

Let us examine these various structural approaches more fully by isolating the several steps in the comparative method.

Analytic problem. The problems posed by structural analysts revolve around the issues of system maintenance and system development, including its various forms, like modernization and industrialization. What functional activities must be performed if the system is going to maintain itself, as well as experience sustained growth? What structural relationships are needed to maintain and modernize the existing system and to transform the society into a different type of system? Considered under these general problems are such topics as the structural relationship between tradition and modernization, the ability of specific concrete groups to further innovation, the role of government in creating entrepreneurship, and the problems of control under the impact of uneven social change in the various sectors of society.

Units for Analysis. Compared with the behavioural approach, the structural approaches study macro-units, that is, whole societies and nations. Also analysed are various parts within a society, such as governmental institutions, political parties, interest groups, kin groups, caste associations, and lineages.[36] The early structural emphasis was on the local community. According to the colonial rationale, the indigenous people were supposed to participate first in units of local government, like village, communal, and town councils. Later they would be granted the right to participate in provincial and territorial governments.[37] However, as the nationalist movement gained greater legitimacy, both the indigenous politicians as well as the scholars shifted their attention to the "nation". A number of studies appeared, describing in considerable detail the history of the nationalist movements first in Asia and later in Africa.

In the middle 1950s the whole area—Latin America, Asia, the Near East, Africa—came to be the unit of analysis. In part, this area studies orientation sprang from the obvious need for cross-disciplinary data and methods to understand the complex relationships between political and social behaviour in the more exotic areas, where the tradition of separation of "state and society" did not hold so true as in Western Europe. The problem with the area studies approach was that the scope for analysis was spread too broad. A scholar had to know everything about an area: its anthropology, economics, geography, history, and, of course, its politics. In failing to specify by what critera data should be included for analysis, the approach was marked by conceptual ambiguity. Often the nations within a particular area had in common only geographic contiguity; the differences among the states were often as noteworthy as the assumed similarities.[38] Recently, the structural approach has witnessed a return to small units for analysis. Most often, the whole nation is studied in breadth, a few selected communities within a nation in depth.

Variables. If structural analysis conceives of concrete membership groups as units, then analytic structures, like structural differentiation, stratification, allocation of goods and services, and allocation of power and responsibility, are variables. Referring to aspects of the behaviour of the unit, variables specify the relationship among the units. Most often, structural analysts consider system maintenance and development as the dependent variable, with some of the analytic structures treated as the independent variables. In recent years, there has occurred a trend toward a more explicit operationalization of structural variables.[39]

Assumptions. The various approaches within the structural dimension make several related assumptions about political development and modernization. For the institutionalists, political development depends upon the establishment of representative institutions identified with Great Britain and the United States. The state machinery operates under structural-legal restraints. The legislature, executive, civil service, and political parties have the capability (power) to respond to public demands and to process these demands into public policies. This decision-making power, however, is constrained by the responsibility owed to several accountability structures—for example, independent courts, representative institutions, and voters whose will becomes revealed in regular elections held under a secret ballot. Thus, the institutionalists associate political development with constitutionalism. They give priority to the rule of law and the separation of powers, rather than to government by widespread popular participation. The "people" fulfil their political role mainly by electing governmental representatives.

The neo-institutionalists, especially Samuel P. Huntington, share many of these institutionalist assumptions, especially the need for political organizations to control social change by dampening popular demands. To avert political decay, the political elites need to establish strong institutions that will control the participation arising from rapid social mobilization (education, urbanization, extension of mass media, incipient industrialization) and that will assimilate the new social groups, both communal and economic. Operating as "gate-keepers", strong parties will bring political order and stability to a situation of social group chaos. By "strong" institutions, Huntington means those which are unified, adaptable, complex (not dependent on a single person), and autonomous from social groups. Only strong institutions can develop the rules for regulating conflicts, provide for succession among elites, expand the resources needed to implement public policies, and in general regulate the effects of rapid social mobilization. In sum, Huntington perceives political organization, not social spontaneity, as the prime requirement for modernization.[40]

Although Huntington, like the older institutionalists, stresses the need for political elites to develop organized means of decision-making, his normative views reflect a different orientation. Whereas the institutionalists identified the public interest with a higher law—the constitution—and upheld legal restraints on executive power, he links the public interest with "whatever strengthens governmental institutions",[41] not with the law, the will of the people, the interests of specific groups, or even the consequences of government policies. He perceives modernization in terms of expanded, centralized power, not a separation of powers. In effect, Huntington has reasserted the primacy of politics with a vengeance.[42]

In contrast to the neo-institutionalists, the structural-functionalists are less likely to equate development with governmental power. For them, development means a balance between structural differentiation and structural integration. According to S. N. Eisenstadt, as the society becomes more functionally specialized—that is, as an individualized family, specialized media of communication, the separation of economic production from consumption, commercialized farming, achievement-oriented stratification systems, and voluntary interest groups that articulate special interests all become more important—then the need arises for integrating mechanisms to balance these tendencies toward differentiation. The structures for integration do not include only political parties or formal legal institutions but professional associations and market organizations. General symbols are also needed to bind together the universal with the particular, the expressive with the instrumental, the traditional with the modern, the local with the central, and the rural with the urban. Only through these integrating structures and values can the political elites of the new nations avert the systemic breakdowns that accompany unbalanced development in different sectors of society. In effect, the conflicts among differentiated structures and between the integrating and differentiating tendencies explain the developmental patterns as a society begins to modernize.[43]

During the 1960s, Gabriel Almond's version of the structural-functional model became the most influential in the structural comparative analyses carried out by political scientists. As chairman of the Comparative Politics Committee of the Social Science Research Council from 1954 through 1962, Almond occupied a strategic role from which he could guide the study of the new nations. Searching for a non-formalistic approach that could be applied to both European states (Almond's speciality) and non-Western areas, Almond and his associates originally began with a focus on concrete groups. They gave an all-inclusive definition to group, distinguishing among four types: (1) anomic: crowds, mobs, rioting and demonstrating groups; (2) non-associational: family, kin group, lineage, clan, tribe; (3) institutional: parties, civil service, church, army; (4) associational: trade unions, business groups, farmers' associations, mass media.[44] Around 1958 the Committee on Comparative Politics decided to expand the foci of inquiry toward more analytical schemes involving a series of functional categories—interest articulation, interest aggregation, socialization, recruitment, communication, rule-making, rule application, and rule adjudication. However, the focus on concrete groups was not lost, for the role of different kinds of groups in the modernizing process became a key concern. Investigated were the ways in which the specific concrete structures performed the

o

general functions. Political development meant a balance between the interest articulation performed by specialized groups and the more general interest aggregation of political parties and representative institutions.[45]

Almond's most recent structural functional model expands upon the basic themes originated in the 1950s, although he now places greater emphasis on the response of government elites to social groups, rather than considering mainly the demands voiced by the groups on government. He sees the causes of development lying in domestic and foreign threats as well as in the general processes of social mobilization. These tendencies encourage groups to make political demands and contribute resources. Depending upon the types of coalitions formed by governmental groups, the personalities of the political elites, and the elite's goals, the government enacts policies in response to these demands. Almond measures political development according to the types of performances demonstrated by the government. A highly developed government possesses the capabilities to effectively regulate social groups, extract resources, distribute goods and services, secure a positive ratio between group demands and public policies, and build up reserves of public support. Presumably, this developed political system reveals a balance between government agencies capable of performing specialized tasks and integrating organizations with power to decide general policies.[46]

Writing within the framework of comparative public administration, Fred Riggs has also concentrated on the role of concrete structures in producing political development and disintegration. For him, "positive" development means a balance between structural differentiation and co-ordination. A modern polity has a balance of power between the bureaucracy, on the one hand, and the elected assembly, electorate, and political parties, on the other. Within this balanced situation, the latter concrete structures formulate public decisions, and the bureaucracy plays the dominant role in implementing decisions. The consequences are responsiveness to public demands and bureaucratic efficiency. In contrast, most modernizing societies reveal unbalanced tendencies. Either the predominantly political agencies, particularly the party and elected assembly, cannot control the bureaucracy, or else the dominant party institutes a spoils system, where the bureaucracy lacks the capability to implement decisions. Alternatively, the head of state—a monarch, a party leader, or a military commander—remains unaccountable to the electorate, assembly, or party. Under these conditions the structures do not effectively perform the functions of making and carrying out public policies for the modernizing society. Stagnation, instability, and low performance result.[47]

The neo-classical political economists, in a partial reaction to the social group "inputism" originally but no longer emphasized by the structural-functionalists have placed policy-making at the centre of their analytic framework. As articulated by Warren Ilchman and Norman Uphoff, the "new" political economy equates politics with the process of choosing among alternative goals and resources. The political leader or "statesman" must decide how to use most efficiently the existing resources (goods and services, authority, status, information, coercion), how to produce more resources, and how to estimate the costs and benefits (the "marginal utility") of alternative uses of resources. Development can take place in three markets: the political, economic, and social. It can be measured both in terms of production and distribution. The territorial centralization of political power, the creation of a national economic market, and social mobilization (greater literacy, urbanization, exposure to mass media) all expand the scope of resource exchange, making possible more specialization, mobility, and hence greater productivity of resources. From the distributive standpoint, popular sharing in political decision-making, more resource equality, and expanded opportunities for social mobility may also create more resources; by feeling more involved in the system, rank-and-file citizens may develop the incentives for greater productivity. In summary, political development means the capacity to bring about change and to process changing demands. This capacity depends upon the creation of new political-administrative structures that will engineer a more efficient pattern of resource flows, so that inputs may be processed into outputs. In this productive process, the political elites assume a dominant role. They act as political entrepreneurs, mobilizing existing resources, integrating these resources into more efficient productive techniques, and creating the new resources needed to implement public policies.[48]

The neo-classical analysts, with their notions of diminishing marginal utility, markets, supply and demand, exchange values, opportunity costs, and price elasticity, have not monopolized the political economy model of development. On the contrary, the neo-Marxists, especially those studying Latin America, have launched a vigorous assault against the existing concepts of development. Why is Marx relevant to the study of political and economic modernization? After all, he wrote over a hundred years ago in an industrialized European setting. The only non-European countries he mentioned were India, China, Persia, Turkey, Morocco, Algeria, Syria, and Mexico. Referring to European "civilization" and Afro-Asian "barbarism", he showed hostility toward peasants and rural life. Marx perceived colonial domination introducing the spark of change to the stagnant Indian society. Despite his Europe-centred focus, both normatively and empirically, today in the new nations, he, not Adam Smith or John Maynard Keynes, is the more widely accepted European philosopher.

What factors explain his appeal to the intellectuals of the Third World? First, Marx posited a dynamic theory of development. For him, rapid fundamental change, not equilibrium, harmony, and stability, is the key concept. Modernization occurs through the dialectical conflict between ideas and between different economic classes. He also perceived the different rates of change in different sectors of society—the economy (village agriculture, for example), the polity (turnover in office of political rulers, including military officials), and the stratification system. Under Asian conditions of common ownership of land and village self-sufficiency, a change in political leaders took place against a basic stagnation in the socio-economic structure.[49] Like contemporary structural-functionalists, Marx had a notion of unintended changes or objective consequences that deviated from the subjective purposes of the actors. For example, in India the British colonialists intended to benefit the ruling class—that is, the British East India Company, the Manchester industrialists, and the administrative elite. Yet by introducing some aspects of modernization to India—a centralized system of authority, a trained army, an educated civil service, legal reforms, and notions of equality transcending caste ties—the British brought about the ultimate downfall of the colonial system. Second, Marx focused on the costs and benefits accruing to specific groups, rather than to the whole society. In the stages of modernization, some groups may benefit far more than others. To understand the dynamics behind change, the social theorist must ascertain those groups resisting moderniza-tion because it threatens their economic interests. Here a key problem is to uncover the empirical links between the preservation of economic interests and the control of political power. Third, intellectuals in the new nations show an ambivalence toward the colonial power, an ambivalence also felt by Marx. On the one hand, the European power exerted a positive consequence, especially during the early stages of modernization. Since Asian societies contained few internal mechanisms for changing the environment, the European colonialists acted as modernizing agents; they introduced a money economy, private ownership of land, secular education, mass media of communication, urbanization, a formalized bureaucracy, and limited features of representative government—all aspects of modernization. On the other hand, Marx recognized the ruthless exploitation carried out by the colonialists. After introducing some modern structural relationships, the imperial power rejected those fundamental changes necessary for the full modernization of the society. In short, colonial rulers, like the bourgeoisie in Europe, played progressive and retrogressive roles at different stages of development.[50]

Today, nearly a century after Marx died, neo-Marxist theories seem most alive in the study of Latin America, rather than in Asia or the Near East, those areas Marx had most heavily stressed. Why does Marxism appeal to Latin American intellectuals and to some young Latin Americanists in the United States? Compared with Africa, Asia, and the Near East, Latin American social structures are more similar to European ones. Especially in Argentina, Chile, Brazil, Venezuela, and Mexico, there is a gap between social modernization and economic industrialization. That is, these societies are fairly urbanized, literate, and penetrated by the mass media. National integration has reached higher levels than in most Afro-Asian territories. When not restricted by the armed forces, political parties and interest groups play a competitive role. Most importantly, incipient industrialization means that class politics assumes relatively greater importance. The conflicts between the landowners, various segments of the bourgeoisie, the emerging working class, and the peasants all take political forms; for the government, allied to foreign investors, controls crucial resources. Thus, neo-Marxist analyses attempt to explain the lag between full scale modernization and retarded industrialization.[51]

The neo-Marxists assert the primacy of economic, rather than political, variables. In their view, economic development is the crucial dependent variable, and the existing domestic and international socio-economic stratification systems become the main independent variables. Their studies explore the structural reasons behind the failure of Third World nations to industrialize. The assumed reasons lie neither in the characteristics of formal representative institutions, the bureaucracy, and political parties nor in the needs, values, attitudes, and personalities of the entrepreneurs. Instead, the stratification system conditions the behaviour of human personalities and political institutions. The neo-Marxists highlight those economic classes controlling the means of political power and occupying the ascendant positions in the stratification system. In the more backward areas, the feudal aristocrats refuse to change the retrogressive land tenure system. In other territories, the national bourgeoisie exercise the dominant political and economic power. Although the new bourgeoisie may spout ideas of African, Arab, or other indigenous forms of socialism, they do not practice real economic equality. Socialism refers to objective structural conditions—to relations among classes—not to the subjective intentions voiced by the political elite. Rather than a classless social structure emerging, a new economic class has taken over control. Often allied with the landowners, it prevents the lower classes from gaining a greater share of the economic resources.[52]

A second closely related assumption made by the neo-Marxists is that the world constitutes one capitalist system, whose parts are not so much interdependent as dependent on the powerful industrial nations. The European capitalist powers and especially the United States make Third World countries dependent on foreign firms. A close linkage occurs between the internal domestic and external international stratification systems. As a consequence, the rural and urban poor become dependent on foreign investors, who are closely attached to some segments of local business. Hence indigenous industrialization is retarded. What specific structural conditions explain the lack of industrialization? Here the neo-Marxists apply the general dependency theory to a specific historical situation. They perceive that contact with the more industrialized nations raises economic aspirations, especially of the middle classes, who become dedicated to the pursuit of "conspicuous consumption". The resulting tendencies toward "embourgeoisement" mean that a smaller proportion of the increase in productivity can be allocated for investment in plants, equipment, and machinery. Indigenous investment requires loans from the industrial nations, but the high interest rates aggravate the foreign debt. Severe balance of payments problems ensure. Moreover, importation of capital goods from the industrial nations also lowers the rate of domestic savings. The imported technology is highly automated, requiring few workers to operate the equipment. Unemployment increases, since the technically unskilled —the majority of the population—can gain few jobs. Finally, although foreign private companies make extensive investments in Latin America, for example, more of the profits return to the industrial nation than are reinvested in Latin America. For all these reasons, indigenous industrialization has lagged; internal structural relations have combined with dependency on foreign countries to produce an allocation of resources that leads to neither rapid economic growth nor to a more equal distribution of economic resources.[53]

Third, the neo-Marxists assume that modernization involves fundamental changes in the social structures. From an analytic perspective, they urge social scientists to focus on the transformations in concrete historical situations, not on static ideal types or formal models. Change results from historical conflicts between opposing economic groups. Thus, the key aspect of social interaction is conflict, not consensus on shared values, harmony of interests, equilibrium, or integration. From a policy perspective, the neo-

Marxists desire fundamental changes in the existing social structure, both to reduce ties of international dependency and to mobilize the lower classes—factory workers, farmers—to play a more influential role in the socio-economic process. Thus mobilization of the déclassé will presumably bring greater distribution of resources, which in turn will lead to greater national autonomy and increased economic productivity.[54]

Techniques for Collecting Data. Those engaged in structural analysis, including the institutionalists, structural functionalists, and political economists, have until recently relied on the observation of concrete structures as the main technique for collecting data. Between the two world wars, anthropologists conducted qualitative field studies long before political scientists. Since 1960, however, there has been a move toward the greater use of data banks, that is, observations collected and recorded by others. In this regard, Karl Deutsch, with his interest in the quantitative indicators of social mobilization, has exercised a profound influence on structural analysis. Partly under his aegis, there has occurred a trend toward the use of computer analysis of aggregate data, for example, ecological data, census materials, and voting statistics. So far, however, no explicit theories to explain these data have emerged. Rather, there has resulted mainly a descriptive treatment of the data.[55] Thus, in the last few years, political scientists have shifted from employing the largely qualitative techniques of anthropologists to more quantitative techniques of economists, but without the latter's deductive theories.

The three aggregate data banks most available to the structural analyst include the Yale Political Data Program, Banks and Textor's *Cross Polity Survey*, and the Human Relations Area File. The Human Relations Area File consists largely of ethnographic data about the economy, religion, family systems, and government of more than four hundred societies. So far political scientists have not extensively used these data. Much of the materials concern small scale societies, rather than modern nations. Cross societal comparisons become difficult because of the poor quality of many of the sources and because different anthropologists depositing data in the H.R.A.F. gave different definitions to the same variables.[56]

For political scientists the most relevant data banks are those compiled by Banks and Textor and by the Yale Political Data Program. The Yale program contains interval data, but mainly of a nonpolitical sort, such as students enrolled in higher education per 100,000 population, daily newspaper circulation per 1,000 persons, and gross national product per capita. Moreover, for many of the tables, data on the African countries are absent.[57] Compared with the Yale bank, the *Cross-Polity Survey* compiled by Banks and

Textor does have information on a number of explicitly political variables. In particular, they classify different countries according to some of the same functional categories employed by Gabriel Almond in his *Politics of the Developing Areas*. Unfortunately, however, most of their data are nominal categories, such as interest articulation and aggregation by political parties and institutions, or else crude rank orderings, like the ranking of bureaucracies by their degree of modernity.[58] From a statistical standpoint, nominal and ordinal variables are analysed by less high powered statistical techniques than are interval variables. In fact, of the three scales, the interval scale is the only really quantitative scale. The common parametric statistics, like means, standard deviations, Pearson correlation coefficients, and F tests, can be used to analyse interval variables. These higher powered techniques are not wholly applicable to nominal and ordinal variables.

What are the advantages and disadvantages of using aggregate data? Compared with survey data, aggregate data are easier and less expensive to obtain. Aggregate data are usually available over a longer period of time. As in the case of the Yale data bank, the data take interval, more objective forms. Since the analyst has direct access to the data for whole populations, he need not worry about the problems of interviewer bias, sampling error, and non-response bias.[59]

What then are the main problems in using aggregate data from the developing nations? First, there is the problem of the accuracy and reliability of the sources. Governments in the new states often publish false statistics for political reasons, as in the case of the Nigerian census, or else produce no statistics at all. Second, as in all comparative analyses, there arises the problem of comparability. How does the analyst compare different types of institutions, like colleges and universities, with a similar label attached to them? Third, the data are not too precise and rigorous, especially in the Human Relations Area File and the Cross-Polity Survey. Banks and Textor have made a number of speculative judgements regarding political conditions in the new states. Fourth, the analyst faces the problems involved in making inferences from his data. He must not lose the distinction between the different units of analysis—the individual and the aggregate. What is true for the aggregate population is not necessarily true of the individual. The presence of authoritarian political structures in the new nations does not necessarily indicate a low percentage of democratic personalities.[60]

Techniques in processing data. Whereas the old techniques for processing one's data were mainly speculative and impressionistic, recent years have seen a trend toward greater quantification of the data. With the advent of high-speed computers, analysis has become less qualitative. Now factor analysis, multiple regression analysis, and correlation coefficients are widely used, especially in the case of interval scales. Future developments in the field of structural analysis portend an increasing use of quantitative, especially aggregate, data. In particular, structural-functionalists, who in the past made largely qualitative statements about political development, will in the future resort to quantitative indicators of development. Attempts will be made to specify more precisely the quantitative indicators of socio-political development and political instability or system break-down.[61] In this respect, comparative structural analysis may move closer to methods used by the economists, who have long relied on quantitative measures of economic output and growth. Thus, the next decade may see a merger of the theoretical insights of structural analysis with empirical validation of their hypotheses.

Critique. As we have seen, the prolific studies carried out by structural analysts deal with the relationships among the parts and also with the interaction between the part and the whole. Despite different terminologies, all these specific structural approaches share many similar assumptions. The most general criticism that can be lodged against the approaches concerns their conception of these structural parts as well as their attempts to link abstract categories with empirical data. The structural-functionalists have found it difficult to establish precise linkages between the highly abstract functions and empirically observable patterns of action. Functions must be inferred from overt activities; yet the *same* activity (pattern) may be seen as performing several *different* functions. For example, during June 1964 four Nigerian labour unions launched a general strike. Can the activity of making wage demands on the governments and private enterprises be considered an illustration of interest articulation, interest aggregation, political communication, political socialization (modelling behaviour), or all four? The linkages between functions and patterns of action thus remain imprecise. Similar comments also apply to other structural-functional categories like system maintenance, equilibrium, and balance, all vague concepts difficult to operationalize. How do we know when a society has established the proper "balance" between structural integration and differentiation that will produce political development? What degree of integration or differentiation is too much or too little? For instance, depending on the specific historical circumstances, like war, a society may require greater integration than differentiation to guarantee system maintenance. By what criteria does the observer decide which functions and which structures are really essential to maintain the system? If the analyst views system maintenance as the dependent variable, then the activities of the parts cannot be regarded as the independent variables, since the units are not empirically separate from the system but rather an integral part of it. Hence, causal explanations become difficult. The structural-functionalist experiences greater difficulties in ascertaining empirically the functional consequences of a concrete structure for the whole society than for the individual or group.[62] Because of all these reasons, structural-functional analysis has become fixated on defining abstract terms and elaborating typologies, rather than on formulating empirically testable hypotheses.

Although taking a more concrete approach to the study of political modernization, the neo-institutionalists also have difficulties conceptualizing the relationships among parts of the social system, especially the links between the political elites and the government institutions. For example, Samuel Huntington's focus on the structural characteristics of institutions—their unity, complexity, adaptability, and political autonomy from social groups—reveals a static orientation. He downplays the concrete individuals who man the institutions, particularly their goals, policies, and the consequences of these policies on groups and individuals within the society. Yet the policies and policy effects are more relevant for assessing the rate of modernization than are the structural characteristics of political institutions. Not all concur with Huntington's assertion: "Just as a strong Presidency is in the American public interest, so also a strong party is in the Soviet public interest."[63] Other structural analysts might query: "Whose interests are affected in what ways by the policies enacted through governmental institutions?" That is, depending upon the cultural values of a society, the personalities of the leaders, their political goals, and the resources available for development programs, similarly "strong" institutions in different societies may exert differential consequences relevant to development.[64]

With an explicit focus on public policies implemented by political elites, the neo-classical political economists avoid the conceptual difficulties faced by Huntington. Yet they, too, offer misleading explanations of the interaction between parts of the society, particularly between the political and economic systems. Rather than focusing on the empirical effects governmental leaders and heads of economic firms exert on each other, they draw a misleading analogy between the economic market and the polity. Ilchman and Uphoff, for example, make comparisons between money and power, monetization and politicization, a corporation and a political party. Analogies, however, do not imply identities but only rough similarities. Crucial differences exist between these supposedly equivalent concepts. Thus, money can be more easily measured than power. Particularly in some new nations, a political party may wield a greater scope of power than a private corporation. Moreover, as applied to the new nations, the analogical use of concepts originally devised to understand the capitalist market economies of Western industrialized societies seems especially misleading. Both the political and economic markets of most non-Western territories operate in only rudimentary form. The exchange notion appears more relevant to diverse private goods than to collective political goods. The neo-classical political economy model also assumes a utilitarian bias applicable mainly to Western capitalism. The decision-makers supposedly engage in a calculated, pragmatic, instrumental weighing of resources to attain alternative ends. Yet in the new states as well as the old, expressive symbols, myths, and political rituals condition the policy process. Political culture has a meaning that transcends its presumed status as a political "infrastructure" facilitating the instrumental exchange of resources.[65] In sum, to predict the effects of political decisions, as the neo-classical political economists justify their approach, it seems more important to ascertain the empirical interaction between the government and economic firms than to formulate an elaborate analogy.

The neo-Marxists claim to explicate the linkages between the political and economic systems; yet they assume this interaction without fully demonstrating its empirical nature. In their models of economic development, political organization becomes an epiphenomenon. Few concrete case studies show the empirical relationships between the processes of political and economic decision-making in particular historical situations. The effects of foreign corporations on domestic policies are established mainly through documentary evidence; the specific normative, structural, and behavioural conditions within each country are usually minimized. Most notably, the values of the political elites, the matrix of a society's primordial and sacred values, and the activities of political parties are downgraded. According to the rather simplistic neo-Marxist motivational assumptions, elites seek to maximize their economic interests; stratification conditions values and attitudes; multinational corporations from industrial countries seek dependence ties so as to maximize their profits. Omitted from this analysis is an empirical focus on crucial behavioural variables leading men to perceive the existing structural situation in particular ways and motivating them to act in complex directions.[66]

IV THE BEHAVIOURAL DIMENSION

Comparative behavioural studies represent the newest orientation to the study of the new nations. While the normative and structural dimensions set internal systemic limits, the behavioural dimension deals with the options selected by political actors, their acceptance or rejection of normative and structural boundaries, and their perceptions of the existing values and structures. As in the case of the structural dimension, there are several analytical approaches, mainly borrowed from the social psychologists.[67] So far, the most frequently used, but least useful, approach employed by political scientists has been psychoanalysis. As revealed in the works of Freud and the neo-Freudians, Alfred Adler and Erik Erikson, psychoanalysis concentrates on unconscious motivations and the origin of these motivations in parent–child conflicts.[68] But most propositions articulated by the psychoanalysts are too general and imprecise to test empirically. Empirical validation becomes especially difficult when leaders of the new states refuse to submit to psychotherapy. The problems are confounded when historical figures are psychoanalysed at a distance. Moreover, with the exception of early childhood experiences, the socio-cultural influences on the personality seem largely ignored by psychoanalysts.

Other social psychological approaches, such as stimulus-response theory, Lewin's field theory, cognitive development models, and attitudinal frameworks will perhaps yield greater explanatory pay-off than psychoanalysis. The stimulus-response approach, with its notions of reinforcement and drive reduction, holds particular relevance to those concerned with political learning. As indicated in the section on structural analysis, political scientists have shown considerable interest in the behaviour of groups in the political process. Kurt Lewin's attention to group norms, reference groups, and the effect of groups on the individual's aspiration level might offer valuable insights, especially in explaining the origins of the need for achievement. Lewinian theory also highlights the perceptual basis behind individual behaviour. A person's "field"—consisting of his past experiences, his present goals, values, needs, knowledge, attitudes toward authority—acts as a cognitive map or perceptual screen through which he views the political world. The cognitive developmental models sketched by Jean Piaget and Lawrence Kohlberg, who focus on the growth toward abstract reasoning and the cognitive processes underlying the formation of moral judgements, suggest theoretical hypotheses about the links between perception and choice behaviour.[69] So far, however, these three approaches have found limited application by political scientists studying the developing nations. At the present time, the behavioural approach has stimulated greater attention to techniques, especially sample surveys, than to theories. Attitude studies have been the most common type carried out overseas. Most of these studies consist of surveys of elite groups, rather than random samples of the national population. The limited data obtained have not yet been interpreted in theoretical terms.

Analytic problem. The various analytic problems posed by the behaviouralists can be classified according to the variables employed, both *traits* and behavioural *processes*: (1) Motivations: How are individuals motivated to seek new goals, to work for the collectivity, and strive for industrialization? What types of personal needs are likely to maximize economic development? Deriving specific hypotheses from his experimental work on motivation, David C. McClelland has presented a provocative interpretation of the relationship between the need for achievement and economic development in a wide range of countries throughout the world. He traces the need for achievement in early childhood experiences.[70] (2) Perceptions: How do individuals perceive the changing world? Diverse stimuli pour in from conflicting sources. Both the colonial and traditional orders are breaking down. In this period of perceptual flux, what is the relevance of ideology to those persons experiencing perceptual confusion? In this regard, two behavioural studies of Malaysian politics have considerable relevance.[71] Influenced by psychoanalytic considerations. Lucian Pye explored the ideological perceptions of Malayan Chinese who joined the Communist party during the 1950s. James E. Scott analysed the perceptions of Malaysian civil servants toward the political universe. In contrast to Pye, Scott placed less emphasis on identity crises and more on the roots of cynical, distrustful orientations in scarce economic resources. (3) Attitudes toward political objects, including the society, government, parties, and leaders: What is the role of dominant personalities in creating new patterns of authority that will lead to political development? How can a positive regard for the national hero be transferred to loyalty toward the political institutions and national societal boundaries? In the future, more survey studies will be carried out to capture the relationship between the personality of the dominant leaders and popular attitudes toward political objects.[72]

The behavioural approaches study not only personal traits but also the processes by which motivations, perceptions, and attitudes become energized in individual development. Here social scientists have shown the greatest concern for learning and socialization processes. How do individuals come to internalize cultural values and norms, both traditional and new ideological values? How do people learn skills, associational sentiments, and motivations? What are the political consequences of the conflicting orientations taught by differing agencies of socialization—the family, school, mass media, and political party? To these questions, Everett Hagen has paid systematic attention. Using a psychoanalytic approach, he explores the relationship between childhood socialization experiences and economic growth. What factors in the socialization of the child led to the formation of the creative (innovational) personality, which produces economic growth, and of the authoritarian personality, which retards economic development? In answering this question, Hagen speculates about the role behaviour of the mother and father in producing innovational personalities.[73]

Units for analysis. Behavioural analysis focuses on micro-units, that is, the individual and the small group. Not the isolated individual apart from society, but the interacting individual as shaped by social influences is the key unit for analysis. Whereas the structural approach does not usually deal with the individual personality, the behavioural approach rarely ignores the aspects of social structure which tend to shape, and be shaped by, the individual.

Variables. The behavioural approach focuses on personality traits —attitudes, needs, perceptions, motivations and emotions—and on behavioural processes—socialization, learning, and adaptation, all of which connote more dynamic activities. Aspects of the personality are conceived of as both dependent and independent variables. In some cases, there is a search for social influences which produce, say, the innovational personality. In other instances, analysts examine the effect of an entrepreneurial personality on expanding production.[74]

Assumptions. What general assumptions do the behaviouralists make about the personal prerequisites of modernization? (1) According to authors like Lucian Pye and Robert Scott, political modernization depends on the political leaders and citizens achieving a clear, stable identity.[75] At present, political leaders are uncertain of their personal identity. They are not sure of the answers to the questions: Who am I? Do I have the requisite self-esteem, political and personal competence to carry out daily tasks? What is my source of recognition from others? These personal anxieties and insecurities deflect energy from problem-solving activities. (2) As Daniel Lerner demonstrated so well for the Near East, modern man shows a basic empathy with other people. Exposed to the modern mass media, he can see himself playing a wide variety of new roles, for he has learned to perceive himself in the other person's situation. Accompanying this capacity for identifying with new aspects of the environment goes the expression of a large number of diverse opinions about a wide range of issues, especially those transcending the immediate surroundings.[76] (3) Working with a sample survey of young men, mainly factory workers in Argentina, Chile, India, East Pakistan, Western Nigeria, and Nigeria, Alex Inkeles and his colleagues have focused on activism as the distinguishing personal characteristic of modern man. He has an open mind, high political information, high political interest, and a national orientation. Conceiving change to be both desirable and possible, he actively participates in politics. Rather than viewing the world in a fatalistic way, modern man believes that the world operates according to law, not arbitrary whim. The world can be understood and transformed by human effort. He also holds that rational, impersonal rules, not traditional authority, should guide political decision-making.[77]

Techniques for collecting data. So far, the most widely used behavioural technique has been the sample survey of individual attitudes. What are the advantages and limitations of conducting sample surveys in the new states? Compared with aggregate data, survey material can better be used to demonstrate causal relationships. Aggregate data refer only to the characteristics of whole populations. They describe what happened but do not explain why a particular individual in the population behaved the way he did. In contrast, survey data can bring to light information on such crucial variables as the meaning of events to an individual, his personal needs, perceptions, and motivations. Moreover, when collecting survey data the analyst often designs a questionnaire and supervises its distribution. Thus, he can search for variables that are left untapped by aggregate data.[78]

Few surveys, however, have yet been conducted in most developing nations, especially outside Latin America, India, and Japan. What then are the difficulties of gathering data through sample survey techniques?[79] First, the social researcher must try to overcome the unwillingness of the host government to co-operate. At times American survey researchers seem ill-informed about the values and social structural patterns found within the new nations. In some cases, collaboration with American intelligence agencies and military organizations may arouse suspicions on the part of Third World political leaders. In other cases, government leaders try to prevent investigations into citizens' political attitudes, for fear that publication of these survey studies will weaken their regimes.

Second, indigenous social scientists may be unwilling or lack the training to carry out survey research with American political scientists. In many of the developing nations, social scientists have been trained in European institutions. From this educational experience, they have gained a humanistic, largely qualitative orientation. They reject the ideas of value neutrality, quantification, and a strong empirical bent associated with modern survey techniques.

Moreover, the curriculum of most colleges and universities in the developing nations stresses the non-quantitative disciplines: aesthetics, literature, law, philosophy, and history. Well-trained political scientists, psychologists, and sociologists are few in number. In Latin America, the developing area with the oldest established universities, economists tend to dominate the social science field. Even in the United States, they rarely work with survey data.

Third, the survey researcher confronts the problems associated with the unwillingness and lack of knowledge of the respondents. Many harbour suspicion of the foreigner. They are not used to the interview situation. Lacking trust in others, the respondents fear being manipulated. Often they will give an answer they think will please the interviewer, especially if they perceive him acting under government sponsorship. In most cases, the interviewer is of higher status than the respondents; this gap in social status may lead to a lack of openness and candour. In some instances, the respondents may have difficulty in answering questions, not because of a lack of candour but because their opinions are unstable, inconsistent, or non-existent. Even in the developed nations, survey researchers are discovering high percentages of individuals holding "non-attitudes". There are also cultural differences in how talkative citizens are when answering questions. At times the interview is not held in private; so others may directly influence the replies.

Fourth, the survey researcher faces difficulties in selecting a random sample. In the developing areas, especially in the less modernized sectors, one rarely finds neatly drawn street boundaries, as in American suburbs. The task of choosing sample units thus becomes vexatious. Rural areas are usually undersampled.[80] Whereas in Asia the men are most accessible for interviewing, in Latin America women are more available than men.[81]

Fifth, there arise the problems associated with adapting question-naires to local dialects and the local context. The questions may be ambiguously worded. Do similar words mean the same thing in different languages? How can concepts devised first in the United States and Europe be translated into the indigenous language? Does the analyst take into account the connotative aspects of political words? For all these reasons, most survey organizations in the United States, like the Survey Research Center of the University of Michigan, have been reluctant to institute sample surveys outside the United States and Europe. Most of the surveying so far has been carried out in Japan, India, Mexico, Argentina, Chile, and Brazil, where there exist indigenous public opinion institutes. The International Data Library and Reference Service, located at the University of California, Berkeley, is increasingly used to store, process and analyse survey data collected in Asia, Africa, and Latin America.[82]

Although the sample survey is the most widely used behavioural technique, behaviouralists have used a number of other techniques to collect data. Oral interviews among select groups have been quite common in the past, as well as today. Usually a small group of important officials, like local politicians and administrators, are given intensive interviews by the researcher. Not of a survey type, these interviews often fall short of methodological precision. In recent years, interviewing carried out in the developing nations has been guided by more explicit methodological considerations. The written word, as well as the spoken word, has also provided a key source of data. Written tests and questionnaires are common. Whereas in the past written documents were analysed in a highly qualitative, sub-jective way, recently content analysis has been widely adopted. In this area, David McClelland's content analyses of children's readers represent especially significant technical contributions. Up to now, the observation of small group settings has remained rather impres-sionistic. But as in the case of the other behavioural techniques, observation methods have recently become more precise and rigorous. In the future, perhaps Bales' methods of observing patterns of communication will be used to analyse political communication within small groups. Experimental techniques are probably most closely associated with behavioural analysis, but so far few experi-ments have found their way into comparative political research. Perhaps an experimental study, like Rokeach's *The Open and Closed Mind*, can be applied in non-Western areas to ascertain the cognitive make-up of so-called "authoritarian personalities".[83]

Techniques to process data. From a technical standpoint, the behavioural revolution in the social sciences has been closely identi-fied with the development of high speed computers. Most survey studies contain literally hundreds of cases and tens of variables. Only a large computer with a large storage capacity can handle this quantity of data. Highly complex statistical techniques have also been associated with behavioural research. Of particular interest to the political scientist has been the emergence of non-parametric statistics to handle nominal and ordinal scales and statistics applicable to small samples.[84]

Critique. As indicated in this review, comparative behavioural studies are still in their infancy. Most behavioural work has been conducted in the United States; few studies have been carried out in the developing nations. Moreover, the behavioural approach has been characterized more by advances in techniques than by efforts to develop empirical theories applicable to the new nations. In effect, there has occurred a gap between theory and techniques. On the

P

one hand, those making the most technical advances have paid least attention to formulating theories to explain the data. Most sample surveys gathering data on public attitudes, unlike experimental studies dealing with attitude change, have not been guided by explicit theoretical assumptions. On the other hand, those most concerned with theory have paid the least attention to devising techniques to empirically validate their theoretical propositions. Psychoanalysis has been the most widely used theory in research on the developing nations, but its assumptions are often difficult to test. It is obviously rather difficult to observe child-rearing practices and parent–child relationships from a distance. Since dead men cannot submit to psychotherapy or experimental investigation, behavioural techniques are difficult to apply to historical situations. David McClelland has made rather imaginative use of content analysis. Although he discovered a high value placed on achievement in certain children's readers, we are unsure if the children reading those textbooks did in fact internalize the need for achievement. Recognizing this limitation, McClelland and his colleagues have integrated findings as from content analyses with information on the actual motivations of businessmen in Mexico and India.[85] Thus, future developments in the behavioural field will see more attempts made to blend theoretical insights with the precise operationalization of variables.

V CONCLUSION

Let us explore more fully the implications of our analysis so far by returning to the four problems—the ethical, policy, technical, and analytic—mentioned in the introduction. What trends and advances in the study of the developing nations can be discerned? In what directions is this field heading? From an ethical standpoint, we have observed a movement from an early postwar emphasis on evaluating political institutions and practices according to Western ideal standards to a more recent concern to specify the explicit criteria by which political life in the developing nations can be evaluated. The older normative orientation assumed without question the innate superiority of Western institutions—the balance of powers system, limited government, social pluralism, the rule of law. Western institutions were models for "primitive" or otherwise unmodern people to follow in building specialized political instruments like ours. Thus the key question became: how can Western parliamentary institutions best be transferred? It was obviously easier to transfer the concrete structures than the attitudes which went along with the operation of these structures in the West.

The most recent ethical orientation does not take so many assumptions for granted. Political science has become a more empirical science, and our ethical concerns reflect this trend. The emphasis now is on evaluating moral hypotheses through empirical methods. The task of formulating ethical evaluations comprises rather specific steps not wholly made explicit by the older approach.[86] First, the analyst clearly delineates the criteria used to define the value under consideration, like democracy or constitutionalism. Second, he tries to find data which relate to these criteria. Third, he devises ways to measure the degree to which this value is being maximized in the performance of particular political systems. How do we find empirical indicators to measure whether or not the values are actualized in political behaviour or institutionalized in the operation of concrete structures? This is the task of operationalizing ethical evaluations.[87]

These ethical concerns are closely associated with the policy problems. How do the ethical positions of American political scientists become institutionalized in the policies pursued by the United States government? If progress is conceived to mean the establishment of democratic institutions, then what policies should the government follow to maximize democracy? Given the increasing economic gap between the rich and the poor nations, what is the relationship between economic development and development of democratic institutions? What economic policies should the United States follow in order to reduce this international gap between the northern and southern hemispheres? Max Millikan, former director of the Center for International Studies at M.I.T. and adviser to the United States government on foreign aid and economic development, assumes a compatibility between political democracy and a private enterprise economy. He encourages the new states to establish a tax structure which will provide private entrepreneurs with the incentives to save and invest. In particular, he urges the avoidance of taxes on high profits and of a progressive income tax, for these taxes reduce the incentive to invest. Instead of directly limiting profits, the new states should rely on high sales and excise taxes on consumer goods and luxury housing. Raising agricultural productivity should take precedence over rapid industrialization.[88]

Among the social scientists dealing with the developing nations, it has been the neo-Marxists who have been most sensitive to the effect of American foreign trade policies on the economic conditions within the Third World. To this question Millikan devotes little attention. The neo-Marxists are quick to point out the quotas and high tariffs placed on goods from the developing nations, the fluctuating world market prices for agricultural exports, the high interest loans, and American control of the International Monetary Fund and World Bank, which encourage foreign private companies to invest in the new nations. As a partial result of these policies, prices for exported agricultural produce have declined, whereas prices for imported manufactured goods have increased. Thus, the trade exchanges do not bring equal benefits to all parties. Moreover, multinational corporations, like Standard Oil of New Jersey, Mobil, Texaco, Gulf, Standard Oil of California, IBM, General Motors, and Ford, are controlled mainly by American officials. Possessing greater resources than most nation-states, these corporations have the ability to dictate economic conditions to many Third World governments. As perceived by the neo-Marxists, North American antipathy for rapid industrialization threatens to increase the dependence of the new nations on Western Europe and the United States. These themes find a sympathetic hearing among scholars, both Marxists and non-Marxists, in the Third World.[89]

The action of the United States military forces in the developing nations constitutes another policy problem faced by the American government. Close involvement of the military in the making and administering of American foreign policy has not only increased the political power of the armies in Latin America, Asia, the Near East, and Africa, but has also threatened American scholarly research in these areas. The Project Camelot case in Chile illustrates the dangers involved in military sponsorship of academic research.[90] The avoidance of such incidents as Project Camelot, which have already affected research in other parts of the world, will in the future require more co-ordination between American research scholars, on the one hand, and foreign governments and educational institutions, on the other. But more than co-ordination, a structural arrangement, is required. Americans should become more sensitive than they have in the past to the different moral concerns of the social scientists within the developing nations. These normative issues in turn are related to policy orientations of the Latin American and Afro-Asian governments. Among both government leaders and social scientists, there remains a pervasive fear of "academic manipulation" and "scientific colonialism". In particular, indigenous social scientists have been critical of the tendency to export data back to the United States, where the information is processed by a computer, analysed, and published. They see in this practice an analogy to economic colonialism, where the more powerful nations purchase cheap labour (interviewers) and raw materials (data) and then sell back finished goods (books).[91] In short, future American policy toward the developing nations will have to take more carefully into account these moral considerations, which involve a policy matter—the compatibility between the American national interest and the national interests of developing nations.[92]

These policy considerations have a direct relevance to the technical revolution now spreading throughout the social sciences. The next decade will find more and more social scientists from the developing areas trained in research techniques now available mainly to scholars working within the United States and Western Europe. Already, the United Nations Educational, Scientific, and Cultural Organization has sponsored individuals from India, Egypt, Nigeria, and Colombia to take training from the Survey Research Center at the University of Michigan. In the next few years, high speed computers will be directly accessible to social scientists in the new nations. Thus collaborative research between American and indigenous researchers will become far more common than heretofore. The greatest innovation in the organization of technical research facilities would be the development throughout the world of large regional centres housing comparative specialists, language centres, and quantitative data banks. One function of these world centres of research would be the co-ordination of research between American and overseas scholars. In these centres, the indigenous social scientists would play a key part in designing a study, gathering information, and processing the data. Of course, the success of this future collaborative research depends in part on the policies pursued by the United States government toward the developing nations.

Another trend in techniques will be a movement toward the combined use of aggregate and survey data, both processed by high-speed computers. The two types of data deal with human behaviour, but one focuses on characteristics of the whole group and the other on aspects of the individual. Aggregate data on whole nations and local communities will be combined with survey data on the attitudes of individuals living in those areas. The task will be to make comparisons between the data arrived at by these two different techniques. The use of both types of data will make it possible to explore the effects of structural characteristics of the nation or local community on individual attitudes. Neither the use of survey or aggregate data alone would enable us to discern this interaction effect.

The technical impact of the computer revolution in the social sciences has made available huge quantities of data never before accessible. Computers facilitate the undertaking of certain types of analytic problems, such as content analyses of verbal materials, which in the past would have involved considerable time, expense, and human labour. However, the possibilities of comparing large numbers of cases via the computer convey certain implications for analysis not always recognized by the social scientist. The computer hardware (machines) and software (programs), as well as the degree of competence of the human programmers, impose certain structural limitations on our analyses. There is always the potential danger that technical considerations will override the theoretical objectives of the researcher. When analytic problems must be adjusted to the capabilities of computer equipment and existing programs, often flexibility is lost. The cost and time involved in replacing old equipment may lead to a certain rigidity, a failure to remain open to environmental changes. By reducing complex, often random, unstructured information to binary choice data, high-speed computers may cause the social scientist to ignore the broader context and meaning of his data.[93]

From a theoretical standpoint, the proliferation of computer-based data banks has also created an information crisis. If this material is not simply to inundate us, it must be organized around conceptual systems capable of codifying, sorting, and making significant theoretical generalizations. Without more explicit attention to analytical approaches, crude empiricism threatens to run rampant. Therefore, the highest priority is to become self-consciously concerned with the management of data according to articulated theoretical principles capable of verification. Hence the immediate relevance of the normative, structural, and behavioural approaches. At the moment, the most progress in comparative politics is being made in the general field of structural analysis, especially in political development and modernization. As we have seen, comparative politics has broadened its scope to include structural models from sociology, particularly as they apply to industrial societies, and anthropology as related to new nations. Work on the behavioural side is most in need of development. Here we need to know the origins and consequences of political socialization, the political effects of differing educational systems, the manner in which ideologies have affected mass beliefs, and the ways in which citizens become motivated to pursue collective goals. These concerns cluster around a more general one pertaining to modernization—namely, the conditions under which people learn to create innovating structures, and come to cope with changes in a framework of popular public participation. Some of the problems involved are structural; others are normative; but the big ones are behavioural. In the next decade, work in comparative political behaviour will increasingly come to occupy the centre of the analytical stage.

In a sense, these three approaches are logical models of analysis. Few scholars work wholly within one approach. Future theoretical break-throughs will come from those attempts to combine two or more of these approaches. An important line of work lies at the point of intersection between the normative and structural dimensions. Here the concern becomes one of investigating how values and norms are institutionalized in concrete structures. The work of Lévi-Strauss and Lipset stand out here. Lévi-Strauss seeks to elucidate unconscious structures of the human mind which explain the relationships within social structures. That is, kinship systems are not only to be understood as objective ties of descent between individuals; rather, they are primarily symbolic systems.[94] Lipset has probed how normative values and structural relationships tend toward a "dynamic equilibrium".[95]

So far, the task of merging the normative and behavioural dimensions has not attracted too much attention from scholars working within the developing areas. This orientation involves the attempt to see how normative values are internalized within the individual. The normative-behavioural intersection involves theories of self-identification and meaning in terms of learning and socialization phases in the individual. The study of symbol formation is particularly important here. Perhaps the work of Erik Erikson best illustrates the merger of these two approaches.[95] Erikson, a non-experimental social psychologist, has revealed the tensions individuals face in modernized societies, where values and norms are in a state of flux. The confusion about one's self-identity partly arises because socialization experiences fail to prepare the individual to deal with social changes.[97]

In our opinion, the structural-behavioural combination represents the frontier of future comparative political studies in the developing nations. Here the works of Daniel Lerner, Alex Inkeles, and Sidney Verba represent significant contributions. In his classic study conducted by the Bureau of Applied Social Research at Columbia University, the early institutional leader in survey research, Lerner combined the structural and behavioural orientations to explain the modernization process in the Near East.[98] He was concerned to demonstrate the profound impact of a modernizing structure, the mass media, on raising popular aspirations and stimulating a feeling of "empathy", the most distinctive personal characteristic of modern man. The survey research of Alex Inkeles and David Smith treats modern attitudes as intervening variables between structural conditions and personality variables like psychic stress, orientation toward change, and feelings of hostility and alienation. Rather than assuming the dominance of structural conditions, Inkeles has empirically weighted their relative effects on modern attitudes. He found that education exerted a slightly more powerful influence on producing modern attitudes (activism, an open mind, high political information and interest, etc.) than did work in a large factory. In contrast to the ideas of Samuel Huntington and Erik Erikson, Inkeles uncovered no correlation whatsoever between psychic stress, as measured by a psychosomatic symptons test, and lengthy exposure to modernizing influences—namely, education, factory employment, urban residence, the mass media, and geographic-social mobility. In fact, those men with greater education and higher exposure to the mass media felt slightly less psychic stress than their less modernized fellows. Similarly, Inkeles' data suggest that hostility, alienation, and a desire for fundamental social changes stem not so much from the personal problems of the individual (his unrealistic aspirations for economic rewards) but instead from the socio-political characteristics of the country. For example, in India the most active citizens—the ones with high political information, interest, and participation— show the greatest sense of alienation from the government institutions. In Argentina and Chile the active citizens give stronger support to total, immediate changes in social and economic institutions than do the less active citizens. In short, Inkeles' research implies that feelings of alienation, anomie, desire for change, and personal stress arise not so much from "identity crises" or exaggerated aspirations produced by exposure to modernizing influences as from the capabilities of the existing concrete structures to satisfy demands.[99] Working within a similar structural-behavioural framework, the Cross-National Program on Political and Social Change seeks to explain the effect of socio-economic changes on personal beliefs and behaviour in Nigeria, India, and Japan, as well as Austria and the United States. This project, directed by Sidney Verba, combines aggregate data on the nation and local community with sample surveys on individual needs and perceptions.[100]

The implications of our analysis should now be clear. In terms of the empirical range of research during the past thirty years, the primary trend in comparative politics has revolved around extending coverage from studies primarily of American and European politics to the new nations. At first, the tendency was to employ national societies as the main units for analysis. However, as more information becomes available, the necessity to probe deeper and explore sub-units grows. New variables have accompanied the discovery of new units. Not only structural differentiation and centralization, but motivation, perception, and socialization come to be emphasized. As more data about more variables becomes accessible, new techniques for processing and analysing this information have developed. Here the effects of computers and advanced statistical methods have been noteworthy. But if these data and techniques are not to overwhelm the scholar and impose a certain mindlessness on the materials, this information must be organized around explicit conceptual systems. Thus, the research area which holds highest priority is not a geographical or technical one, but a theoretical sphere. As we have seen, promising contributions include structural-behavioural analysis and normative-structural analysis. In the next decade or two, comparative studies of the new nations will increasingly come to explore more deeply the theoretical implications of these approaches, while at the same time they will employ quantitative data and computer programming. Analytical sophistication, quantitative technique, and descriptive area knowledge will need to be more effectively integrated in a theoretical context.

REFERENCES

1　Such books as Alexander Leighton's *The Governing of Men* (Princeton: Princeton University Press, 1945) and Ruth Benedict's *The Chrysanthemum and the Sword* (Boston: Houghton Mifflin, 1956) were examples. Early Viking Fund publications, such as S. S. Sargent and M. W. Smith, eds., *Culture and Personality* (New York: Viking Fund, 1949), were also relevant and particularly among young political scientists who had been in O.W.I. and O.S.S. projects during World War II. People like Morris Janowitz, Harold Lasswell, Heinz Eulau, Gabriel Almond and many others carried on full-time operations research in an interdisciplinary context.

2　See the discussion of these institutionalists in David E. Apter, "Comparative Politics and Political Thought: Past Influences and Future Developments", in Harry Eckstein and David Apter, eds., *Comparative Politics: A Reader* (New York: The Free Press, 1963), pp. 730–32.

3　Some early monographic studies include George McT. Kahin, *Nationalism and Revolution in Indonesia* (Ithaca, N.Y.: Cornell University Press, 1952); David E. Apter, *The Gold Coast in Transition* (Princeton, N.J.: Princeton University Press, 1955); James S. Coleman, *Nigeria: Background to Nationalism* (Berkeley: University of California Press, 1958); Keith Callard, *Pakistan: A Political Study* (New York: Macmillan, 1957). Although monographic in character, most of these studies drew heavily on relevant insights and resource materials developed by anthropologists.

4　Daniel Lerner and his associates made explicit comparisons in six Near East countries on such problems as communications and modernization. See Daniel Lerner, *The Passing of Traditional Society: Modernizing the Middle East* (Glencoe, Ill.: The Free Press, 1958). The work of the Comparative Politics Committee of the Social Science Research Council located political development as the focal problem for comparison. Edited by Gabriel Almond and James S. Coleman, *The Politics of the Developing Areas* (Princeton, N.J.: Princeton University Press, 1960), provided comparative analyses of the politics of five areas: South-east Asia, South Asia, Sub-Saharan Africa, the Near East, and Latin America. The introductory and concluding essays by Gabriel Almond and James Coleman presented functional overviews drawing upon the findings of the area studies. The Comparative Politics Committee sponsored a series of successive volumes which dealt with various aspects of political development. Issued by Princeton University Press, these include *Communications and Political Development,* ed. Lucian W. Pye (1963); *Bureaucracy and Political Development*, ed. Joseph LaPalombara (1963); *Political Modernization in Japan and Turkey*, ed. Robert E. Ward and Dankwart A. Rustow (1964); *Education and Political Development*, ed. James S. Coleman (1965); *Political Culture and Political Development*, ed. Lucian W. Pye and Sidney Verba (1965); *Political Parties and Political Development*, ed. Joseph La Palombara and Myron Weiner (1966). During the 1960s a number of works appeared attempting to synthesize the development process in Afro-Asia with conditions in Latin America, Europe, and the United States. Some of the best known of these are David E. Apter, *The Politics of Modernization* (Chicago: The University of Chicago Press, 1965); Samuel P. Huntington, *Political Order in Changing Societies* (New Haven, Conn.: Yale University Press, 1968); Dankwart A. Rustow, *A World of Nations* (Washington, D.C.: The Brookings Institution, 1967); C. E. Black, *The Dynamics of Modernization: A Study in Comparative History* (New York: Harper and Row, 1966); A. F. K. Organski, *The Stages of Political Development* (New York: Knopf, 1965); S. N. Eisenstadt, *Modernization: Protest and Change* (Englewood Cliffs, N.J.: Prentice-Hall, 1966); Reinhard Bendix, *Nation-Building and Citizenship: Studies of Our Changing Social Order* (New York: Wiley, 1964); Barrington Moore, Jr., *Social Origins of Dictatorship and Democracy* (Boston, Mass.: Beacon Press, 1966); Irving Louis Horowitz, *Three Worlds of Development* (New York: Oxford University Press, 1966). Nearly all these syntheses about the processes of development and modernization take a historical view of sociopolitical change. For a critical review of the volumes by Huntington, Black, and Moore, see Lester M. Salamon, "Comparative History and the Theory of Modernization", *World Politics*, 23 (October 1970), 83–103.

5 Two efforts to formulate classifications of governments relevant to both modernized and modernizing societies include David E. Apter, "Political Systems and Developmental Change", *Some Conceptual Approaches to the Study of Modernization* (Englewood Cliffs, N.J.: Prentice-Hall, 1968), pp. 329–50 and two essays by Fred W. Riggs, "The Comparison of Whole Political Systems", in Robert T. Holt and John E. Turner, eds., *The Methodology of Comparative Research* (New York: The Free Press, 1970), pp. 73–121; "Systems Theory: Structural Analysis", in Michael Hass and Henry S. Kariel, eds., *Approaches to the Study of Political Science* (Scranton, Penn.: Chandler, 1970), pp. 194–235.

6 In "From Social Darwinism to Current Theories of Modernization", *World Politics*, 21 (October 1968), 69–83, Ali Mazrui elaborates the value assumptions underlying Western notions of modernization.

7 For a different review of the several different facets of political "development", see Samuel P. Huntington, "The Change to Change: Modernization, Development, and Politics", *Comparative Politics*, 3 (April 1971), 298–313.

8 In much of the exploratory work of political scientists, the hypotheses emerge during and after the data are collected, rather than before. Psychologists and quantitative sociologists take more care to pose specific hypotheses before data gathering begins.

9 Neil Smelser, *Theory of Collective Behavior* (New York: The Free Press, 1963), pp. 25–27.

10 Those most identified with the sociology of knowledge tradition have held deep moral convictions. Despite the fact that Max Weber is identified with "value-free" sociology, in reality he was a man "passionately involved in the events of his day". See Reinhard Bendix, *Max Weber: An Intellectual*

Portrait (Garden City, N.Y.: Doubleday Anchor Books, 1962), p. 266 Weber's study of the development of legal rationality in the West reflects his early legal career and training in the law. His view of nationalism as the highest form of civilization can only be understood in light of his personal position as a fervent German nationalist. Arthur Mitzman in *The Iron Cage: An Historical Interpretation of Max Weber* (New York: Knopf, 1969) uses psychoanalytical insights to explain the relationship between Weber's intellectual values and his personal experiences. In one sense, the approach of the normative analyst resembles that of the psychoanalyst. From the standpoint of the French anthropologist Claude Lévi-Strauss, who has studied small-scale societies, field work becomes comparable to psychoanalysis. Just as in psychoanalysis, the intern comes to understand better himself and others, so through field work the observer perceives the higher, organic meaning of events which before held only fragmentary significance. See Claude Lévi-Strauss, *Structural Anthropology* (New York: Basic Books, 1963), p. 373.

11   For several general critiques of the "traditional vs. modern" dichotomy, see Edward Shils, "Tradition", *Comparative Studies in Society and History*, 13 (April 1971), 122–59; S. N. Eisenstadt, "Some Observations on the Dynamics of Tradition", *Comparative Studies in Society and History*, 11 (October 1969), 451–75; Reinhard Bendix, "Tradition and Modernity Reconsidered", *Comparative Studies in Society and History*, 9 (April 1967), 292–348; Joseph R. Gusfield, "Tradition and Modernity: Misplaced Polarities in the Study of Social Change", in Jason L. Finkle and Richard W. Gable, eds., *Political Development and Social Change*, 2nd ed. (New York: Wiley, 1971), pp. 15–26; Joseph R. Gusfield, ed., "Tradition and Modernity: Conflict and Congruence", *The Journal of Social Issues*, 24 (October 1968), 1–158; C. S. Whitaker, "A Dysrhythmic Process of Political Change", *World Politics*, 19 (January 1967), 190–217; Ralph Braibanti and Joseph Spengler, eds., *Tradition, Values, and Socio-Economic Development* (Durham, N.C.: Duke University Press, 1961). For specific case studies about the process by which traditional values can be adapted to modern situations and to the requirements of modernization, see Lloyd I. Rudolph and Susanne Hoeber Rudolph *The Modernity of Tradition: Political Development in India* (Chicago: The University of Chicago Press, 1967); Rajni Kothari, *Politics in India* (Boston: Little Brown, 1970), especially pp. 1–99, 250–92; Milton Singer, "Beyond Tradition and Modernity in Madras", *Comparative Studies in Society and History*, 13 (April 1971), 160–95; R. S. Khare, "Home and Office: Some Trends of Modernization among the Kenya-Kubja Brahmans", *Comparative Studies in Society and History*, 13 (April 1971), 196–216; S. N. Eisenstadt, "Tradition, Change, and Modernity: A Study of China's Encounter with Modernity", *Hamizrah Hehadash*, 18 (Nos. 1–2, 1968), 64–78, English summary pp. vii–ix; John T. McAlister, Jr., and Paul Mus, *The Vietnamese and their Revolution* (New York: Harper and Row, 1970), especially pp. 78–92, 140–66; C. S. Whitaker, Jr., *The Politics of Tradition: Continuity and Change in Northern Nigeria, 1946–1966* (Princeton, N. J.: Princeton University Press, 1970); Donald N. Levine, *Wax and Gold: Tradition and Innovation in Ethiopian Culture* (Chicago: University of Chicago Press, 1965); David E. Apter, *The Political Kingdom in Uganda* (Princeton: Princeton University Press, 1961); Ali A. Mazrui, "Borrowed Theory and Original Practice in African Politics", *Patterns of African Development*, ed. Herbert J. Spiro (Englewood Cliffs, N.J.: Prentice-Hall, 1967), pp. 91–124; and several essays in Lucian W. Pye and Sidney Verba, eds., *Political Culture and*

Political Development, especially the articles on Japan, Turkey, India, and Ethiopia.

12 See Rupert Emerson, *From Empire to Nation* (Boston: Beacon Press, 1960), pp. 89–209; John Kautsky, *Political Change in Underdeveloped Countries* (New York: Wiley, 1962), pp. 30–56.

13 Rupert Emerson has posed these questions. See *From Empire to Nation*. pp. 272–292.

14 See Claude Lévi-Strauss, *Structural Anthropology*; Max Gluckman, *Politics, Law and Ritual in Tribal Society* (Oxford, England: Basil Blackwell, 1965).

15 Seymour M. Lipset, *The First New Nation* (New York: Basic Books, 1963), Chapter 1.

16 See Barrington Moore, Jr., *Social Origins of Dictatorship and Democracy*, pp. 484–87.

17 For a lucid, brief account of the dialectical manner of perceiving social behavior, see Pierre L. Van den Berghe, "Dialectic and Functionalism", *American Sociological Review*, 28 (October, 1963), 695–705.

18 See Clement Henry Moore, *Politics in North Africa: Algeria, Morocco, and Tunisia* (Boston: Little, Brown, 1970), pp. 33–90.

19 Leonard Binder, *Iran: Political Development in a Changing Society* (Berkeley: University of California Press, 1962), p. 16.

20 Leonard Binder, *The Ideological Revolution in the Middle East* (New York: Wiley, 1964); *Religion and Politics in Pakistan* (Berkeley: University of California Press, 1961).

21 Max Weber took this position. See Reinhard Bendix, *Max Weber: An Intellectual Portrait*, p. 266; Dennis Wrong, ed., *Max Weber* (Englewood Cliffs, N.J.: Prentice-Hall, 1970), pp. 17–25.

22 See Clifford Geertz, "Religion as a Cultural System", *Anthropological Approaches to the Study of Religion*, Vol. 3, ed. Michael Banton (London: Tavistock, 1965), pp. 1–46; "Ideology as a Cultural System", *Ideology and Discontent*, ed. David E. Apter (New York: The Free Press, 1964), pp. 47–76. In *The Religion of Java* (Glencoe, Ill.: The Free Press, 1961) and *Islam Observed: Religious Development in Morocco and Indonesia* (New Haven, Conn.: Yale University Press, 1968), Clifford Geertz explores the ways in which people use religious values to gain meaning and find a sense of cultural solidarity. For analyses of the links between modernization and ideology as an energizer of human behaviour, see Mary Matossian, "Ideologies of Delayed Industrialization", *Economic Development and Cultural Change*, 6 (April 1958), 217–28; Irving Leonard Markovitz, *Léopold Sédar Senghor and the Politics of Négritude* (New York: Atheneum 1969); Richard R. Fagen, *The Transformation of Political Culture in Cuba* (Stanford: Stanford University Press, 1969); Charles W. Anderson, Fred R. von der Mehden, and Crawford Young, *Issues of Political Development* (Englewood Cliffs, N.J.: Prentice-Hall, 1967), pp. 175–235. The links between religious values and modernization are explored in S. N. Eisenstadt, ed., *The Protestant Ethic and Modernization: A Comparative View* (New York: Basic Books, 1968) and in Donald Eugene Smith, *Religion and Political Development* (Boston: Little, Brown, 1970).

23 See Gabriel Almond and G. Bingham Powell, *Comparative Politics: A Developmental Approach* (Boston: Little, Brown, 1966), pp. 50–63, 315–22.

24 A number of articles have appeared which report on the Vicos project. For examples, see the March 1965 issue of *The American Behavioral Scientist*; the summer 1962 issue of *Human Organization*; and Harold Lasswell, *The Future of Political Science* (New York: Atherton Press, 1963), pp. 105–15.

25 See Ole Holsti, "An Adaptation of the 'General Inquirer' for the Systematic Analysis of Political Documents", *Behavioral Science*, 9 (October 1964), 382–88; "Content Analysis", in Gardner Lindzey and Elliot Aronson, eds., *The Handbook of Social Psychology*, 2nd ed., Vol. 2 (Reading, Mass.: Addison-Wesley, 1968), pp. 596–692; *Content Analysis for the Social Sciences and Humanities* (Reading, Mass.: Addison-Wesley, 1969).

26 For criticisms of the methodology for analyzing values, see Robert Marsh, *Comparative Sociology* (New York: Harcourt, Brace, and World, 1967), pp. 28–29; Robert T. Holt and John M. Richardson, Jr., "Competing Paradigms in Comparative Politics", in Robert T. Holt and John E. Turner, eds., *The Methodology of Comparative Research*, pp. 48–49. Two critiques of the concept of values held by Talcott Parsons include Brian M. Barry, *Sociologists, Economists, and Democracy* (London: Collier-Macmillan, 1970), pp. 75–98, and Alvin W. Gouldner, *The Coming Crisis of Western Sociology* (New York: Basic Books, 1970), 246–85.

27 For this distinction between concrete and analytic structures, see Marion J. Levy, Jr., *The Structure of Society* (Princeton: Princeton University Press, 1952), pp. 88–89; *Modernization and the Structure of Societies* (Princeton: Princeton University Press, 1966), pp. 20–26.

28 See Almond and Powell, *Comparative Politics*, p. 42; Fred W. Riggs, *Administration in Developing Countries* (Boston: Houghton Mifflin, 1964), pp. 23–24, 29–30; David E. Apter, *The Politics of Modernization*, pp. 243–45.

29 Lloyd Fallers, "Political Sociology and the Anthropological Study of African Polities", *Archives Européennes de Sociologie* 4 (1963), 326.

30 For illustrative examples of this approach in the African case, see R. L. Buell, *The Native Problem in Africa* (New York: Macmillan, 1928; reprinted Frank Cass, London, 1965); Lord Lugard, *The Dual Mandate in Tropical Africa* (London: Blackwood, 1929; 5th ed., with a new introduction by Margery Perham, 1965); Margery Perham, *Native Administration in Nigeria* (London: Oxford University Press, 1937).

31 Gabriel A. Almond, "Introduction: A Functional Approach to Comparative Politics", *The Politics of the Developing Areas*, p. 8.

32 See Pierre van den Berghe, "Dialectic and Functionalism", *American Sociological Review*, 28 (October 1963), 696; Arthur L. Stinchcombe, *Constructing Social Theories* (New York: Harcourt, Brace, and World, 1968), pp. 80–93.

33 Samuel P. Huntington, *Political Order in Changing Societies*, pp. 1–92, 397–461, especially p. 37: "Modernization thus tends to produce alienation and anomie, normlessness generated by the conflict of old values and new. The new values undermine the old bases of association and of authority before new skills, motivations, and resources can be brought into existence to create new groupings." Compare the views of Hegel and Huntington. Both perceive society as a centre of conflict among social groups. However, whereas Hegel saw the state civil service as a "universal class" transcending the social conflict, Huntington assigns this role to the political party.

34 See Joseph LaPalombara, "Macrotheories and Microapplications in Comparative Politics: A Widening Chasm", *Comparative Politics*, 1 (October 1968), 52–78; Roy Macridis, "Comparative Politics and the Study of Government: The Search for Focus", *Comparative Politics*, 1 (October 1968), 79–90, especially Macridis' discussion of "the fallacy of inputism", pp. 84–86. These criticisms apply mainly to the functional approach of Gabriel Almond. Other structural functionalists like David Apter, Fred

Riggs, and S. N. Eisenstadt have concentrated more on concrete structures, including government.

35 For a general outline of the neo-classical approach to political development, see Warren F. Ilchman and Norman Thomas Uphoff, *The Political Economy of Change* (Berkeley: The University of California Press, 1969). Specific applications of neo-classical ideas, especially as they relate to making and implementing public policies, include Charles W. Anderson, *Politics and Economics in Latin America* (Princeton, N.J.: D. Van Nostrand, 1967); Charles W. Anderson, *The Political Economy of Modern Spain: Policy-making in an Authoritarian System* (Madison: The University of Wisconsin Press, 1970); Ronald D. Brummer and Garry D. Brewer, *Organized Complexity: Empirical Theories of Political Development* (New York: The Free Press, 1971); J. S. Nye, "Corruption and Political Development: A Cost-Benefit Analysis", *The American Political Science Review*, 61 (June 1967), 417–27; Karl de Schweinitz, Jr., "Growth, Development, and Political Modernization", *World Politics*, 22 (July 1970), 518–40. Two neo -Marxist critiques of the existing literature on political and economic development include Susanne J. Bodenheimer, "The Ideology of Developmentalism: American Political Science's Paradigm-Surrogate for Latin American Studies", *Berkeley Journal of Sociology*, 15 (1970), 95–137, reprinted in *Sage Professional Papers in Comparative Politics*, 1971; and Henry Bernstein, "Modernization Theory and the Sociological Study of Development", *Journal of Development Studies*, 7 (January 1971), 141–60.

36 The behavioural approach concentrates on micro-units, that is, the individual and small group. Of course, the designation of a concrete structure as a macro-unit or a micro-unit is a relative matter. In relationship to a geographic area, the nation is a micro-unit. But in relationship to an individual, the nation is a macro-unit.

37 See Fred Riggs, "Bureaucrats and Political Development: A Paradoxical View", *Bureaucracy and Political Development*, ed. Joseph La Palombara, p. 131.

38 In Latin America, for example, note the differences between Chile, Argentina, Uruguay, and Costa Rica, on the one hand, and Haiti, Ecuador, Peru, and Paraguay, on the other.

39 For attempts to operationalize the variables of "societal differentiation" and "political complexity", see Robert Marsh, *Comparative Sociology*, pp. 31–38, 329–74; Mark Abrahamson, "Correlates of Political Complexity" *American Sociological Review*, 34 (October 1969), 690–701. For a study trying to measure political variables related to development, see Raymond F. Hopkins, "Aggregate Data and the Study of Political Development", *Journal of Politics*, 31 (February 1969), 71–94. Using the Cross-polity Survey, the World Handbook, the Dimensions of Nations study, and the Cutright data bank, Hopkins applied the structural theories of Gabriel Almond and Samuel Huntington to aggregate data from 85 countries. He located through factor analysis five dimensions of political development: power sharing, executive stability, domestic violence, participant political socialization, and territorial integrity. See also Irma Adelman and Cynthia Taft Morris, *Society, Politics, and Economic Development* (Baltimore: The Johns Hopkins Press, 1967). In "Soldiers in Mufti: The Impact of Military Rule upon Economic and Social Change in the Non-Western States", *The American Political Science Review*, 64 (December 1970), 1131–48, Eric A. Norlinger uses the Adelman and Morris data to test Huntington's hypothesis about the relationship between the size of the middle class, the

degree of civilian power exercised by the military officers, military orientations, and the rate of economic modernization.

40 Samuel Huntington, *Political Order in Changing Societies*, pp. 1–92, 397–461. In a re-analysis of Huntington's assumptions about the relationship between social mobilization and political stability, Paul R. Brass has used aggregate voting statistics in Indian elections to demonstrate that in certain Indian provinces, contrary to Huntington's predictions, political stability and high institutionalization were related to *high* political participation and *high* social mobilization and that low institutionalization and low stability correlated with low political participation and low social mobilization. See his "Political Participation, Institutionalization, and Stability in India", *Government and Opposition*, 4 (Winter 1969), 23–53.

41 Samuel Huntington, *Political Order in Changing Societies*, p. 25.

42 Not all neo-institutionalists go so far as Huntington in equating political modernization with the strength of governmental organizations. They link politics more with a bargaining model and give greater importance to other concrete structures like interest groups. See, for example, Joseph LaPalombara. "Political Power and Political Development", *Yale Law Journal*, 78 (June 1969), 1253–75.

43 S. N. Eisenstadt, *Modernization: Protest and Change*, pp. 1–15, 142–61. Neil Smelser, *The Sociology of Economic Life* (Englewood Cliffs, N.J.: Prentice-Hall, 1963), pp. 106–12, also views development as a balance between the forces of structural differentiation and integration.

44 Gabriel Almond, "Introduction: A Functional Approach to Comparative Politics", *The Politics of the Developing Areas*, pp. 33–34.

45 See Gabriel Almond and G. Bingham Powell, Jr., *Comparative Politics: A Developmental Approach*, pp. 73–163, 299–332. Almond and Powell place greater emphasis on differentiation than on integration as an indicator of political development.

46 Gabriel Almond, "Political Development: Analytical and Normative Perspectives", *Comparative Political Studies*, 1 (January 1969), 447–69; "Determinancy-Choice, Stability-Change: Some Thoughts on a Contemporary Polemic in Political Theory", *Government and Opposition*, 5 (Winter 1969/70), 22–40.

47 See the several writings by Fred Riggs; over the years his interpretations of political development have undergone some changes, at least in terminology. Compare *Administration in Developing Countries*, pp. 23–40, with *Thailand: The Modernization of a Bureaucratic Polity* (Honolulu, Hawaii: East-West Center Press, 1966), pp. 376–86, with "The Dialectics of Developmental Conflict", *Comparative Political Studies*, 1 (July 1968), 197–226, especially page 207, with "Bureaucratic Politics in Comparative Perspective", *Journal of Comparative Administration*, 1 (May 1969), 5–38.

48 See Warren F. Ilchman and Norman Thomas Uphoff, *The Political Economy of Change*, pp. 3–48, 256–86; Norman Uphoff, "Ghana and Economic Assistance: Impetus and Ingredients for a Theory of Political Development", paper delivered at the 66th Meeting of the American Political Science Association, Los Angeles, California, 1970.

49 Although not taking an explicit neo-Marxist position, John Kautsky and Merle Kling have focused on the tensions between an unchanging society and changes in political leadership. See John Kautsky, *Political Change in Underdeveloped Countries*, pp. 3–119; Merle Kling, "Towards a Theory of Power and Political Instability in Latin America", *Political Change in Underdeveloped Countries*, pp. 123–39.

50 In *Karl Marx on Colonialism and Modernization* (Garden City, New York: Doubleday Anchor, 1969), Shlomo Avineri, ed., presents a succinct, lucid account of Marx's ideas about modernization and about the unintended consequences effected by colonial expansion in India and North Africa. See pages 1–31, as well as the newspaper articles and letters written by Marx.

51 For an account of the differences in development between Latin America and Afro-Asia, see Edward J. Williams, "Comparative Political Development: Latin America and Afro-Asia", *Comparative Studies in Society and History*, 11 (June 1969), 342–54. Works applying neo-Marxist assumptions to the Latin American situation include Andre Gunder Frank, *Latin America: Underdevelopment or Revolution* (New York: Monthly Review Press, 1969); Andre Gunder Frank, *Capitalism and Underdevelopment in Latin America: Historical Studies of Chile and Brazil* (New York: Monthly Review Press, 1967); James O'Connor, *The Origins of Socialism in Cuba* (Ithaca, N.Y.: Cornell University Press, 1970); James Petras, *Politics and Social Forces in Chilean Development* (Berkeley: University of California Press, 1969); Pablo González Casanova, *Democracy in Mexico*, trans. Danielle Salti (New York: Oxford University Press, 1970); Rodolfo Stavenhagen, *Les Classes Sociales dans les Sociétés Agraires* (Paris: Editions Anthropos, 1969); Fernando Henrique Cardoso, *Sociologie du Développement en Amerique Latine* (Paris: Editions Anthropos, 1969); James Petras and Maurice Zeitlin, eds., *Latin America: Reform or Revolution? A Reader* (New York: Fawcett, 1968), especially the essays by Rodolfo Stavenhagen, Teotonio dos Santos, and Luis Vitale. Fewer neo-Marxist analyses of African and Asian countries have appeared; examples include Robert Fitch and Mary Oppenheimer, *Ghana: End of an Illusion* (New York: Monthly Review Press, 1966); Samir Amin, *Le développement du capitalisme en Côte d'Ivoire* (Paris: Editions de Minuit, 1967); Samir Amin, *Le monde des affaires Sénégalaises* (Paris: Editions de Minuit, 1969); Giovanni Arrighi and John S. Saul, "Nationalism and Revolution in Sub-Saharan Africa", in Ralph Miliband and John Saville, eds., *The Socialist Register, 1969* (London: Merlin Press, 1969), pp. 137–88; Giovanni Arrighi and John S. Saul, "Economic Development in Tropical Africa", *The Journal of Modern African Studies*, 6 (No. 2, 1968), 141–69; Charles Bettelheim,¹ India Independent, trans. W. A. Caswell (London: MacGibbon and Kee, 1968).

52 For these themes, see Irving L. Horowitz, *Three Worlds of Development*, especially his chapter on "mending and smashing", pp. 195–224; Robert Fitch and Mary Oppenheimer, *Ghana: End of an Illusion*; Andre Gunder Frank, *Latin America: Underdevelopment or Revolution*, pp. 21–94.

53 See Keith Griffin, *Underdevelopment in Spanish America* (London: Allen and Unwin, 1969); Susanne J. Bodenheimer, "The Ideology of Developmentalism: American Political Science's Paradigm-Surrogate for Latin American Studies", *Berkeley Journal of Sociology*, 15 (1970), 95–137; Philip Ehrensaft, "Semi-Industrial Capitalism in the Third World", *Africa Today*, 18 (January 1971), 40–67.

54 Egil Fossum, "Political Development and Strategies for Change", *Journal of Peace Research*, 7 (No. 1, 1970), 17–31; Theotonio dos Santos, "La crise de la théorie du développement et les rélations de dépendance en Amerique Latine", *L'Homme et la Société*, (No. 12, Avril-Mai-Juin 1969), pp. 43–68.

55 Karl Deutsch has evinced an interest in both cybernetic and economic models to explain these vast quantities of data. See *The Nerves of Government* (New

York: The Free Press, 1966); "Some Quantitative Constraints on Value Allocation in Society and Politics", *Behavioral Science*, 11 (July 1966), 245–52.

56 For a brief description of the contents of the H.R.A.F. and some of its inadequacies, see Robert Marsh, *Comparative Sociology*, pp. 261–70. Carl J. Friedrich and Morton Horwitz, "Some Thoughts on the Relation of Political Theory to Anthropology", *The American Political Science Review*, 62 (June 1968), 536–45, point out that most investigators depositing data with the H.R.A.F. fail to clarify the differences between power and authority or between law and custom, crucial variables for political scientists.

57 See Bruce Russett, *et al.*, *World Handbook of Political and Social Indicators* (New Haven: Yale University Press, 1964).

58 See Arthur S. Banks and Robert B. Textor, *A Cross-polity Survey* (Cambridge: The M.I.T. Press, 1963); Arthur S. Banks, *Cross-polity Time Series Data* (Cambridge: The M.I.T. Press, 1971).

59 For a discussion of the uses of aggregate data, see Austin Ranney, "The Utility and Limitations of Aggregate Data in the Study of Electoral Behavior", *Essays on the Behavioral Study of Politics* (Urbana: University of Illinois Press, 1962), pp. 91–102; Ralph H. Retzlaff, "The Use of Aggregate Data in Comparative Political Analysis", *The Journal of Politics*, 27 (November 1965), 797–817; Edward Tufte, "Improving Data Analysis in Political Science", *World Politics*, 21 (July 1969), 641–54; Charles L. Taylor, ed., *Aggregate Data Analysis: Political and Social Indicators in Cross-National Research* (Paris: Mouton, 1968).

60 Everett E. Hagen fallaciously argues, "The structure of traditional society has lasted as long as it has because the personalities of the simple folk are authoritarian". See Everett E. Hagen, *On the Theory of Social Change* (Homewood, Illinois: The Dorsey Press, 1962), pp. 73–74. This relationship between structure and personality *may* be true, but without an examination of the personalities of individuals in traditional societies we cannot be sure of the validity of this generalization. For an illuminating discussion of the fallacies involved in using aggregate data, see Erwin K. Scheuch, "Cross-national Comparisons Using Aggregate Data: Some Substantive and Methodological Problems", *Comparing Nations*, ed. Richard L. Merritt and Stein Rokkan (New Haven: Yale University Press, 1966), pp. 131–67.

61 For a series of aggregate data studies exploring the relationship between domestic political instability and indicators of development, see John V. Gillespie and Betty A. Nesvold, eds., *Macro-quantitative Analysis* (Beverly Hills, Calif.: Sage Publications, 1971). See also Ivo K. Feierabend and Rosalind Feierabend, "Aggressive Behaviors within Polities, 1948–1962: A Cross-national Study", *The Journal of Conflict Resolution*, 10 (September 1966), 249–71; Ivo K. Feierabend, Rosalind L. Feierabend, and Betty A. Nesvold, 'Social Change and Political Violence: Cross-National Patterns", in *The History of Violence in America*, ed. Hugh Davis Graham and Ted Robert Gurr (New York: Bantam, 1969), pp. 632–87; Ivo K. Feierabend, Betty Nesvold, and Rosalind L. Feierabend, "Political Coerciveness and Turmoil: A Cross-national Inquiry", *Law and Society Review*, 5 (August 1970), 93–118. Samuel Huntington has used some of the Feierabend-Nesvold aggregate data to illustrate the links between modernization and political violence. See *Political Order in Changing Societies*, pp. 39–59.

62 For critiques of Almond's structural-functional assumptions, see S. E. Finer, "Almond's Concept of 'The Political System,': A Textual Critique",

Q

Government and Opposition, 5 (Winter 1969/70), 3–21; Alexander J. Groth, "Structural Functionalism and Political Development: Three Problems", *The Western Political Quarterly*, 23 (September 1970), 485–99. In "Bureaucratic Politics in Comparative Perspective: A Commentary and Critique", *Journal of Comparative Administration*, 1 (May 1969), 39–46, Richard Sisson reviews Fred Riggs' rather neological structural approach. John C. Harsanyi, "Rational-choice Models of Political Behavior vs. Functionalist and Conformist Theories", *World Politics*, 21 (July 1969), 513–38, criticizes structural-functional assumptions from a neo-classical economic standpoint.

63   Samuel P. Huntington, *Political Order in Changing Societies*, p. 25. See the review of Huntington's book by Joseph LaPalombara, "Political Power and Political Development", *Yale Law Journal*, 78 (June 1969), 1270–74. LaPalombara, a fellow neo-institutionalist, criticizes Huntington for his normative, metaphysical views, i.e. the equation of the public interest with strong political institutions, rather than for his structural concern for legal institutions.

64   Huntington has recently paid greater attention to exploring the interaction between different components of the political system—especially the interaction between the "power" and "content" of cultural values, formal organizations, social groups, leaders, and policies. This more complex focus of inquiry may obviate some of the difficulties in giving exclusive priority to the structural characteristics of political institutions and social groups. See "The Change to Change: Modernization, Development, and Politics", *Comparative Politics*, 3 (April 1971), 316–19.

65   Warren Ilchman and Norman Uphoff, *The Political Economy of Change*, p. 215.

66   Kalman H. Silvert, "Much Conflict, Little Power", *Comparative Politics*, 3 (April 1971), 447–62, suggests some deficiencies in the neo-Marxist political economy model as applied to Latin America: "The theories of dependency posit a people helplessly acted upon—man as a dependent variable with a vengeance. Such ideologies promote helplessness by seeing human beings as the passive products of industries, cities, power blocks, 'forces'." p. 461.

67   Three summaries of behavioural theories include Morton Deutsch and Robert M. Krauss, *Theories in Social Psychology* (New York: Basic Books, 1965); Marvin E. Shaw and Philip R. Costanzo, *Theories of Social Psychology* (New York: McGraw-Hill, 1970); Gardner Lindzey and Elliot Aronson, eds., *The Handbook of Social Psychology*, 2nd edition, Vol. I (Reading, Mass. Addison-Wesley, 1968), especially the essays on stimulus-response theory, Freudianism, cognitive theories, field theory, and role theory. See also the discussions of behavioural theories in David E. Apter and Charles F. Andrain, eds., *Contemporary Analytical Theory* (Englewood Cliffs, N.J.: Prentice-Hall, 1972), pp. 459–682.

68   For two examples, see E. Victor Wolfenstein, *The Revolutionary Personality: Lenin, Trotsky, Gandhi* (Princeton, N.J.: Princeton University Press, 1967); Erik H. Erikson, *Gandhi's Truth* (New York: Norton, 1969).

69   See Lawrence Kohlberg, "Stage and Sequence: The Cognitive-Developmental Approach to Socialization", in David A. Goslin, ed., *Handbook of Socialization Theory and Research* (Chicago, Ill.: Rand McNally, 1968), pp. 347–480. Kohlberg, who bases his ideas on a revised Piagetian framework has explored his theories of cognitive-moral development in the United States as well as Yucatan, Mexico, Taiwan, and Turkey.

70   David C. McClelland, *The Achieving Society* (New York: Free Press Paper-

back, 1967); David C. McClelland and David G. Winter, *Motivating Economic Achievement* (New York: Free Press Paperback, 1971).

71 Lucian W. Pye, *Guerrilla Communism in Malaya* (Princeton, N.J.: Princeton University Press, 1956); James E. Scott, *Political Ideology in Malaysia: Reality and the Beliefs of an Elite* (New Haven: Yale University Press, 1968).

72 For examples of attitudinal research in this socialization area, see Robert D. Hess, "The Socialization of Attitudes toward Political Authority", *International Social Science Journal*, 15 (1963), 542–59; Akira Kubota and Robert E. Ward, "Family Influence and Political Socialization in Japan", *Comparative Political Studies*, 3 (July 1970), 140–75; M. Lal Goel, "Distributions of Civic Competence Feelings in India", *Social Science Quarterly*, 51 (December 1970), 755–68; Samuel J. Eldersveld, V. Jagannadham, and A. P. Barnabas, *The Citizen and the Administrator in a Developing Democracy: An Empirical Study in Delhi State, India, 1964* (Glenview, Ill.: Scott, Foresman, 1968); Richard W. Wilson, *Learning to Be Chinese: The Political Socialization of Children in Taiwan* (Cambridge, Mass.: M.I.T. Press, 1970); Kenneth Prewitt and Goren Hyden, "Voters Look at the Elections", in Lionel Cliffe, ed., *One Party Democracy: The 1965 Tanzania General Elections* (Nairobi, Kenya: East African Publishing House, 1967), pp. 273–98; Kenneth Prewitt, George von der Muhll, and David Court, "School Experiences and Political Socialization: A Study of Tanzanian Secondary School Students", *Comparative Political Studies*, 3 (July 1970), 203–25; David Koff and George von der Muhll, "Political Socialization in Kenya and Tanzania: A Comparative Analysis", *The Journal of Modern African Studies*, 5 (May 1967), 13–51; Daniel Goldrich, "Political Organization and the Politicization of the Poblador", *Comparative Political Studies*, 3 (July 1970), 176–202; Read Reading, "Political Socialization in Colombia and the United States: An Exploratory Study", *Midwest Journal of Political Science*, 12 (August 1968), 352–81. In exploring attitudes toward political objects, most of these studies draw on voting variables, such as party identification, feelings of political efficacy, civic obligation, and degree of politicization. In a somewhat different type of study based on psychoanalytic principles, Lucian Pye has attempted to link attitudes of the Chinese toward their parents with the type of authority exercised by Mao tse-tung. See his *The Spirit of Chinese Politics: A Psychocultural Study of the Authority Crisis in Political Development* (Cambridge: The M.I.T. Press, 1968).

73 See Everett C. Hagen, *On the Theory of Social Change*, pp. 137–232.

74 In "Personality and Structural Dimensions in Comparative International Development", *Social Science Quarterly*, 51 (December 1970), 494–513, Irving Louis Horowitz points out the lack of congruence between structural indicators and attitudinal patterns in countries like Argentina. In his view, social scientists should place greater emphasis on the structural conditions and consequences of holding particular attitudes. David C. McClelland recognizes, like Horowitz, that structural opportunities condition the expression of personal variables such as the need for achievement: "No matter how high a person's need to Achieve may be, he cannot succeed if he has no opportunities, if the organization keeps him from taking initiative, or does not reward him if he does." See "The Two Faces of Power", *Journal of International Affairs*, 24 (No. 1, 1970), 31. Yet, compared with Horowitz, McClelland has greater faith that the innovative personality will create the opportunities for successful achievement. According to his view of the interaction between the subjective motivations of man and the objective structural conditions, "Whatever a generation wants, it gets." See "To Know Why

Men Do what they Do: A Conversation with David C. McClelland and T. George Harris", *Psychology Today*, 4 (January 1971), 75.

75   See Lucian Pye, *Politics, Personality, and Nation-Building: Burma's Search for Identity* (New Haven, Conn.: Yale University Press, 1962); Robert Scott, "Mexico: The Established Revolution", *Political Culture and Political Development*, ed. Lucian Pye and Sidney Verba, pp. 330–95.

76   See Daniel Lerner, *The Passing of Traditional Society*, pp. 43–75.

77   See David H. Smith and Alex Inkeles, "The OM Scale: A Comparative Socio-psychological Measure of Individual Modernity", *Sociometry*, 29 (December 1966), 353–77; Alex Inkeles, "The Modernization of Man", *Modernization: The Dynamics of Growth*, ed. Myron Weiner (New York: Basic Books, 1966), pp. 138–50; Alex Inkeles, "Making Men Modern: On the Causes and Consequences of Individual Change in Six Developing Countries", *The American Journal of Sociology*, 75 (September 1969), 208–25; Alex Inkeles, "Participant Citizenship in Six Developing Countries", *The American Political Science Review*, 63 (December 1969), 1120–41; Alex Inkeles and David H. Smith, "The Fate of Personal Adjustment in the Process of Modernization", *International Journal of Comparative Sociology*, 11 (June 1970), 81–114.

78   For an analysis of the strengths and limitations of survey data gathering, see Angus Campbell, "Recent Developments in Survey Studies of Political Behavior", *Essays on the Behavioral Study of Politics*, ed. Austin Ranney, pp. 31–46.

79   For perceptive answers to this question, see three articles by Robert Edward Mitchell: "Barriers to Survey Research in Asia and Latin America", *American Behavioral Scientist*, 9 (November 1965), 6–12; "Survey Materials Collected in the Developing Countries: Sampling, Measurement, and Interviewing Obstacles to Intra- and Inter-national Comparisions", *International Social Science Journal*, 17 (No. 4, 1965), 665–85; "Survey Materials Collected in the Developing Countries: Obstacles to Comparisons", in Stein Rokkan, ed., *Comparative Research across Cultures and Nations* (Paris: Mouton, 1968), pp. 210–38. The most comprehensive account of the methods for carrying out cross-national survey research appears in Frederick W. Frey, "Cross-cultural Survey Research in Political Science", in Robert T. Holt and John E. Turner, eds., *The Methodology of Comparative Research*, pp. 173–294. See in particular his discussion of procedures for securing greater validity, reliability, and equivalence of meaning. Other useful discussions can be found in Frank Bonilla, "Survey Techniques", *Studying Politics Abroad*, ed. Robert E. Ward (Boston: Little, Brown, 1964), pp. 134–52; Prodipto Roy and Frederick C. Fliegel, "The Conduct of Collaborative Research in Developing Nations: The Insiders and the Outsiders", *International Social Science Journal*, 22 (No. 3, 1970), 505–23; Charles E. Osgood, "On the Strategy of Cross-national Research into Subjective Culture", *The Social Studies: Problems and Orientations* (Paris: Mouton, 1968), pp. 475–507; John DeLamater, Robert Hefner, and Remi Clignet, eds., "Social Psychological Research in Developing Nations", *The Journal of Social Issues*, 24 (April 1968), 1–268. Of all the continents in the Third World, Latin America has experienced the greatest number of survey studies. For illustrative studies of Latin American surveys of subnational groups, see Kalman H. Silvert and Frank Bonilla, *Education and the Social Meaning of Development* (New York: American Universities Field Staff, 1961); Daniel Goldrich, *Sons of the Establishment: Elite Youth in Panama and Costa Rica* (Chicago: Rand McNally, 1966); Wendell Bell, *Jamaican Leaders* (Berke-

ley: The University of California Press, 1965); Charles Moskos, Jr., *The Sociology of Political Independence* (Cambridge, Massachusetts: Schenkman, 1967); Maurice Zeitlin, *Revolutionary Politics and the Cuban Working Class* (Princeton, N.J.: Princeton University Press, 1967); Joseph Kahl, *The Measurement of Modernism: A Study of Values in Brazil and Mexico* (Austin: University of Texas Press, 1968); Everett M. Rogers and Lynne Svenning, *Modernization among Peasants: The Impact of Communication* (New York: Holt, Rinehart and Winston, 1969); Frank Bonilla and Myron Glazer, *Students and Politics in Chile* (New York: Basic Books, 1970); Arthur L. Stinchcombe, "Political Socialization in the South American Middle Class", *Harvard Educational Review*, 38 (Summer 1968), 506–27; Frank Bonilla, "Promoting Political Development Abroad: Social Conditions and Attitudes of Latin American Intellectuals", *Studies in Comparative International Development*, 4 (No. 1, 1968/69); Daniel Goldrich, Raymond B. Pratt, and C. R. Schuller, "The Political Integration of Lower-class Urban Settlements in Chile and Peru", *Studies in Comparative International Development*, 3 (No. 1, 1967/68).

80 See the Mexican sample in Gabriel Almond and Sidney Verba, *The Civic Culture* (Princeton, New Jersey: Princeton University Press, 1963), pp. 514–16.

81 In *The Civic Culture* study, 64% of the Mexican sample is composed of women; yet women constitute only 52% of the population sampled. In India women are unwilling to be interviewed; they defer to their husbands. In the surveys conducted by the Indian Institute of Public Opinion, the Gallup Associates in India, women comprise only 20% of the samples. See M. Lal Goel, "Distribution of Civic Competence Feelings in India", *Social Science Quarterly*, 51 (December 1970), 755.

82 See the discussions of Robert E. Mitchell, "A Social Science Data Archive for Asia, Africa, and Latin America", *Social Sciences Information*, 4 (September 1965), 85–103; Robert E. Mitchell, "Information Storage and Retrieval: Information Services", *International Encyclopedia of the Social Sciences*, Vol. 7 (New York: Macmillan, 1968), pp. 304–14; David Nasatir, "Social Science Data Libraries", *The American Sociologist*, 2 (November 1967), 207–12.

83 Milton Rokeach, *The Open and Closed Mind* (New York: Basic Books, 1960).

84 See Sidney Siegel, *Nonparametric Statistics for the Behavioral Sciences* (New York: McGraw-Hill, 1956).

85 In Mexico, the United States, Bombay, and three small Indian cities, David McClelland and David Winter established a training course and institute to educate businessmen in the need for achievement. See their *Motivating Economic Achievement*. For a critique of McClelland's assumptions, especially as they apply to Japanese economic development, see George A. de Vos, "Achievement and Innovation in Culture and Personality", in Edward Norbeck, Douglass Price-Williams, and Williard M. McCord, eds., *The Study of Personality: An Interdisciplinary Appraisal* (New York: Holt, Rinehart and Winsteon, 1968), pp. 348–70. See also the discussion of the need for achievement in John H. Kunkel, *Society and Economic Growth: A Behavioral Perspective of Social Change* (New York: Oxford University Press, 1970), pp. 94–101.

86 For a discussion of the newer trends of evaluation, see Robert A. Dahl, "The Evaluation of Political Systems", *Contemporary Political Science*, ed. Ithiel de Sola Pool (New York: McGraw-Hill, 1967), pp. 166–81.

87 See the attempts of Russell Fitzgibbon over the last twenty years to measure the degree of democracy in Latin American states. His most recent report can be found in "Measuring Democratic Change in Latin America", *Journal of Politics*, 29 (February, 1967), 129–66. In a study measuring the degree of "polyarchy" (electoral equality, effectiveness of control of leaders by non-leaders, and freedom of competition between elites), Deane Neubauer found that Japan ranked third on this scale of ten countries; Chile, 6·5 along with Italy; the United States, eighth; India, ninth; and Mexico, tenth. The European countries of Sweden, Great Britain, West Germany, and France all ranked above the United States in the degree to which they maximized the value of polyarchy. See Deane E. Neubauer, *On the Theory of Polyarchy: An Empirical Study of Democracy in Ten Countries* (Yale University: unpublished doctoral dissertation, 1966). In "Some Conditions of Democracy", *The American Political Science Review*, 61 (December 1967), Neubauer found that the United States ranked sixteenth out of twenty-three countries on a scale of "democratic performance", as measured by the percentage of the population eligible to vote, equality of representation, information equality, and electoral competition. The older, more speculative evaluative approach would have been unlikely to reach these conclusions.

88 See Max F. Millikan, "Equity versus Productivity in Economic Development", *Modernization: The Dynamics of Growth*, ed. Myron Weiner, pp. 307–20. Those working on the Committee on Comparative Politics of the Social Science Research Council—namely, Lucian Pye, Joseph La Palombara, Myron Weiner, and Gabriel Almond—take a similar position about the need to decentralize the economy and political institutions. For example, according to La Palombara, the role of government in furthering economic development should be to create a framework for private enterprise, that is, provide law, order, and security for private entrepreneurs and engage in limited economic planning. See Joseph La Palombara, "Bureaucracy and Political Development: Notes, Queries, and Dilemmas", *Bureaucracy and Political Development*, ed. Joseph La Palombara, pp. 55–60. In *The Politics of Scarcity* (Chicago: The University of Chicago Press, 1962), Myron Weiner also comes out for decentralized government and private entrepreneurship. To alleviate the economic gap between the rich and poor nations, Lucian Pye supports population control and concentration on agriculture, rather than industrialization. See Lucian Pye, "The International Gap", *Modernization: The Dynamics of Growth*, ed. Myron Weiner, pp. 340, 344. Against those who claim that a less openly competitive political system will stimulate economic growth, Pye argues that political and social pluralism will more likely result in economic development than will a more autocratic system. See *Aspects of Political Development* (Boston: Little, Brown, 1966), pp. 72–74.

89 For a critique of American economic policy towards the Third World, especially Latin America, see Irving L. Horowitz, *Three Worlds of Development*, especially pp. 164–224; "United States 'Policy' in Latin America", *New Politics*, 9 (May 1971), 74–83. Two Latin American economists working with the United Nations who have paid attention to the economic gap between the rich and poor nations are Raúl Prebisch, *Nueva Política Comercial para el Desarrollo* (Mexico, Buenos Aires: Fondo de Cultura Economica, 1964); Celso Furtado, "Development and Stagnation in Latin America", in Irving Louis Horowitz, ed., *Masses in Latin America* (New York: Oxford University Press, 1970), pp. 29–64. For an analysis of the effects of multinational oil companies in the developing nations, see Michael Tanzer,

The Political Economy of Oil and the Underdeveloped Countries (Boston: Beacon Press, 1969). For a view stressing the more positive effects of American-dominated multinational corporations on economic development in underdeveloped countries, see Robert L. Heilbroner, "The Multinational Corporation and the Nation-State", *The New York Review*, 16 (February 11, 1971), pp. 20–25. Heilbroner argues that these corporations, compared with local businesses, pay higher wages, contribute higher taxes, and operate more efficiently. They also provide a channel for the importation of advanced technology, thus increasing economic productivity.

90 For an incisive indictment of American social scientists dealing with Latin America, see Kalman H. Silvert, "American Academic Ethics and Social Research Abroad: The Lessons of Project Camelot", *Background*, 9 (November, 1965), 215–36. This project, sponsored by the Department of the Army under the aegis of American University, sought to discover the causes of and cures for "internal war" in Chile, as well as in a number of other Latin American countries. Silvert notes that Chilean newspapermen had great fun twisting "Camelot" around to read "Camelo"—joke or jest, and "Camello"—camel.

91 See the article by Johan Galtung, "Scientific Colonialism", *Transition*, 6 (April/May 1967), 11–15.

92 As Charles C. Moskós, Jr. and Wendell Bell point out, "The possibility is seldom broached that the national interests of the United States, *as presently constituted*, and its role in the economic division of the world may not be compatible with the future political progress of the underdeveloped areas." See "Emerging Nations and Ideologies of American Social Scientists", *The American Socioligist*, 2 (May 1967), 71. Moskós and Bell demonstrate how the moral assumptions of many American social scientists implicitly affect the concepts they develop to explain the new nations' performance.

93 For a probing critique of the effect of computer technology on social science research strategy, see Robert Boguslaw, *The New Utopians* (Englewood Cliffs, New Jersey: Prentice-Hall, 1965).

94 Claude Lévi-Strauss, *Structural Anthropology*, pp. 50–51.

95 Seymour Martin Lipset, *The First New Nation*, p. 7.

96 See Erik Erikson, *Childhood and Society* (2nd ed., New York: Norton, 1963); Erikson, *Young Man Luther* (New York: Norton, 1958); and especially *Gandhi's Truth*. See also "On the Nature of Psycho-historical Evidence: In Search of Gandhi", *Daedalus*, 97 (Summer 1968), 695–730.

97 According to Erikson, "Industrial revolution, world-wide communication, standardization, centralization, and mechanization threaten the identities which man has inherited from primitive, agrarian, feudal, and patrician cultures. What inner equilibrium these cultures had to offer is now endangered on a gigantic scale. As the fear of loss of identity dominates much of our irrational motivation, it calls upon the whole arsenal of anxiety which is left in each individual from the mere fact of his childhood. In this emergency masses of people become ready to seek salvation in pseudo identities." See *Childhood and Society*, pp. 412–13.

98 Daniel Lerner, *The Passing of Traditional Society*.

99 See in particular Alex Inkeles, "Making Men Modern", *American Journal of Sociology*, 75 (September 1969), 208–25; Alex Inkeles, "Participant Citizenship in Six Developing Countries", *The American Political Science Review*, 63 (December 1969), 1120–41; Alex Inkeles and David H. Smith, "The Fate of Personal Adjustment in the Process of Modernization", *International Journal of Comparative Sociology*, 11 (June 1970), 81–114.

Whereas Huntington argues (*Political Order in Changing Societies*, pp. 34–35, 47) that education raises man's *aspirations*, Inkeles points out that education also gives man the *capabilities* to cope with the modernizing situation.

100 See Sidney Verba, Norman Nie, and Jae-on Kim, "The Modes of Democratic Participation: A Cross-National Comparison", *Sage Professional Papers in Comparative Politics* (Beverly Hills, Calif.: Sage Publications, 1971).

Index

Adams, Henry, 88
Adler, Alfred, 210
Africa, 121; development of comparative analysis of, 181
Agency for international development in U.S.A., 152
Aggregate date, 158; instructural analysis, 205–06; and survey data, 219
Aid, 147–57; as assistant for development in modernizing countries, 147; characteristics of U.S.A. aid, 162; as a marginal interest, 157; original conceptions in U.S.A., 148; representative of theories and ideologies, 147; types and results of, 147–49; 150–52
Algeria, 150, 201; under Ben Bella, 95; nationalist development in, 190
Almond, Gabriel, 160, 194, 199, 206
Alvear, Marcelo, 36
"Americanism", 31, 32, 33
Analysis; comparative, 180–222; of choice, 25; of government, 75; of independent variables of government, 107; indicator and trend, limitations of, 164; levels of, 7; of norms, 5, 8; of role, 159; of social and economic prerequisites of polis, 152; structural, 5, 8, 182
Anarchism; acceptance of violence in, 19, 20; as doctrine of role rejection, 18; as liberator, 19; old and new, 11–22; revived and modified in U.S.A., 33; role of theory in, 11, 14–16; as wanderer, 22; in universities, 22; as a youth counter culture, 17, 18
Andrain, Charles, 161
Anti-roles, 18, 21; and rebirth of innocence, 18, 19
Antonov-Ovseenko, Vladimir, 40
Argentina, 4, 27, 134, 149, 163, 168, 203; comparison with U.S.A., 34–36, 38; reconciliation and the failure to industrialize, 34–38
Aristotle, 77, 103
Australia, 181

Babeuf, François Emile, 39
Bakunin, Michael, 11, 15, 17
Baran, Paul, 162
Barker, Sir Ernest, 180
Behavioural approach to comparative analysis, 210–16; analytic problem of, 211–12; critique of, 215–16; techniques of data collection of, 213–15; techniques of data processing of, 215; units for analysis, 212; variables and assumptions of, 212–13
Behavioural approach, in the analysis of choice, 25
Behaviourism, 3
Belgium, 194
Bellah, Robert, 160
Bentham, Jeremy, 76; Benthamites, 90; equitable utilitarianism, 76
Bentley, A. F., 97
Bernstein, Eduard, 39
Besant, Annie, 12
Binder, Leonard, 160, 190
Bipolarity; development since World War II, 183
Black Power, 28, 34
Bloch, Marc, 24
Bolivia, 149
Bourgeois radicals, 29
Bourguiba, Habib, 190
Brazil, 149, 160, 203
British East India Company, 202
Bruce, Lord, 75
Bukharin, Nikolai, 40
Bureaucracy defined, 28
Bureaucratic system, 106, 108, 110–13, 127, 134

240   POLITICAL CHANGE

Burma, 113
Busia, Kofi A., 48

Campbell, Angus, 158
Canada, 181
Ceylon, 172
Chenery-Hollis, absorption theory, 157
Chile, 4, 86, 149, 167, 203
China, 44, 53, 79, 163, 168, 169, 201
Choice, 25, 105; elements of, 8, 105;
relationship to allocation, 106; in
societies during modernization, 126
Coercion; in decision-making, 41;
relationship with information (see
information); relationship with
information in U.S.A., 33
Coleman, James, 194
Colonial administrative system, 132
Colonialism, 181, 189; early comparative analysis of, 181; as modernizing
agent, 202; terminal, 194; as
unifying force of African nationalism, 189; scientific, 218
Columbia, 149
Combination analysis, 172; versus
eclecticism, 163-66
Combination theories, 165-68; 170;
criteria of, 165-66; hypotheses for,
166-67; political system change as
base for, 170; strategies of, 171-72;
theoretical constructs for, 168-69
Committee on comparative politics,
199
Communist governments, 82-84
Comparative analysis, 180-81; behavioural approach, 210-16; computer technology and, 183-87, 192,
219-20, 222-23; ethical values of,
183; evolution of, 181-83; norma-
tive approach, 185-92; structural
approach, 193-210
Computer technology, 219-20
Conflict in neo-marxism, 204
Congo, 121
Congruence theory, 161
Constitution; characteristics of 118-
20; in colonial societies, 119; in
Ghana, 122-24, a plan for, 118-45;
in Uganda, 122-24
Constitutionalism in political develop-
ment; 170-71
Consummatory values, 35, 48
Convention People's Party, 4, 45, 50
Creativity, 13

Cross-cultural data, in micro-
component analysis, 158
Cuba, 1
Czechoslovakia, 39, 43

Dahl, Robert, 158
Daniel, Yuli, M., 42
Darwinism, 13
Data banks, 172-73; problems of
220; use in structural analysis,
205-06
Daya; aggregate, 159, 205-06, 219;
cross-cultural, 158; survey, 213-14,
219
Democratic types of government, 76,
91-93; intervening variables relating
to, 93
Deutsch, Karl, 98, 158, 182; influence
on structural analysis, 205
Development; achievement motivation in, 154; in comparative analysis
184-85; as constitutional engineering, 152; as defined by political
economists, 201; control of, 1;
education as an agent in, 154-55;
expansion of choice, 1; hypotheses
in the study of, 167; Marx's theory
of, 202; political, 152; and the
political process, 118-45; as the
prerequisite of viability, 120-22;
religion as an agent in, 154; single
party as instrument for, 132; of
social science policy, 173; using
political system types, 7; viability
relationship, 125-28; welfare
expenditures in, 125
Development upper house in development constitution; framework and
duties of, 136-38; 141-43; relationship with lower house, 141-45
Development constitution, 121, 126,
170; characteristics of, 126; colonial
system bearing on, 121; information-
coercion relationship 127; as interim
measure, 144; objects of, 133-34;
structural arrangements for, 135-45;
values in, 128
Development ideologies in U.S.A., 152
Development team, 173; organization
of, 173-75
Development theorists and practitioners, 156; split between, 156-58
Durkheim, E., 2, 67, 159

Easton, David, 160, 161
Ecological analysis, 158; in micro-component analysis, 158
Economic development, 13, 148, in behaviourist approach, committee for, 149; in neo-marxist theory, 203–04
Economism plus constitutionalism, 152
Education as means for political development, 154–55
Egypt, 95
Eisenstadt, S. N., 160, 194, 199
Electicism verses combination analysis, 163–66
Elites; function in government, 107, 111; functional criteria, 26; as a maximal unit, 110; participation in decision-making, goal specification, central control, institutional mediations, 26, 29; relationship to government and society, 105; in unions, 32
Embourgeoisement, 9, 167; and neo-marxism; problem of, 105; and radicalization, 23–57; of working class
Emotionality, 13
England, 152, 194
Equity in government, 105–06, 111; order relationship in society, 110
Equity constitution, 144
Erikson, Erik, 210, 222
Evans-Pritchard, E. E., 2

Fallers, L. A., 2, 160
Fascist governments, 84–86
Finer, Herman, 75, 180
Firth, Raymond, 2
Fortes, Meyer, 2
France, 125, 194; aid from 150
Franco, Generalissimo, 85
Friedrich, Carl, 75, 118, 180
Freud, Sigmund, 13
Frey, Frederick, 158
Fromm, Eric, 14
Functional requisites 107, 109–11; accountability and consent, 107; authoritative decision-making, 107

Gap theory, 175–76
Geertz, Clifford, 2, 154, 160
Germany, 168; fascist government, 84–85; national socialist party, 85
Ghana, 4, 6, 27, 48, 49, 50, 95, 115,

119, 155, 169; constitutional changes in, 122–24; independence for, 1, 45; parallels with Argentina 47; rapid change in political systems, 45–47
Gluckman, Max, 189
Goodman, Paul, 14
Government; analysis of independent variables of, 107–09; behavioural aspects of, 75, 77; centralized authority, 81; as a concept, 103–05; decentralized authority, 81; as a dependant variable, 76, 79; as an educational body, 77; functions of, 106–10; as an independent variable, 78–79, 94; normative aspects of, 74, 77; relationship to elites in society, 105; sovergin, 73; structural principals of, 74, 77; structural requisites of, 107, 109–11; theory in, 75–79; types of, 74
Government contemporary research and theory in, 96–99; organismic analogy, 97; mechanistic tradition, 97
Government in new nations, 93–96; in pluralistic single party state, 95
Government, theories of, 75–79; mechanistic, 75–77; organic, 77–79
Government, types, 82–93, 109
Great Britain, 198
Greece, 79
Green, Thomas Hill, 78
Greenstein, Fred, 161
Guinée, 47, 50, 115; Parti Démocratique de, 50

Hagen, Everett, 212
Happenings, as substitute for programs, 12, 16–18
Hegel, G. F., 77, 190
Herzen, Alexander, 39
Hierarchical authority, 114–15
Hirschmann, Albert, 155
Hitler, Adolph, 109
Hobbes, John, 75
Holland, 194
Holmberg, Allan, 192
Homans, George, 24
Human Relations Area File, 205
Hungary, 39, 83
Huntington, Samuel P., 167, 195, 198, 208, 222
Hypotheses, 165–67; as guide to

combination theories, 166–67; in political development, 167

Ilchman, Warren, 201, 208
India, 12, 49, 201; effect of colonialist modernization on, 202
Indonesia, 6, 154
Industrialization; in societies, 105, 176; as a variable, 107; in Latin America, 203
Information, in government, 169, 141–42; key variable in development, 147; planning, 131; popular, in constitution, 129–30; populist and technical, 135–36, 139–40; technical in constitution, 129–30
Information-coercion relationship, 6, 7, 9, 27, 33, 107, 113–16, 126–27, 129, 133, 169
Infrastructure development, 156
Inkeles, Alex, 182, 213, 221
Innocence, in American life, 30; relation to violence, 19
Institution building, 156
Institutional change, value prerequisites for, 153
Institutionalist, defined as structural approach in comparative analysis 194–94; neo-institutionalists, 195, 208; method of data-collection of, 205–6
Institutional theories, 75
International Monetary Fund, 218
Irigoyen, Hipólito, 36, 37
Italy, 125, fascist government in, 84–5

Japan, 12, 181, 154, 168

Kamenev, Lev, 40
Kautsky, Karl, 39
Kennedy, J. F., assassination of, 30
Kenya, 121, 156
Khrushchevism, 38, 39
Kohlberg, Lawrence, 210
Korea, North, 163
Kropotkin, Peter, 11, 15, 17, 20

Laing, R. D., 14
Langton, Kenneth, 161
La Palonbara, Joseph, 160
Laski, Harold, 75, 180
Lasswell, Harold, 191

Latin America, foreign investment in* 204; military in, 218; neo-marxism in, 203–04
Latreille, André, 176
Law, 104
Lefebvre, Georges, 24
Lenin, Nikolai, 16, 39
Leninism, 38, 39, 83
Lerner, Daniel, 182, 212, 221
Lévi-Strauss, Claude, 24, 189, 192, 221, 162
Levy, Marion, 3, 194, 160
Lewin, Kurt, 98, 210
Lewis, Arthur, 155
Liberalism, 16
Linz, Juan, 158
Lippitt, R., 98
Lipset, Seymour, M., 30, 166, 189
Litvinov, Pavel, M. 42
Locke, John, 76, 128
Lugard, Lord, 193
Lunacharsky, A. V. 40

McClelland, David C., 153, 211, 215, 216
Macro-component approach, 159–61, 165, 172; characteristics of 159–60; political socialization as a variant of, 161
Maine, Henry Summer, 2
Maitland, Frederic William, 2, 24
Malatesta, Errico, 20
Malaysia, behavioural study of, 211
Mali, 6, 50, 115, 175
Malinowski, B., 159
Mannheim, Karl, 97
Mao Tse-tung, 16, maoism, 33, 34
Marcuse, Herbert, 14
Marginals, functionally superfluous, 29
Mariana, Juan de, 88
Marx, Karl, II, 13, 39, 77, 78, 128; theory of development, 202; and use of history, 23
Marxism, 2, 14, 16, 20, 21, 33, 38, 42, 62–67, 71, 80, 152; theocratic goal of, 140; weaknesses of theory, 2 (see Neo-Marxists)
Mead, George Herbert, 3
Meinecke, Friedrich, 24
Meritocracy, 33; 105, problem of in U.S.A., 47
Merritt, Richard, 158
Merton, Robert, K. 3

Mexico, 149, 201, 203

Micro-component approach, 158–59, 165, 169, 172; activities of, 158; characteristics of 158–59, 161

Military, as an instrument for internal development, 137–38

Mill, John Stuart, 90

Millikan, Max, 217; and Rostow, emphasis on development loans, 157

Mobilization systems, 50–54, 106, 108, 168, 172; difference between traditional and, 51; industrializing of, 52–54; information coercion relationship in, 110–13; modern forms, 51; modernizing of, 50–52; reasons for change in, 110–13

Models, abstract, of development, 182, 195

Modernization; and change in political systems, 116–17; choice in society during, 126; as creator of universal values, 153; and neo-Marxism, 204–5; in society, 105, 170; theories of; 61–71, as a variable, 106

Moore, Barrington, 189

Moore, Clement Henry, 160, 190

Morocco, 154, 201; nationalist development in, 190

Nadel, S. F., 3

National building, 150

Nationalism, as focus for comparative analysis, 181, in North Africa, 190

Neo-institutionalists, as critics of structural functionalists 195; critique of, 208

Neo-Marxists, 165, 217, 196; and economic development, 203–04; and modernization, 204–05; critique of, 209; theory of developmental assistance, 162–63

Netherlands, social and economic council, 124–25

Newcomb, T. M., 3, 98

Nigeria, 113, 115, 121, 137, 172

Nkrumah, Kwame, 4, 45, 46

Normative, aspects of comparative analysis, 184, 185–92

Normative approach, analytic problems of, 188–89; assumptions of, 190–91; ideology and religion in, 191; techniques of data collection and processing, 191–92; to develop-

ment constitution, 128; units for analysis of, 189; variables of 189–90

Ostrogorskii, M., 75

Pakistan, 113, 119, 156

Panama, 149

Pareto, V., 2

Parsons, Talcott, 3, 159, 194

Perón, Juan, 37, 47, 168; government of, 38, 86

Persia, 201

Peru, 4, 149, 167

Petras, James, 162

Piaget, Jean, 210

Plato, 75, 77, 103

Poland, 34, 39, 83

Policy research, 157

Political economic approach, 161–63

Political economists, as critics of structural functionalists, 195; data collection techniques of, 205–06; critique of, 208–09; neo-classical, 201

Political groups, and structural-functionalists, 199–200, types of, 199

Political infrastructure, 16

Political institution, in structuralist approach, 197–98

Political norms, sacred, 79–80; secular, 80–81

Political science, 61–67; comparative studies, 70; critique of, 67–69

Political system types, 7, 26; change in 25, 133–35, 110–13; change in Argentina, 36; change in Ghana, 45–47; in U.S.S.R., 40; stratification categories of, 26; theories of, 105, 106

Political typologies, derivation of, 82

Pool, Ithiel, 158

Populist autocracy, 122

Populist politics, 30

Proudhon, P. J., mutualist doctrines, 17

Prussia, 168

Psychoanalysis, use in political science, 210

Pye, Lucian, 211, 153

Pyramidal authority, 113, 114

Radcliffe–Brown, A. R., 159

Radicalization, 9, 167; and embourgeoisement, 23–57

Rationality, 13; in anarchism, 11

Reconciliation system, 48–50, 106, 108, 172; characteristics of, 49–50; information-coercion relationship in, 110–13; modernizing of, 49; reasons for change in, 110–13

Reich, Wilhelm, 14

Religion, as agent for development, 154; in normative approach, 191

Riesman, David, 27

Riggs, F., 194, 200

Roco, General Julio, 36

Rokkan, Stein, 158

Rolelessness, 18–19

Role relationships, 159–60

Rorschach radicals, 16

Rosa, Juan, military regime of, 18, 52, 35

Rousseau, Jean Jacques, 76, 128

Ruskin, John, on Ghandi, 12

Russell, Bruce, 158

Russia, see U.S.S.R.

Sacred and centralized government, 82–86; communist, 82–84; fascist, 84–86

Sacred and decentralized government, 87–89

Saint Simon, Claude Henri de, 39

San Martin, José de, 34

Sarmiento, Domingo, 36

Sartre, Jean-Paul, 162

Schurmann, Franz, 162

Scientific colonialism, 218

Scott, James, E., 211

Scott, Robert, 212

Secular and centralized government, 86–87

Secular and decentralized government, 90–93

Sinyavsky, Andrei, 42

Smelser, Neil, 150

Smith, Adam, 202

Sokolnikov, Grigority, 40

Spain, fascist government, 84; Falange in, 85

Stalin, 83, 109; Stalinism, 38, 39, 41

Structural approach; analytic problem of, 196; assumptions of, 197; critique of, 207–09; data collection of, 205–06; data processing of, 206–07; to comparative analysis, 193–210; to development constitu-tion, 128–29; units for analysis, 197, variables of, 197

Structural-functional approach, 194–95, 199; critique of, 207–08; data collection of, 205–06

Structural requisites of government, 107, 109–11

Sudan, 113

Sullivan, Henry Stack, 3

Survey data, and aggregate data, 219; in behavioural approach, 213–14

Syria, 201

Systems for aiding development, 157–63; macro-component dimension, 159; micro-component dimension, 158–59; political economic approach, 161–63

Tanzania, 135, 175; under Nyerere

Tarrow, Sidney, 161

Technology; effect on policy and analysis, 183

Theocratic system, 54–55, 106, 108; reasons for change in, 110–13

Theosophist movement, 12

Third World Liberation Front, 28, 33

Toennies, F., 2

Tolstoy, his primitive Christianity, 17

Totalitarian government, 109

Trade Unions, 199; organization of, 32

Troeltsch, Ernst, 24

Trotsky, Leon, 39–40

Truman, H., 150–51

Tsarism, 38, 39

Tunisia, nationalist development in, 190

Turkey, 201

Uganda, 119–75; Bantu–Nilotic con-flict, 121; constitutional changes in, 122–24

Uphoff, Norman, 201, 208

Uraguay, 149

U.S.A., 12, 27, 181, 198, 204; com-parison with U.S.S.R., 47, 48; development ideologies in, 152; development problem, 27; immi-grant problem, 31, 33; as an industrial reconciliation system, 27–34; overseas aid from, 147–9, 150–52; pattern of stratification, 29; policy needs of, 183; revival of ideologies, 33; revival of utopian-ism, 33

U.S.S.R., 6, 12, 27, 48, 83; aid to developing countries, 149, 151; comparison with U.S.A., 44, 47, 48; from mobilization to bureaucracy, 38–44

Values, consummatory, 35, 45; in normative approach to development in constitution, 128; as variable in normative approach in comparative analysis, 189–90, 192
Venezuela, 134, 144, 203
Verba, Sidney, 161, 222
Viability, approach to constitution, 120; breakdown of, 132; development as prerequisite of, 120–22; development relationship, 125–28
Vietnam, North, 163; war, 30

Vinogradoff, Paul, 2, 24
Voltaire, 76

Wallas, Graham, 75
Ward, Barbara, 175
Washington, George, 35
Weber, Max, 2, 23, 24, 67, 97, 128, 154, 159
Weiner, Myrom, 160
Wilson, Woodrow, 120
World Bank, 218

Yale Political Data Program, 205
Youth, 17–18; counter-culture, 17; subcultures, 12, 16, 19, 22
Yugoslavia, 34, 39, 43, 83, 124–25

Zeitlin, Maurice, 162